To my dear FRIEND
Julian Edison

Happy Chanukah

EMS

104 Gen 12:3

מסורה

ArtScroll Mesorah Series®

Expositions on Jewish liturgy and thought

Rabbis Nosson Scherman / Meir Zlotowitz
General Editors

Chanukah

CHANUKAH — ITS HISTORY, OBSERVANCE, AND SIGNIFICANCE / A PRESENTATION BASED UPON TALMUDIC AND TRADITIONAL SOURCES.

Published by

Mesorah Publications, ltd

History and Laws by
Rabbi Hersh Goldwurm

Ritual and Insights by
Rabbi Meir Zlotowitz

Overview by
Rabbi Nosson Scherman

FIRST EDITION
First Impression ... November, 1981

Published and Distributed by
MESORAH PUBLICATIONS, Ltd.
Brooklyn, New York 11223

Distributed in Israel by
MESORAH MAFITZIM / J. GROSSMAN
Rechov Bayit Vegan 90/5
Jerusalem, Israel

Distributed in Europe by
J. LEHMANN HEBREW BOOKSELLERS
20 Cambridge Terrace
Gateshead
Tyne and Wear
England NE 1RP

ARTSCROLL MESORAH SERIES®
"CHANUKAH" / Its History and Observance
© Copyright 1981 by MESORAH PUBLICATIONS, Ltd.
1969 Coney Island Avenue / Brooklyn, N.Y. 11223 / (212) 339-1700

ISBN
0-89906-185-0 (hard cover)
0-89906-186-9 (paperback)

סֵדֶר בְּמִסְגֶּרֶת
חֶבְרַת אַרְטְסְקְרוֹל בע״מ

Typography by Compuscribe at ArtScroll Studios, Ltd.
1969 Coney Island Avenue / Brooklyn, N.Y. 11223 / (212) 339-1700

Printed in the United States of America by Moriah Offset

Table of Contents

יעקב קמנצקי

RABBI J. KAMENECKI

38 SADDLE RIVER ROAD

MONSEY, NEW YORK 10952

בע״ה

כבוד ידידי הרב הגאון הנעלה מוה״ר צבי הירש גאלדוואורם שליט״א

מה מאד שמחתי לשמוע שכב' משתתף בחיבור ספר על עניני חנוכה בשפה המדוברת שיצא לאור אי״ה על ידי החברה הדגולה ״ארטסקרול״ שכבר יצאו לה מוניטין כמרביצי תורה על פי מסורת חז״ל ומקרבים לבבות אחבנ״י לתורה ולתעודה. דבר חשוב מאד קיבל כב' על עצמו לחבר פרק מיוחד על ההיסטוריה של תקופת הנס ערוך על הדרך שהביע כב' לפני. התקופה יש בה הרבה ענינים סתומים ומסובכים המעוררים תמיהות והיא אינה ידועה אף לרוב יודעי ספר ותלמידי חכמים. ועל כן יישר חילו שיעמול לברר המקורות ויסדר דבר דבור על אופנו לתועלת המון בני תורה. המשתתפים עמו בהחיבור ידידי הרה״ג הנעלה מוה״ר נתן שערמאן שליט״א וידידי הרה״ג הנעלה מוה״ר מאיר יעקב זלאטאוויץ שליט״א ינדבו הקדמה כללית על השקפה המוסרית של נס חנוכה וג׳״כ פירוש על תפלות החג הנשגב מלוקט מדברי חז״ל וחכמי הדורות.

לזה הנני מברך ומעודד את כב' והמשתתפים עמו בעבודת הקדש, שהיא מצוה רבה של הרבצת והפצת התורה ברבים, שתזכו לברך על המוגמר ולהתחיל ולסיים גם שאר ספרים שבדעתכם להוציא לאור לזכות את הרבים.

[signature]

[signature]

﹏§ Preface

Mesorah Publications is proud to present "Chanukah," a book that will give its readers, scholar and layman alike, a heightened sensitivity and increased understanding of the festival, its historical background, its underlying significance, and its prayers and ritual.

Alone among all the festivals in the Jewish calendar, Chanukah has no Scriptural basis. We lack the authoritative narrative of Scripture and there is very little Talmudic and Midrashic narrative and interpretation. It is not surprising, therefore, that when people ask the question 'What is Chanukah?' not many of us have more than a superficial answer.

That question inspired this book. Indeed, what is Chanukah? Who were the Maccabees? Whom did they fight? Did the miracle of the oil and the liberation of Eretz Yisrael from foreign domination come at the same time? What does Chanukah say to the modern era when revolts against tyranny are almost an everyday affair? Why do so many people say that Chanukah was a war against Greece when the villain was King Antiochus of Syria? What are the prayers: what do they mean, and how were they chosen? What are the laws of Chanukah?

The list of questions goes on and on, but until now it was longer than the list of answers. It was to provide the public with a well-rounded and solidly founded understanding of Chanukah that this book was written. Its several sections touch upon all aspects of the celebration:

□ The **Overview**, like the others in the ArtScroll Series, presents a hashkafah/philosophical perspective on the miracle in terms of the full scope of Jewish history.

□ The **History** draws upon all the authoritative material, some of it obscure, to present a full review of the events, from background to climax. In addition, it offers the famous stories of Chanah and her seven sons, and the brave woman who demoralized an entire army.

□ The **Insights** presents a fascinating collection of rabbinic thought, homilies, and interpretation.

□ **Dinim/Laws** gives a concise review of the relevant laws and procedures.

□ Finally, the **Ritual** presents the Blessings, hymns, and prayers, complete with the original translation and anthologized commentary that are unique to the award-winning ArtScroll Series.

The History section of this book was written by RABBI HERSH GOLD-WURM, a talmid chacham and scholar of rare distinction. His earlier contribution of the ArtScroll Series — the Book of Daniel and several tractates of the Mishnah — stamp him as a man of rare depth, breadth, and judgment. His vast knowledge of Jewish history has been acknowledged by scholars and lecture audiences, but this is the first time it has appeared in print. In addition, nearly the entire book bears his scholarly imprint, the fruit of his careful reading and many suggestions and additions.

We are deeply grateful to one of the venerable Torah authorities of our time MARAN HAGAON HARAV YAAKOV KAMINETZKY שליט״א for his warm encouragement of the ArtScroll Series and particularly for his invaluable guidance to Rabbi Goldwurm in preparing the History. Despite the Rosh Yeshiva's heavy responsibilities, he graciously offered his time and sage counsel to review and discuss the presentation and help resolve the problems inherent in the contradictory sources. It is our fervent prayer that the Jewish People may benefit from his sagacity and guidance for many years to come, עמו״ש.

We are especially grateful, too, to HARAV DAVID FEINSTEIN, HARAV JOSEPH ELIAS, and HARAV DAVID COHEN, living repositories of Torah knowledge and hashkafah, who have lent their support to this project, and given generously and graciously of their time to review, crystallise, and enhance whenever we call upon them.

RABBI MENACHEM WELDLER, principal of the Yeshiva Rabbi Samson Raphael Hirsch High School has done considerable research on various aspects of Chanukah. He kindly made his notes available to us. It is gratefully appreciated.

There is one individual to whom the z'chus of this publication must be credited. Our dear friend, MR. AARON L. HEIMOWITZ, a tireless askan and man of rare vision and dedication, has perceived the importance of this volume as a Harbotzas Torah contribution, and undertaken personal responsibility for its wide dissemination through an impressive list of yeshivos and Torah institutions throughout the country. His only goal is to bring Torah knowledge — often for the first time — to thousands of his fellow Jews — הקב״ה ישלם שכרו.

Our associate, REB SHEAH BRANDER, has again demonstrated his graphics expertise as evidenced in the cover and every page of this volume. His skills raise the level of the Series and his great artistry is totally dedicated to the service of Torah.

RABBI AVIE GOLD assisted materially in producing a volume worthy of the expectations of ArtScroll readers; MR. STEVEN BLITZ bears gracefully the responsibility of disseminating the ArtScroll Series to the reading public. The Mesorah staff — MRS. SHIRLEY KIFFEL; MRS. FAYGIE WEINBAUM, CHANEE FREIER; MRS. SHEVI ASIA; EDEL STREICHER; ESTHER GLATZER — has again responded cheerfully to the pressures of publication. Their diligence again find expression in this sefer.

To all of the above — and others too numerous to mention — we owe our profoundest gratitude, and not least to the public that makes our work possible.

May the Almighty — Who has allowed us to serve as His quill — privilege us to continue bringing the world of Torah to His children. ויהי נעם ה׳ אלקינו עלינו ומעשה ידינו כוננה עלינו ומעשה ידינו כוננהו.

Rabbi Nosson Scherman / Rabbi Meir Zlotowitz
GENERAL EDITORS

Kislev, 5742

✒️ An Overview/
Light Banishes Darkness

An Overview/
Light Banishes Darkness

מַאי חֲנֻכָּה? ... שֶׁכְּשֶׁנִּכְנְסוּ יְוָנִים לְהֵיכָל טִמְּאוּ כָּל
הַשְּׁמָנִים שֶׁבְּהֵיכָל וּכְשֶׁגָּבְרָה מַלְכוּת בֵּית
חַשְׁמוֹנַאי וְנִצְּחוּם בָּדְקוּ וְלֹא מָצְאוּ אֶלָּא פַךְ אֶחָד
שֶׁל שֶׁמֶן שֶׁהָיָה מוּנָח בְּחוֹתָמוֹ שֶׁל כֹּהֵן גָּדוֹל ...

What is Chanukah? ... When the [Syrian-]
Greeks entered the Sanctuary they contaminated all the [flasks of] oil that were in
the Sanctuary. When the dynasty of the
Hasmoneans grew strong and conquered
them, they searched and found only one
flask of oil that was emplaced with the seal
of the High Priest ... (Shabbos 21b).

כְּשֶׁעָמְדָה מַלְכוּת יָוָן הָרְשָׁעָה עַל עַמְּךָ יִשְׂרָאֵל
לְהַשְׁכִּיחָם תּוֹרָתֶךָ ... וְאַתָּה בְּרַחֲמֶיךָ הָרַבִּים ...
מָסַרְתָּ גִבּוֹרִים בְּיַד חַלָּשִׁים וְרַבִּים בְּיַד מְעַטִּים
וּטְמֵאִים בְּיַד טְהוֹרִים ...

When the wicked Greek kingdom rose up
against Your people Israel to make them
forget Your Torah ... You in Your great
mercy ... delivered the strong into the
hands of the weak, the many into the
hands of the few, the impure into the
hands of the pure ... (Al HaNissim
Liturgy).

I. The Oil's Lesson

Events   To understand events, one must understand the
and   people who brought them about and were af-
Meaning fected by them, otherwise he confronts a tangled,
often confusing jumble of facts with no unifying
structure. When Israel left Egypt, did it do so as the
children of the Patriarchs going to receive the Torah
and build a society according to its dictates, or did it

flee as a slave-nation escaping its oppressor and seeking a piece of real estate it could call its own? Similar questions are raised about more modern settings as well. Did nations fight revolutionary wars to gain liberty or was it a case of rising commercial interests losing patience with the old order? Were leaders motivated by 'ethics and idealism' or did they use platitudes to justify selfish grabs for power?

More often than not, people see what they choose to see, and they arrange the facts to suit their thesis.

More often than not, people see what they choose to see, and then arrange the facts to suit their thesis. There is nothing mysterious or abstract about this notion. We see it every day in discussions of issues, from the international scene to the personal one. People of equal intelligence, experience, and knowledge will disagree sharply. Even when events seem to support one side, the other will persist: 'If we had done more of this or less of that, things would have turned out.' 'If we hadn't given up so easily before my strategy had a chance to succeed ...' 'If only outside factors had not interfered just when the tide was about to turn *my* way!'

This is no less true in the spiritual realm than in the temporal one: choices are seldom easy. Indeed, in this world it can be no other way. If the way to the 'good life' were too obvious — if sinners were struck by lightning as soon as they transgressed and the righteous showered by heavenly bounty — people would rush to do good, both because of the tangible results and because all sincere doubts would be resolved. Then man would be little more than an automation doing the obvious. He would be as unworthy of reward as a child whom experience has taught to keep his hands in the cooky jar but out of the oven *(Derech Hashem.* See Overview to ArtScroll *Bereishis* I and *Ezekiel).*

If sinners were struck people would rush to do good.

The miracle of Chanukah is one of the great events in Jewish history — the only miracles singled out by the Sages for commemoration by festivals are Chanukah and Purim. When it occurred, however, it was not absolutely clear whether a miracle had indeed taken place or what it was. Only through the spiritual perspective of the Sages could that be deter-

When it occurred, however, it was not absolutely clear whether a miracle had indeed taken place or what it was.

Those connoisseurs of the eternal understood the factors underlying the heroics of the Jews and the sadism of the Syrians.

mined. Those connoisseurs of the eternal understood the factors underlying the heroics of the Jews and the sadism of the Syrians; they knew the inner dynamics of the struggle between Greek culture and Jewish sanctity. In a struggle that began three years before the Chanukah miracle, and continued for more than a generation after it, they knew how to pinpoint the critical events, how to interpret them, which to celebrate, and how.

Secular historians would have interpreted the events differently — and certainly proclaimed a different national holiday. Such pundits would have put gaudy markers on many trees, but the Divinely inspired Sages saw the forest.

The famous 'miracle of the lights,' took place three years after the beginning of the Hasmonean revolt. That is the only miracle that the Talmud mentions.

As outlined in 'A History of the Chanukah Period' later in this volume, the famous 'miracle of the lights,' when a one-day supply of pure olive oil burned for eight days, took place three years after the beginning of the Hasmonean revolt. That is the only miracle that the Talmud (*Shabbos* 21b) mentions in its brief description of the Chanukah events. The *Al HaNissim* liturgy, however, which recounts the festival's origin and which is inserted into the Chanukah prayers, tells a different tale. There, the eight-day miracle of the oil is not even mentioned. There, the emphasis is on the miracles of the military triumph. *Al HaNissim* tells how the Syrian-Greeks conquered the Jews and sought to wrest them from the Torah and commandments and how God came to Israel's defense, enabling them to overcome 'the strong, the many, the impure, the wicked, and the wanton,' bringing about 'a great victory and salvation.'

Perspective Provided

Maharal (Chiddushei Aggados) notes the discrepancy between the Talmud's emphasis on the oil and the liturgy's emphasis on the war. He explains that even at the time of the miracle it was necessary for a Divine intervention to show the victorious Jews that their military triumph had indeed been miraculous. As we read of the Maccabean victories over the Syrian-Greeks [see History], we can marvel at their

faith in God and at their courage in the face of impossible odds. A band of devout Jews defeated one of the superpowers of the day. But one who reads the history without knowing from faith, tradition, and study that God was in their ranks might be forgiven if he wonders. Even in modern times we have seen mighty armies of apathetic mercenaries defeated by bands of rebels, fighting for their own homes and to defend the dignity of their wives and children. If guerrillas can defeat huge armies equipped with twentieth century armaments, why couldn't an ancient Jewish force do the same against Syrian horsemen with spears? Surely the triumph was immense, but was it a miracle? Yehudah the Maccabee, who succeeded his father, Mattisyahu, as leader of the revolt, was a master tactician as well as a devout and righteous *tzaddik* — couldn't the victory be attributed to his tactics and the bravery of his men?

Surely the triumph was immense, but was it a miracle? Couldn't the victory be attributed to his tactics and the bravery of his men?

The Sages of the time asked these same questions. Jewish tradition does not proclaim festivals lightly; communities and individuals have the right and obligation to thank God and celebrate their salvation from death or danger, but only Scripture, prophecy, or some other Divine message allows us to proclaim that a day has been invested with holiness.

For the Sages who exulted at the liberation and purification of the Temple but wondered how miraculous it had been, God performed an unmistakable miracle to prove that the entire process had occurred only through His intervention. A lone flask of pure oil was found, still bearing the unbroken seal of the *Kohen Gadol.* How did it happen that the Syrian-Greeks failed to contaminate it? Why did it have the *Kohen Gadol's* seal when it had never been the Temple practice for him to seal or even supervise the flasks of oil? Strange. Extraordinary. But still not necessarily miraculous. Then they lit the oil, and it burned and burned and burned. For eight days it burned until fresh oil could be prepared and brought.

Then they lit the oil, and it burned and burned and burned. For eight days it burned until fresh oil could be prepared and brought.

This was undeniably a miracle.

To the Jewish Sages, trained in perception and

refined in spirit, the glow of the Menorah was a Heavenly answer to all their doubts. *Yes!* Miracles *had* taken place. Not only for eight days, but throughout the three years that old Mattisyahu and then his loyal, vigorous sons fought and defeated the best generals and most daunting forces that King Antiochus could hurl at them. True, similar victories might have been won by the strong right arm of man, but this war had been won by the Supreme Warrior.

The Talmud speaks of the miracle of the oil and it is that event that our Menorah-lighting ritual symbolizes but, as our prayers make plain, the entire process leading up to it — skirmish, battle, and onslaught — was the primary miracle. We celebrate the oil because it was God's means of showing us what we would otherwise not have known — that it was He Who delivered the strong, many, and wanton into the hands of those who were weak and few but who fought for the sake of God's Torah.

We celebrate the oil because it was God's means of showing us what we would otherwise not have known.

II. The Second Temple*

Written and Oral Torah

The lesson of the oil goes further. Not only did it reveal that a miracle had occurred, it revealed *why* Israel was worthy of such a phenomenon. As many of the classic commentators write, the structure and service of the Tabernacle symbolize a microcosm of all creation; just as God intended the universe to be a vehicle for people to recognize His holiness and thereby be worthy of His Presence, so He commanded Israel to fashion a structure where His Presence could rest among them. In the Tabernacle itself, there were two vessels that represented the Torah: the Ark and the Menorah.

In the Tabernacle itself, there were two vessels that represented the Torah: the Ark and the Menorah.

The Ark contained the Tablets of the Law, the Written Torah given by God. The Ark was separated from the physical presence of Israel by the *Paroches*, the curtain beyond which no human being was permitted to venture (except for the few moments on

---

*Except where othewise noted, the rest of the Overview is based on the thoughts of *Harav Gedaliah Schorr* ל״צז, many of which are collected in *Ohr Gedaliahu.*

Yom Kippur when the *Kohen Gadol* offered incense in the Holy of Holies). From the time the Tabernacle was erected, Moses went there to receive commandments and communications from God; he stood outside the *Paroches* and God's Voice emanated from atop the Ark. The Ark, therefore, symbolized God's communication to Israel by means of תּוֹרָה שֶׁבִּכְתָב, *the Written Law*. Man has the duty to study the Written Torah and master it, but he has neither the right nor the capability to add to it. Only the Giver of the Torah can formulate its contents.

The Menorah, too, represents Torah, but it symbolizes תּוֹרָה שֶׁבְּעַל פֶּה, *the Oral Law*, the companion of the Written Torah; the part that man can derive, embellish, and — in a sense — 'create' by using his own diligence and intelligence in accord with the God-given hermeneutical principles [מִדּוֹת שֶׁהַתּוֹרָה נִדְרֶשֶׁת בָּהֶם]. This is not to suggest that the Oral Law is the creature of human invention and creativity. The Oral Torah was taught to Moses along with the written one and, indeed, one could not exist without the other. The Torah itself cannot be understood properly — and much of it cannot be understood at all — without the explanations, laws, and amplifications that form the Oral Law. In addition, within the rules of rabbinic discourse and inquiry, students may question and elucidate, and the product of their intellectual inquiry acquires the sanctity and status of Torah.

Although the Oral Law allows man to exercise his creative, inquisitive abilities, its essence was transmitted by God to Moses, for every authentic addition to the store of Torah knowledge flows from the principles of the God-given law. A halachic ruling regarding tomorrow's electronic technology or medical breakthrough will be decided according to the eternal principles of Halachah; consequently, that ruling will be part of the Sinaitic tradition.

This concept is symbolized by the Menorah. It was placed outside the *Paroches* where it was accessible to everyone — the Halachah provides that one need not even be a *Kohen* to light it — and it was kindled by

The Menorah, too, represents Torah, the Oral Law, the companion of the Written Torah.

A halachic ruling regarding tomorrow's electronic technology or medical breakthrough will be decided according to the eternal principles of Halachah.

means of wicks, oil, and flame that were all produced by man. For this is the essence of the Oral Law: when man acts as God commands him to, he can create new wisdom that becomes a part of the Torah, just as man's wicks, oil, and flame, when added to the Menorah, became a holy part of the Temple.*

The Second Temple Era

The greatest blossoming of the Oral Law began with the period of the Second Temple. Then the Mishnah was composed and the principles of Scriptural exegesis and Talmudic reasoning were utilized to articulate, derive, and develop the immense body of law and logic that became the Talmud and from which the infinite body of Rabbinic literature began to flow. Nor was it a coincidence that a new era of Torah knowledge began then.

The אַנְשֵׁי כְנֶסֶת הַגְּדֹלָה, *the Men of the Great Assembly*, who were the leaders of Israel, knew that the *Shechinah* [the Divine Presence] would not rest upon the Second Temple as it had upon the First, and that after the death of the few living prophets the age of prophecy would be over and God would no longer speak directly to Israel through His emissaries. The people were deeply distressed, not only because they longed for these sacred gifts, but because they realized that the nation's renewed vigor required some form of spiritual grandeur to compensate for the loss of the *Shechinah* and prophecy. So they prayed, insisting that they could not go ahead with the construction of the Temple unless the generation was granted an intensified degree of insight into the Torah:

The people realized that the nation's renewed vigor required some form of spiritual grandeur to compensate for the loss of the Shechinah and prophecy.

אע״פ שֶׁלֹּא שָׁרְתָה שְׁכִינָה בְּבַיִת שֵׁנִי, מ״מ עִיקַּר הַתּוֹרָה וְזִיוָהּ וַהֲדָרָהּ לֹא הָיָה אֶלָּא בְּבַיִת שֵׁנִי שֶׁלֹּא רָצוּ לִבְנוֹת עַד שֶׁהִבְטִיחָם השי״ת לְגַלּוֹת לָהֶם רָזֵי תוֹרָה

Even though the Divine Presence did not rest on the Second Temple, nevertheless, the main part of Torah, its splendor and its glory, was only in the period of the Second

*The concept of the Written and Oral Torah are discussed at length in an Overview, ArtScroll *Genesis* I p. XXVII.

> *Temple, for they [i.e. the Men of the Great Assembly] did not wish to build it until HASHEM, Blessed is He, promised that He would reveal to them the secrets of the Torah (Pirkei Heichalos 27).*

The Menorah's Message That period's uniqueness as the era of the Oral Law was foreshadowed in a prophetic vision of Zachariah, in which he was shown that Israel would soon be privileged to erect a Temple (Zachariah 4:11-14). He was shown a Menorah flanked by two olive trees.

'What are these two olive trees, to the right of the Menorah and its left?' asked Zechariah.

God answered, אֵלֶּה שְׁנֵי בְנֵי הַיִּצְהָר, *these are two people who are likened to olive oil.*

The Talmud (*Sanhedrin* 24a) explains that Zachariah was shown a vision of the far-off future. Olive oil symbolizes the knowledge of Torah, which provides spiritual illumination just as oil burning in a lamp gives physical light.

The future of Israel would depend on two sets of scholars — the scholars of Eretz Yisrael and the scholars of Babylonia. The future of Israel, Zachariah was shown, would depend on two sets of scholars who would illuminate their people and the world with their study and teaching of Torah — the scholars of *Eretz Yisrael* and the scholars of Babylonia.

The history of Israel's Second Commonwealth proceeded from Persian to Greek to Egyptian domination, and — after only a seventy-year period of independence and power — back to dominion status under the Roman Empire that would eventually destroy the Temple. It was not a happy history, but for all its degradation and tragedy, its darkness was relieved by brilliant light — the illumination of Torah coming from *Eretz Yisrael* and Babylonia. Now Zachariah's Menorah takes on a deeper meaning.

He foresaw that the joy of the Second Temple era would be the product of the Menorah that symbolized the Oral Law. He foresaw that the joy of the Second Temple era would be the product of the Menorah that symbolized the Oral Law, flanked, expounded, and given fulfillment by the scholars of Israel. The time when the scholars of Israel and Babylonia would be most fruitful was more than two centuries in the future,

but Zachariah was shown that they would be the Temple era's main accomplishment.

As noted earlier, the Tabernacle parallels the universe and this is true not only in the symbolism of its structure, but in its goals. The first specific command uttered by God in His creation of the universe was יְהִי אוֹר, *Let their be light (Genesis 1:2)*. The Midrash (*Bamidbar Rabbah* 15:18; *Tanchuma, B'haalos'cha*) teaches that after the construction of the Tabernacle was done and it was enveloped with the holy cloud of the Divine Presence, God gave Moses the first commandment of actual service:

בְּהַעֲלֹתְךָ אֶת הַנֵּרוֹת ... יָאִירוּ שִׁבְעַת הַנֵּרוֹת
When you kindle the lights ... the seven lights shall glow (Numbers 8:2).

The Menorah was the fulfillment of God's command that there be light in His universe. The Menorah — which would illuminate Jewish minds and hearts with its spiritual glow, by inspiring them to contribute to the riches of the Oral Law — was the fulfillment of God's command that there be light in His universe. It was the first thing He desired for His world, for a world without the light of Torah is mired in darkness.

Chanukah's Light

They had been waging the war of light against darkness, and bringing about the fulfillment of God's command Let their be light! Chanukah is the festival when oil produced a light that illuminated the true nature of a major slice of Jewish history. The war against the Syrian-Greeks had been won through miracles. But more. The fact that the struggle was climaxed with the miracle of the oil and that God chose to stamp His salvation with a miracle of light was a proof to the leaders of Israel that their struggle was more than a fight for self-respect and freedom — they had been waging the war of light against darkness, and bringing about the fulfillment of God's command *Let their be light!*

Harav David Feinstein notes that Zachariah's vision was chosen as the *haftarah* of the Sabbath of Chanukah (*Zachariah* 2:14-4:6). Zachariah was shown a Menorah of seven lamps, fueled by seven pipes flowing with oil. The oil was coming into the Menorah without any human hand to produce or deliver it. Zachariah asked what this Menorah symbolized and he was told, לֹא בְחַיִל וְלֹא בְכֹחַ כִּי אִם בְּרוּחִי

אָמַר ה' צְבָאוֹת, *Neither through might nor through power, but through My spirit, says HASHEM of legions* (4:6). As the commentators (*Rashi; Radak; Mahari Kara*) explain, Zachariah was told to assure the leaders of Israel, Zerubabel and Joshua the *Kohen Gadol*, that the means to build the Second Temple would be provided by God without need for Jewish interventions or struggles. God would see to it that the Persian kings volunteered all necessary help.

This is the *haftarah* of Chanukah, Harav Feinstein explains, because its message foreshadowed the miracle of Chanukah as well as the entire history of the Second Commonwealth. Almost throughout its existence, Israel was militarily and politically weak, but spiritually and intellectually it thrived, because the fuel for its brilliant light was given it by God. Even when it took up arms, as it was forced to against Syria, its triumph was put in perspective by the miracle of a Menorah whose oil gave light even after it should have been consumed. *Neither through might nor through power, but through My spirit.*

Almost throughout its existence, Israel was militarily and politically weak, but spiritually and intellectually it thrived.

III. Greece is Darkness

A historian without the spiritual perceptions of our Sages would think that darkness is the least apt characterization of the Syrian-Greek domination. Greed, cruelty, oppression, intolerance, impurity, yes — but *darkness?*

Antiochus carried the banner of Greek culture and he was its missionary. His was the wave of progress, of light, surely not of darkness.

Antiochus carried the banner of Greek culture and he was its missionary. His was the wave of progress, of light, surely not of darkness. In his wake came gymnasiums, academies, art, sport, philosophy. He could justly be condemned for the greed with which he looted *Eretz Yisrael* and the Temple to finance his ill-conceived foreign adventures and the gluttonous hedonism of his court. He could be abhorred for slaughtering children and elders who refused to bow to his idols and enjoy the flesh of his sacrifices, castigated for his decrees against the chastity and self-respect of young women and men. But instead of decrying him for such crimes, the Sages chose a

seemingly rhetorical characterization — darkness — which could hardly be more inapt.

If it were only the cruel, mad Antiochus we could agree that the black clouds of his baseness obscured the glimmers of his past.

If it were only the cruel, mad Antiochus who was so described, we could agree that the black clouds of his baseness more than obscured the glimmers of light that he inherited from the Alexanders and Aristotles of his past. But the Sages are far more sweeping. The second verse of *Genesis* tells that before the creation of light, vegetation, and life — when the universe was still a raw, formless mass of unrealized potential — וְהָאָרֶץ הָיְתָה תֹהוּ וָבֹהוּ וְחֹשֶׁךְ, עַל פְּנֵי תְהוֹם, *The earth was astonishingly empty, with darkness upon the surface of the deep.* The Sages perceive this forboding description to refer not only to those temporary primeval conditions, but also to stages in the human condition that man, and particularly Israel, must pass on the road to carrying out the purpose of creation. As *Ramban* (*Genesis* 2:3) sets forth, everything that happened in the first six days of creation is indicative of what would take place in the first six thousand years of the earth's existence.

Just as God created a finished universe from a total vacuum, humanity was to take creation and nurture it through the infinite stages of development that inexorably lead to the completion of God's master plan.

When history has played out its final scene, man will understand the script; until then we can only follow the stage directions set forth in the Torah.

When history has played out its final scene, man will understand the script; until then we can only follow the stage directions set forth in the Torah and the Oral Law. [Major aspects of this idea are discussed at length in *Daas Tevunos* by R' Moshe Chaim Luzatto.]

External Beauty

In analyzing the verse describing the emptiness and desolation of creation's earliest state, the Sages teach that it refers to the four nations under whom Israel would endure exile from the destruction of the First Temple until the ultimate redemption: Babylonia, Persia, Greece, and Rome.

ר׳ שִׁמְעוֹן בֶּן לָקִישׁ פָּתַר קְרָא בְּמַלְכִיּוֹת ...
׳וְחֹשֶׁךְ׳ זוֹ מַלְכוּת יָוָן שֶׁהֶחְשִׁיכוּ עֵינֵיהֶם שֶׁל
יִשְׂרָאֵל בִּגְזֵרוֹתֵיהֶן ...

R' Shimon ben Lakish interpreted the verse with regard to the kingdoms ... [the phrase] 'and darkness' refers to the kingdom of Greece, for it darkened the eyes of Israel with its decrees (Bereishis Rabbah 2:4).

It is inappropriate to say that someone 'created' darkness at *midnight* or prevents a *blind* man from seeing; the conditions of darkness and sightlessness already existed. Only when someone extinguishes an existing light can he be accused of plunging his victim into darkness. During the times when Babylonia, Persia, and Rome enjoyed their greatest power over Israel, our source of spiritual light, the Temple, did not exist. Those nations thrust Israel into emptiness and the deep abyss of hopelessness, but they did not 'darken the eyes of Israel' — Israel's eyes were darkened because its source of light was gone. But the Temple *did* stand during Israel's Grecian exile.

Only when someone extinguishes an existing light can he be accused of plunging his victim into darkness.

Not only that — neither Greeks nor Syrian-Greeks had any plans to destroy the Temple. To the contrary, the people of the Acropolis, amphitheaters, gymnasia, and the pagan temples of Mount Olympus had no grievance against the existence of Israel's Holy Temple as the center of Jewish culture. It was not the *seat* of Jewish culture that galled Greece — it was the *kind* of culture it espoused. Other enemies of Israel might direct their hatred against Jews rather than Judaism, but the nature of Greece required it to do the opposite. The philosophers and Olympians of Greece vented their rage against Israel's stubborn allegiance to the Torah and its teachings.

It was not the seat of Jewish culture that galled Greece — it was the kind of culture it espoused.

More than any other monarch of his dynasty, King Ptolemy II Philadelphius of Egypt respected Israel and he proved his interest by compelling seventy Jewish Sages to translate the Torah into Greek. The product of their labor was the famous Septuagint and it made the Divine wisdom of the Torah available to all. But the Sages mourned. When the Torah was translated יָרְדָה חֹשֶׁךְ לָעֹלָם, *darkness descended to the world* (Megillas Taanis). Why?

King Ptolemy II Philadelphius of Egypt respected Israel but the Sages mourned.

Shem and Yapheth Let us go back to the ancestors of Israel and Greece, Noah's sons Shem and Yapheth. The Torah tells us that Noah became drunk and uncovered himself in his tent — and, even worse, was ridiculed by his own son, Ham. Shem and Yapheth draped a garment over their shoulders and, walking backwards to avoid seeing their father's shame, went into the room and covered him. When Noah learned what had happened, he blesssed his two loyal sons, saying:

יַפְתְּ אֱלֹהִים לְיֶפֶת וְיִשְׁכֹּן בְּאָהֳלֵי שֵׁם

May God extend Yapheth, but He will dwell in the tents of Shem (Genesis 9:27).

Although both Shem and Yapheth did the same compassionate, respectful deed, Noah gave them different blessings. Although both Shem and Yapheth did the same compassionate, respectful deed, Noah gave them different blessings. Obviously Shem's blessing was superior — or was it? Yapheth's boundaries were vastly expanded, it is true: Alexander and his successors ruled the world. His esthetic boundaries, too, were extended. The Talmud (*Megillah* 9b) derives both Yapheth's name and the word with which he was blessed, יַפְתְּ, from יָפֶה, *beautiful.* He was blessed not only with territory but with beauty, and that blessing endures to this day wherever Greek philosophy is studied, Greek plays are performed, and Greek athletic events are emulated. These and other manifestations of Greek culture all flowed from Noah's blessing.

Shem was blessed with none of these. He was rewarded with the promise that God's Presence would find a home in his tents. Abraham, as Shem's primary descendant, produced the nation that accepted the Torah, built the Temples, and remained loyal to their teachings and concepts even in the darkest moments of many exiles.

Mental, no less than physical, gymnastics are essentially superficial in comparison with the Godliness of the Divine Presence. What is the essential difference between the two blessings? Yapheth's was an *external* gift. Mental, no less than physical, gymnastics are essentially superficial in comparison with the Godliness of the Divine Presence. The architect of physical beauty, the composer of scores that meld the talents of a hundred musicians — even the playwright and philosopher — do not approach the inner depth of one whose mind

is engaged with the wisdom of God, whose heart tingles with love of God, whose limbs are sanctified by the acts ordained by God.

Which blessing is greater — Yapheth's or Shem's? the world has more Yapheths than Shems.

Which blessing is greater — Yapheth's or Shem's?

Propriety may require one to say emphatically that Shem's is greater, but is that an honest answer? Coming from the Shems and Abrahams of the world it surely is, but the world has more Yapheths than Shems. Superficial people prefer superficial blessings. That is why Noah allocated his blessings as he did. Although both his sons participated equally in their commendable act, there was a world of difference between them. Yapheth took pains to cover his father's shame because it was *unseemly* that his flesh and blood — *his own father* — should lay about so disgracefully. In today's parlance, Yapheth would have exclaimed horrifiedly, 'What will the neighbors say!'

Surely Shem had that consideration as well, but his driving emotion was more fundamental. His feelings for Noah's honor were deeper and unselfish — and closer to the striving toward the 'image of God' in which man was created. Each was properly rewarded, in keeping with the quality of his deed. Yapheth received a great but superficial blessing, and Shem became the bearer of God's mission.

Yapheth received a great but superficial blessing, and Shem became the bearer of God's mission.

So Ptolemy Philadelphius had the Torah translated. He and his subjects rejoiced that another book had been added to the library shelves of human knowledge, but the Sages grieved, for Ptolemy had divorced the *words* of Torah from its spirit, its deeper, true meaning. Instead of capturing the Oral Law and the soul of the Torah, he ignored them and prided himself in a Septuagint of rolling cadences, social legislation, ritual and history.

Antiochus did not wish to exile the High Priest or destroy the Holy Temple, but let them declaim his culture, worship his gods, eat of his sacrifices.

Antiochus IV, too, had a feel for beauty. He did not wish to exile the High Priest or destroy the Holy Temple. To the contrary — let Jerusalem be a mother city, its Temple a magnet, its *Kohen Gadol* an inspiration, but let them declaim *his* culture, worship *his* gods, eat of *his* sacrifices.

Wisdom, Not Torah

Even vastly different sorts of people do not find themselves in conflict unless their difference are in like matters.

It is a familiar facet of human nature that even vastly different sorts of people do not find themselves in conflict unless their differences are in like matters. Carpenters and engineers, doctors and accountants, physicists and lawyers may be as dissimilar as can be, but their differences seldom cause animosity because their respective courses do not impinge on one another. But two lawyers, or two doctors, or two carpenters, having different opinions about the *same* project can easily reach the point of animosity.

So it was when the offspring of Shem and Yapheth came into conflict. Antiochus and his Syrian-Greeks saw in the Judaism of *Eretz Yisrael* nothing more than another culture, and one that could not compare to the grandeur of Greece. Antiochus had no interest in changing Jewish methods of agriculture, but Jewish wisdom was something he could not countenance — because it was in direct contradiction to his own. His was the wisdom of the body and its was the wisdom of the soul. Judaism

Judaism could not submit to Antiochus, and Antiochus would not acknowledge the superiority of Torah.

could not submit to Antiochus, and Antiochus would not acknowledge the superiority of Torah. The Sages commonly refer to Greek and other cultures, as well as other forms of intellectual activity and applied science, as חָכְמַת חִצוֹנִיוֹת, *external* (or superficial) *knowledge*. This is not to imply that such pursuits are unimportant; rather it must be understood in the light of the Talmudic dictum:

אִם יֹאמַר לְךָ אָדָם יֵשׁ חָכְמָה בַּגּוֹיִם תַּאֲמִין, תּוֹרָה בַּגּוֹיִם אַל תַּאֲמִין

If someone will tell you there is wisdom among the nations — believe it. [If someone will tell you] there is Torah among the nations — do not believe it (Eichah Rabbassi 2:13).

The exercise of intellect and amassing of wisdom are commendable and often essential pursuits, but they are not comparable to the development of *inner* wisdom, the Godly wisdom of Torah for which man was created. The artist who seeks and creates beauty is sensitive and easily moved, but just as he can distort the human body to fit the dictates of style,

dance, or whatever else the contemporary definition of elegance happens to be, so he can distort the mind, mold the conscience, twist morals and values to suit his perception of the 'needs of the times.' Modern political man is proudest of a constitution that allows itself to be reinterpreted and stood on its head. This is good, for no man-made convention, be it in fashion or law, can ever be perfect and therefore it should never be unchangeable. But if the mortal, error-prone humans who do the changing have no rudder of truth to guide them, who is to prevent them from being driven by the tyranny of lust, demagogues, or mobs?

Modern political man is proudest of a constitution that allows itself to be reinterpreted and stood on its head.

The scientist, too, is not immune to a similar, though different, danger. In the human sciences we have learned, sometimes at enormous cost, that yesterday's 'revealed truth' becomes tomorrow's cant, yesterday's guaranteed solutions were the source of today's problems, tinkering and tampering with the social and economic order has often created misery on a vast scale, and the surveys on which public policy is based are often formulated — without malice or dishonesty — in accordance with the deeply held preconvictions of the tester. In the physical sciences man's achievements have not been without awesome moral dilemmas. The ability to terminate, extend, and perhaps even to create life, for example, demands that one have a perspective on the *meaning* of life, otherwise the sanctity of man is exchanged for a collection of organs, electrical impulses, and grist for the mills of experimentation. No wonder intelligent people grapple with the specter of technologies that cannot be controlled by their creators.

In the physical sciences man's achievements have not been without awesome moral dilemmas.

When Yapheth lets his sensitivity and knowledge be guided by the Presence that rests in the tents of Shem, then he too becomes a chariot for God's glory. But if he perceives the Torah as his competitor, he will drag it down to the level of just another ancient literary classic as Ptolemy did, or he will wage war against it as Antiochus did.

When Yapheth perceives the Torah as his competitor, he will drag it down to the level of just another ancient literary classic.

Three　With the reign of Antiochus and the Syrian Greeks,
Targets　a *kulturkampf* came to *Eretz Yisrael*. The Syrian-
Greek bearers of Yapheth's blessing imposed their
culture upon Israel and attempted to destroy its allegiance to God. They defiled the Temple and chose
three commandments as their prime targets: שַׁבָּת,
חֹדֶשׁ, וּמִילָה, *the Sabbath*, the proclamation by the
Sanhedrin of the *New Moon*, and *circumcision*.

The Sabbath is the eternal witness that in six days
God created יֵשׁ מֵאַיִן, existence *from absolute*

If God is the　*nothingness*, and He rested on the seventh. If God is
eternal Creator　the eternal Creator and continuous Resuscitator of
then Greek culture　the universe, and if His Torah formed the blueprint
would have to　and formula for the existence and purpose of Crea-
stand aside.　tion, then Greek culture would have to stand aside
and bow humbly before the tents of Shem. This, Antiochus could not countenance.

The New Moon is　**The New Moon** is the symbol of man's obligation
the symbol of　to instill holiness into time, for when the Sanhedrin
man's obligation to　proclaims Rosh Chodesh it makes possible the time-
instill holiness into　related festivals like Rosh Hashanah and Passover
time.　that cannot exist without a calendar. Man's power to
proclaim the New Moon proves that time, the symbol of nature's tyranny over man, can be subjugated.
When the Sanhedrin hallows the New Moon, the
festivals — the appointed meeting places in time
between God and man — enter the calendar and raise
it from a record of material pursuit and struggle to a
vehicle of holiness. Antiochus had to fight this concept, for it meant that culture had value only as a
means toward a higher purpose.

Circumcision demonstrates that the physical and
The body must　the spiritual must be intertwined. The body must
bear the mark of　bear the mark of allegiance to God's covenant, the
allegiance to God's　restraining mark that says, 'You are a servant, not a
covenant.　master; you are host to a soul and you must elevate
yourself to its exalted level. Beauty and pleasure are
not the independent virtues Antiochus says they are.
They are regulated by the Torah or they are nothing.'

A world without a Creator, a calendar without
holiness, a body without restraint — these were the
goals of a culture that had accepted the gifts but not

the goals of Noah's blessing to Yapheth, a culture of grace and splendor covering a corrosive emptiness. To this had the potential of Yapheth's beauty been pulled down.

Small wonder that the Midrash comments that the primeval חֹשֶׁךְ, *darkness*, (1:2) signifies יָוָן, Greece. A tragic miscarriage of purpose! Greece should have placed its culture at the service of Shem, used it to help provide a glorious dwelling place for the Divine Presence. Instead, its splendor became darkness.

it did w. P.

Of all the periods described as exiles, only that of Greece took place while Israel was in its land and the Temple stood. Thus, in a sense it was the most damaging kind of exile, for it happened when Israel's potential for greatness was highest, when it could have illuminated the world, especially since the vaults of the Oral Torah had been opened wide. Over this splendor, Antiochus cast his impure pall. This was darkness.

And this was why the victory of the Hasmoneans was symbolized both at the time and in our annual commemoration by the flames of the Menorah, the glow of Torah, the spiritual presence that illuminated the tents of Shem — whether they are on the Temple Mount or in the humblest Jewish home that holds the Torah sacred.

IV. Understanding Chanukah

What Was Won?

The only victory won by Yehudah and his brothers was the right to resume the Temple service and to practice their religion.

Let us not forget that the Hasmoneans had *not* won their independence when they proclaimed the festival of Chanukah. As the History of Chanukah shows (see next section of this book), the *only* victory won by Yehudah and his brothers was the right to resume the Temple service and to practice their religion. Not only was Antiochus still their ruler, his Syrian troops and Jewish-Hellenist lackeys still occupied *Eretz Yisrael* and even most of Jerusalem. Many bloody battles and more than a generation would pass before Shimon, the only Maccabee not

The margin note: • *Of all the periods described as exiles, only that of Greece took place while Israel was in its land and the Temple stood.*

killed in war, was proclaimed ruler of *Eretz Yisrael* and more years went by pass before his son Yochanan Hyrkanos declared himself free of any foreign domination.

Nevertheless, the Sages declared the festival of Chanukah after the miracle of the oil, even though Israel did not enjoy independence or political and military ascendancy. And even after Shimon and Yochanon won independence, our festival remains a commemoration of the miracle of lights.

Even after Shimon and Yochanon won independence, our festival remains a commemoration of the miracle of lights.

Why a celebration while still under foreign rule? Because Israel knew that the goal of the Second Temple era was the kingdom of Torah and the commandments — and the kindling of a small Menorah that could banish the darkness of Greece. When that happened, it was time to celebrate; let the eventual triumphs of diplomats and generals be greeted with joy and then consigned to the historians.

If this is the significance of Chanukah, then its proper observance demands an uncommon degree of serious thought into the true nature and lesson of the miracle. *Sfas Emes* notes the halachah that if one was unable to light or participate in the lighting of the Menorah, and then he sees someone else's Menorah, he may recite two of the Chanukah blessings: 1) שֶׁעָשָׂה נִסִּים לַאֲבוֹתֵינוּ, *Who did miracles for our ancestors*; and 2) *Shehecheyanu*, the blessing of thanks to God for permitting us to live to enjoy this new event in our own lives.

That the first blessing may be recited *only* upon seeing Chanukah flames is quite logical; the flames are our tangible means of publicizing the fact that such miracles occurred. But it is surprising that the *Shehecheyanu* blessing may not be recited unless one sees the flames. In the case of other festivals, even if one is ח״ו placed in a situation where he cannot pray or observe any of the festival commandments, he still recites that blessing in thanks for the mere arrival of the holy day.

Merely being alive on the twenty-fifth of Kislev is not enough; one must see the flame, remember what it represents.

It would appear that Chanukah is different. Merely being alive on the twenty-fifth of Kislev is not enough; one must *see* the flame, *remember* what it

represents, *know* that we are grateful for the triumph of Torah's light over Greece's darkness.

In that early verse in *Genesis* that alludes to the Four Kingdoms, the Torah says וְחֹשֶׁךְ עַל פְּנֵי תְהוֹם, *and darkness was on the surface of the deep.* Apparently there is a connection between the darkness of Greece and the תְּהוֹם שֶׁאֵין לָהּ חֵקֶר, *the [apparently] endless depths* of the Roman exile. Rome was epitomized by brute, selfish force rather than pseudo-enlightenment, but the Torah seems to be suggesting that even the unfathomable deep is more chilling if it is blanketed with darkness.

Even the unfathomable deep is more chilling if it is blanketed with darkness.

The heroic Jews of the Hasmonean era dispelled darkness with the light of Torah. May we be granted the wisdom and the courage to 'see' the Menorah they kindled, to thank God for allowing us to be guided by the Divine wisdom it symbolizes — and to let its lesson illuminate our road to the final redemption.

Nosson Scherman

ב׳ מרחשון תשמ״ב

❧ Background:

A History of the Chanukah Period

✑§ Preface

The central events of the Chanukah story are the miracle of the one-day supply of pure olive oil that burned for eight days, and the military victory of the weak over the mighty, the few over the many, the pure over the impure, the righteous over the wicked. That triumph was climaxed, as the Chanukah liturgy stresses, with the liberation and purification of the Temple after its desecration and contamination by the Syrian-Greek forces of King Antiochus IV. The miracle of the lights is commemorated in the ritual observance of Chanukah, for the Sages ordained that every Jewish home attest to the miracle by lighting the Menorah night after night for eight nights, and the miraculous victory over the foe is the subject of עַל הַנִּסִּים [Al HaNissim], the liturgical thanksgiving that is inserted into the Chanukah prayers.

In the popular mind, the celebration of Chanukah is linked with the establishment of an independent Jewish state under the Hasmonean kings — a Jewish state unsurpassed in size, influence, and power since the days of David and Solomon. Indeed, as outlined in "The Dating of Chanukah" (p. 81), this view is held by many of the early chroniclers. However the most detailed and completely documented history of the period available to us — the books of Maccabees (also known as Chashmonaim) I and II and Josephus Flavius' Antiquities — show quite the contrary*. Although the events of Chanukah were surely the catalyst that led to the eventual establishment of a powerful Hasmonean dynasty, it was not until many years after the miracle that Israel became an independent, powerful nation. The victory of the Hasmonean brothers at the time of Chanukah was not total, nor did it even succeed in removing Syrian-Greek influence from Eretz Yisrael.

What, then, did occur on Chanukah? If independence was still far off, why did the Sages ordain a festival? What is the historical mosaic in which the Chanukah miracle took place? What happened before it and what happened afterward?

---

* See "The Dating of Chanukah" (p. 81) for a full discussion of both these views. This approach in our history is the one held by the ancient chronicle *Seder Olam Zuta* and is adopted by most history texts used in Orthodox schools. Although *Doros HaRishonim,* by R' Yitzchok Isaac HaLevi, does not deal with the Chanukah period, it is clear tht he too held that view (see vol. I, pp. 168,177, ed. Israel). In his discussions with this writer, *Maran Harav Yaakov Kaminetzky,* שליט"א, concurred with this approach.

Through an understanding of the history of the period, we can gain a deeper insight into the significance of Chanukah itself. With this goal, we shall approach our historical inquiry into the events of the period.

For information, we are indebted primarily to the books of Maccabees I and II the authors of which lived relatively close to the time of the miracle (in the case of I Maccabees), or drew upon contemporary sources. The authorship of these books is unknown, but they were undoubtedly written by staunchly loyal Jews. Although there is evidence that I Maccabees was originally written in Hebrew, both books were available only in Greek and Latin for over 1500 years and came down to us through gentile hands. For this reason, the two books were largely unknown to Jewish chroniclers and commentators until fairly recent times. The first known Hebrew translation was not published until 5590 (1830) in Kesuvim Acharonim. Despite the fact that the books of Maccabees are not mentioned in virtually any early classic Rabbinic work, we may assume that Jewish scholars would have accepted them, because they are cited by the great commentator to the Mishnah, R' Yom Tov Lipmann Heller (Tosefos Yom Tov, Megillah 3:6), and by the great halachist R' Eliyah Shapiro of Prague in his magnum opus Eliyah Rabbah to Orach Chaim 671:1. I know of only three other relatively early Jewish scholars who had access to Maccabees: R' Azariah min HaAdomim (De Rossi) in his Me'or Einayim; (Imrei Binah ch. 16, 25, 26, 51, 55); and the disciple of R' Moshe Isserles (רמ״א), R' David Ganz (in Tzemach David, part I, year 3590). Nevertheless, it is fair to assume that such scholars would not have cited the books of Maccabees unless they were convinced of its reliability.[11]

The reader should bear in mind that the period of Scripture was sealed prior to the events of Chanukah. No later book, even if it were historically accurate and true to the underlying spiritual theme of the events it chronicled, could have been canonized. Consequently, the status of Maccabees as an apocryphal work does not, in and of itself, prove that it is not reliable.

[Josephus Flavius' account of this era is probably based on the books of Maccabees (see Antiquities 12:5-13:7), but his books, too, were not available in Hebrew until modern times and were thus not available to most Jewish scholars. The Hebrew counterpart of Josephus — Yossipon — contains much material found in Maccabees, but dates are lacking and in some places the historical sequence is different, thus making it difficult if not impossible to use Yossipon as an exclusive source for the recreation of a historical framework.]

We have also referred to Megillas Taanis, whenever possible. Composed by Chananiah ben Chizkiah ben Garon around the time

of the Second Temple's Destruction (Shabbos 13b), it is an authoritative chronicle of minor festivals that were observed in commemoration of miracles performed on behalf of the Jewish people. [Megillas Taanis is cited by the Mishnah (Taanis 2:8) and is quoted extensively by the Talmud (Taanis 17b-18b; Rosh Hashanah 18b-19a; Yoma 69a; and Shabbos 13b, 21b). The Talmud (Rosh Hashanah 19b) concludes that the post-Temple Sages abrogated observance of the holidays enumerated in Megillas Taanis, except for Chanukah and Purim.] Several events that occurred during the battles of the Hasmoneans against the Syrian-Greeks are recorded in Megillas Taanis and we have drawn upon it, where possible, for our chronicle of this period.

It must be mentioned that there are discrepancies among the various sources and that the dating system used in ancient times was much different from contemporary dating systems. In "The Dating of Chanukah," p. 84, footnote 1, we will explain briefly the method used to synchronize the calendar of Maccabees with the contemporary one. We shall also endeavor to show that the time frame assigned by Maccabees to the Chanukah story does not conflict with that given in the Talmud and Seder Olam Rabbah. To further assist the reader in understanding the events of Chanukah in the context of the general history of the era, we have appended a table of important dates of the Second Temple era (p. 90).

In the books of the later prophets, world history is envisioned as consisting of four epochs, in each of which a major power holds sway over *Eretz Yisrael* and the Jewish nation. These 'Four Kingdoms' are: (1) Babylon; (2) Medea and Persia; (3) Greece;

Alexander the Great and his Successors

and (4) Edom-Rome. These four periods will be followed by a fifth, in which the world will achieve perfection and the Kingdom of God will be established by the King Messiah.

Ramban (Genesis 10:4) explains that the concept of the Four Kingdoms is not meant to embrace all of mankind's history, but is to include, in outline form, the history of the Jewish exile. Therefore only the kingdoms considered responsible for the exile are mentioned. Other nations, no matter how great their might, are not named. The era of the Second Temple is considered part of

this exile for several reasons: most of the Jews did not return to the Holy Land, the Temple was not rebuilt to perfection, the *Shechinah* [Divine Presence] was missing, and for the greater part of this period the Jews were not autonomous (see *Ramban* to *Leviticus* 26:23). Babylon, responsible for the first exile, is the first of the Four Kingdoms. Persia, successor to the Babylonian empire, is considered the second kingdom and Greece the third, because it succeeded Persia. Rome is identified as the fourth kingdom for two reasons: Its conquests included *Eretz Yisrael*, the center of Jewry; it was directly responsible for the subsequent exile from the Holy Land.

So long as no new empire arises which, by its conquests, can be considered successor *in toto* to Rome's power, we are still considered to be mired in the 'Roman' exile. Though Islam later conquered *Eretz Yisrael*, the Arabic empire did not succeed Rome in the scope of its conquest. Furthermore, Rome's influence in the formation of Arab and Turkish empires also allows them to be considered extensions or outgrowths of the Roman empire. *Abarbanel* (*Mashmia Yeshuah* 3:7) points to the influence of Christianity in the formation of Islam as another factor in considering this exile to be an extension of Rome's.

According to the commentators, in the heavenly vision seen by Daniel and explained by the angel (*Daniel* chap. 7), Rome undergoes a metamorphosis from the secular power of the old empire into the religious power of Christianity. The struggling faith adopted by the mighty empire, originally by Emperor Constantine I and later by his successors, grew up to utilize its unique position as state religion of the Roman Empire and moved on to a period of unprecedented growth. Its power, whether temporal or spiritual, eclipsed that of kingdoms and empires. Thus throughout our exile, the Fourth Kingdom is represented by the Christian Church, conceived of, despite all its diverse forms, as one unit (see ArtScroll comm. to *Daniel* 2:40).

The third of these epochs was ushered in by Alexander the Great's meteoric conquest of the Persian Empire and the entire civilized world. Although he originated in Macedon, north of Greece, the Sages regard Alexander as the initiator of the Greek kingdom, because Greece was his power base and because he spread its culture in the wake of his conquests. Divine Providence willed that much of the Second Temple era be spent under the Greek hegemony of Alexander and his successors. Some commentators find allusion to this in Noah's blessing to Japheth, the primogenitor of the Greek tribes: יַפְתְּ אֱלֹקִים לְיֶפֶת וְיִשְׁכֹּן בְּאָהֳלֵי שֵׁם, *May God*

extend Japheth, but he will dwell in the tents of Shem (Genesis 9:27). Abarbanel interprets this as a reference to the Japhethian Alexander's expanding boundaries, that eventually made him master of the Temple, the tent of Shem's primary descendants, Israel. Indeed, the Sages understand that the Greek rule over the Temple was to repay Japheth for the honor he did Noah, his father, at the time of the latter's humiliation at the hands of Ham (Midrash Zuta, see ArtScroll Genesis 9:23-27).

Eretz Yisrael at the time was in the shaky control of the newly established Jewish communities built by returnees from the Babylonian Exile, who were still subjects of the Persian Empire. They had recently rebuilt the Temple, in 3408 (353 B.C.E.), with the permission of the Persian kings Cyrus and Darius, but the young, struggling Jewish community was by no means secure. Surrounded by hostile enemies, it was subject to their constant aggression and political intrigue. Although Alexander easily conquered Eretz Yisrael and there were people in his entourage who sought to persuade him to make drastic restrictions in the freedom of the Jews and the Temple service, a miracle occurred that caused the monarch to grant special dispensations to Eretz Yisrael in general and the needs of the Temple in particular.

The Talmud (Yoma 69a; Tamid 27b; and Megillas Taanis ch. 10) relates that Shimon HaTzaddik, the Kohen Gadol [High Priest], led a delegation of elders to greet Alexander as he advanced upon Jerusalem at the head of his army. Upon seeing Shimon, Alexander dismounted and prostrated himself. To his astonished men, the great conqueror explained that every time he went into battle, he would see an apparition in the likeness of this Kohen Gadol leading the Greek troops to victory. To Alexander it was clear that all his conquests were due to the saintly Shimon, resplendent in the sacred vestments of the Kohen Gadol, who stood at the head of the army. God had shown Alexander this vision to assure that he would not treat Israel as just another vassal state, but as the repository of enormous spiritual power.

The Talmud continues that Alexander asked Shimon why such an impressive array of elders had gone to the trouble of meeting him at the approaches to Jerusalem. Shimon answered, 'Can it be that idolaters will convince you to destroy the Temple where we pray that you and your empire not be destroyed?'

Outraged, Alexander asked who would dare conspire to destroy the Temple. Shimon pointed at the king's Cuthean [Samaritan] advisors who were sworn enemies of the Jews. That marked the end

of the long string of Cuthean conspiracies and harassment of the Jews. Josephus Flavius *(Antiquities* 11:8) adds that Alexander canceled Jewish taxes during Sabbatical years and gave animals to be sacrificed on his behalf in the Temple.

Benevolent though Alexander was to the Jews, his conquest is regarded as the start of the Greek Exile, because from that time on, the Jewish inhabitants of *Eretz Yisrael* were under the dominion of exponents of Greek culture.

At the zenith of his life and with all the world at his feet, Alexander the Great died a sudden and untimely death at the age of only thirty-three. No successor was powerful enough to hold the entire kingdom together, so Alexander's vast empire was divided among his four leading generals in 3448 (313 B.C.E.).

Ptolemy I took Egypt as his fiefdom while Seleucus I founded the Seleucid dynasty, which ruled Syria. *Eretz Yisrael* became part of Seleucus' territory, but, geographically, it was a buffer between the two newly founded kingdoms of Egypt and Syria, and, like many small states situated between large, ambitious ones, it was to suffer from the caprices of both. Before long, Alexander's heirs began quarreling among themselves. Antigonas, ruler of Asia Minor, wanted to annex Babylonia, Iraq and the neighboring lands, *Eretz Yisrael* among them, to his kingdom. War broke out between him and Seleucus. The Syrian king was forced to seek an alliance with Egypt. Ptolemy and Seleucus defeated Antigonas at Gaza in 3448 (313 B.C.E.), but as the price of Ptolemy's assistance, Seleucus was forced to cede *Eretz Yisrael* to Egypt.

In general, the Jews suffered much under the oppressive Ptolemaic regime. The only exception was the comparatively benevolent reign of Ptolemy II (Philadelphius) under whom there was a brief respite. It was under him that seventy Jewish sages were compelled to translate the Torah into Greek, as related by the Talmud *(Megillah* 9a; see also *Soferim* 1:8, *Megillas Taanis* ch. 10, *Yossipon* ch. 17, *Antiquities* 12:2). The translation is known as the Septuagint.

We do not know exactly how *Eretz Yisrael* was governed under the Ptolemies. Since Egypt's major concern was the collection of tribute and taxes, it is reasonable to assume that the Jews had a great deal of autonomy over local matters. The *Kohen Gadol* was held responsible for tax collection, which implies that he had considerable secular powers and that he headed the existing administrative and executive apparatus. Shimon HaTzaddik held both of Israel's major offices, as *Kohen Gadol* [High Priest] and *Av*

Beis Din [President of the Great Sanhedrin of seventy-one members]. The fact that two such august offices were invested in one person naturally lent him great stature and strengthened the impression of foreign rulers that the *Kohen Gadol* was supreme both in matters of faith and in secular administration. This impression was to become pivotal in the years leading up to the Hasmonean rebellion and the Chanukah miracle. Naturally, many or most internal matters were under the jurisdiction of the Great Sanhedrin (see *Doros HaRishonim* vol. I, p. 182, ed. Israel).

A lthough the Jewish community in *Eretz Yisrael* at this time was considerable, it was by no means the preponderant majority in the land, especially since the majority of the Jews had chosen to stay in Babylon rather than return to their ancestral lands. The heaviest Jewish concentration was in the Jerusalem region, and many towns, especially in the coastal regions, were peopled primarily by gentiles. Samaria was populated by the Cutheans [Samaritans], sworn enemies of the Jewish nation. The Jewish community itself was fragmented by various ideologies, and its members had to have continuous contact with the heathen world surrounding it.

Seeds of Destruction — Hellenizers and Sadducees

Naturally, one result of such contact, then as in all generations, was that many weak Jews would try to emulate the gentile culture surrounding them and to appear more Grecian than the Greeks, with a parallel weakening of their commitment to Torah and its values. This tendency, known as Hellenism [from *Hellas,* the ancient Greek name for Greece], was strongest in the upper strata of society — the rich and those in the employ of the heathen government. It must be remembered that during the Babylonian Exile of the not too distant past, intermarriage had been rampant in this group, and the observance of the Sabbath and some other *mitzvos* surprisingly lax (see *Ezra* chs. 9-10, *Nechemiah* chs. 9-10, 13). Only the influence of personages as Ezra, Nechemiah and others of their stature — the Sages of the Great Assembly (אַנְשֵׁי כְּנֶסֶת הַגְּדוֹלָה) — had been able to stem the tide and insure the continuity of Jewish life at that time.

The Sages set up safeguards to control and limit the influence of the alien surroundings. The prohibitions against using food cooked by gentiles and wine handled by them — aimed at curtailing social

intercourse — were promulgated in this period, but even they could not entirely eradicate the problem. [See *Avodah Zarah* 35b, *Chiddushei HaRamban* there; ArtScroll to *Daniel* 1:8.] Such precautions had not been necessary in the First Temple era, and during the early years of the Second Temple. As long as Shimon HaTzaddik — the last remaining member of the Great Assembly, head of the Sanhedrin and *Kohen Gadol* — was alive, he was able to inspire his people to remain at the spiritual plane to which his predecessors had elevated them (see *Yoma* 39a), but with his demise, a spiritual regression set in and the negative influences began to make inroads.

Shimon HaTzaddik's successor as head of the Sanhedrin was his illustrious disciple Antigonas (*Avos* 1:3). It was during the latter's tenure that the Hellenistic tendency was provided with an ideology to cloak the transgression of the Torah in the garb of respectability. This heresy in sheep's clothing was spearheaded by none other than two of Antigonas' own disciples, Zaddok and Boethus [צָדוֹק וּבַיְתוֹס], whose followers were called Sadducees and Boethusians [צְדוֹקִים וּבַיְתוֹסִים]. They declared their belief that there was no retribution for sin nor reward for virtue in the World to Come; indeed they denied its existence. The logical conclusion of this philosophy was that one's first priority should be the pursuit of self-gratification in this world (*Avos* 1:3, *Avos D' Rabbi Nasssan* ch. 5). They denied both the validity of the Oral Tradition and the authority of the Sages to interpret the Torah and to promulgate decrees. Consequently, they refused to accept any law not stated explicitly in the Torah.

This so-called theology was only a front for the real aim of this movement — total abrogation of the Torah. By denying the authority of the Sages, they robbed the Torah of any definitive meaning, and gave the individual's transgression of the Torah an aura of legitimacy (see *Rambam's* comm. to *Mishnah, Avos* 1:3). Josephus Flavius' description of the Sadducees (*Wars* 2:8:14) implies that basically they were irreligious. No doubt, at this period of history they swelled the ranks of the Hellenists from whom they did not differ to a great extent.[2]

During the rule of Ptolemy III Euergetes (3515-40/246-221 B.C.E.), an event occurred that was to have far-reaching political implications and would strengthen the Hellenists. From the

beginning of the Greek period, the Ptolemies had regarded the

The Children of Toviyah

Kohen Gadol as the Jewish people's representative to them. As much autonomy as was allowed their subject peoples was vested in him. As noted above (see preface) this impression was based on the great prestige of Shimon HaTzaddik. The Greek rulers held the *Kohen Gadol* responsible for the collection of taxes, a responsibility that presupposes a governmental bureaucracy possessing a police arm, without which it is impossible to collect taxes. In addition, many other governmental functions were performed by the apparatus headed by the *Kohen Gadol*. Shimon HaTzaddik (son of Chonyo I) was succeeded by his brother Elazar *(Ant.* 12:2:5) who was succeeded by another brother, Menasheh *(Ant.* 12:4:1). After Menasheh's death, the *Kehunah Gedolah* [High Priesthood] reverted to Shimon's son, Chonyo II (ibid.; see *Menachos* 109a-b; R' S. Rottenberg, *Toldos Am Olam,* vol. 2, p. 111). Thus, when Ptolemy Euergetes made his annual demands for taxes from the Jews, his notification was sent to Chonyo.

One year Chonyo refused to pay the tribute. Why he did so is not clear. Josephus claims that his motive was simple greed; one version of Josephus has it that his father and uncles had customarily paid the national tribute out of their personal fortunes, apparently to spare their people this onerous burden *(Ant.* 12:4:1). Neither contention seems valid. The annual tribute was twenty talents of silver (approx. 28.8 kg.) and it seems most unlikely that any *Kohen Gadol* could pay from his own pocket every single year what was a huge fortune in ancient times. Furthermore, since the penalty for non-payment would be an Egyptian invasion and severe reprisals — as, indeed, Ptolemy threatened to impose when informed of Chonyo's refusal — it would seem to have been foolish beyond belief to have taken such a risk by avoiding the payment of taxes. Some modern historians theorize that Chonyo favored a takeover of *Eretz Yisrael* by the Seleucid kings of Syria and hoped to provoke it by antagonizing Egypt. In any case, while we do not know the reason for Chonyo's resistance, it is clear that Ptolemy regarded it as tantamount to rebellion and threatened to invade Judea and punish its inhabitants.

In this dangerous situation, Chonyo's nephew, Joseph ben Toviyah volunteered to meet with the irate king and to placate him with extravagant presents. Joseph succeeded greatly in his mission; not only did he remove the threat of military sanctions by the government, but he also obtained from the king the right to collect

the taxes for the entire region, including the whole of *Eretz Yisrael*, and Phoenicia (Lebanon).

This was more than a diplomatic triumph for Joseph; it was a highly profitable arrangement for him. In ancient times, an entrepreneur purchased the right to collect taxes. He would pay the king a fixed amount, and keep any excess collections. Unscrupulous people collected exorbitant amounts for personal profit. Joseph, unfortunately, was such a person. To facilitate the collections, Ptolemy provided a battalion of 3,000 soldiers, and Joseph did not hesitate to use this force to demonstrate his resoluteness.

The first city he visited was Ashkelon on the border of *Eretz Yisrael*. When the townspeople refused to admit him, he captured twenty of its most prominent citizens and had them hanged. He punished ruthlessly the citizens of other towns when they refused to pay the extortionate tax placed upon them. In this manner, he terrorized the entire region and raised the tax collection to seven times what it had been. Thus with one swoop Joseph had usurped a degree of power not possessed by any of the previously recognized local authorities and completely stripped the office of *Kohen Gadol* of its governmental function. A new bureaucracy of tax collectors, (מוֹכְסִין) culled in the main from the ranks of the Hellenists, arose in the name of the king, and terrorized and oppressed their own countrymen. This sort of behavior explains why the Talmud condemns most tax collectors as thieves. It is quite proper to collect legally imposed taxes, but not to use force to extort money for personal gain.

The Seleucids

In the year 199 B.C.E. (3562) Antiochus III the Great, a scion of the Seleucid dynasty, defeated the armies of Ptolemy V Philopator, and detached Judea and Phoenicia from Egyptian domination. The Jews welcomed Antiochus, for they were weary of the oppressive reign of the Ptolemies.

The rule of Antiochus III was benevolent in comparison to the persecution the Jews had suffered under Ptolemy III and IV. Israel welcomed Antiochus and assisted him in his siege of the Egyptian garrison stationed in the citadel in Jerusalem (*Ant.* 12:3:3). He granted special privileges to the Jewish inhabitants of Jerusalem and exempted the *Kohanim* from certain taxes. He set aside a yearly stipend for sacrifices and provided for the completion of parts of the Temple complex that were under

construction at this time. Antiochus III was succeeded by his son Seleucus IV (3574-86/187-75 B.C.E.). Under him the simmering rivalry between the Hellenizers and Torah-true Jewry erupted into outright confrontation, starting the process that became the catalyst for Antiochus IV's oppression of the Jewish religion and brought - about the Hasmonean struggle for independence.

At this time, Chonyo II, Shimon HaTzaddik's son, had long been dead, and his successor, Shimon II, was also no longer alive. The latter's son, Chonyo III, was a righteous man who hated all evildoers; he was a worthy successor to the post once held by his revered great-grandfather, Shimon HaTzaddik (II Macc. 3:1). Chonyo aroused the enmity of a Temple official named Shimon of the tribe of Benjamin, when he opposed the latter's bid to administer the markets of Jerusalem. No doubt Shimon was but one of many officials appointed under Joseph ben Toviyah's scandalous rule, and had been the victim of a campaign by the saintly new *Kohen Gadol* to do away with the venality and extortion that were Joseph's legacy (see *Doros HaRishonim*, vol. 1, p. 186). Seeking vengeance, Shimon went to Apollonius, the Syrian governor of Phoenicia, and informed him that the Temple treasury contained fabulous amounts of money over and above the amount needed for its maintenance and the purchase of sacrifices. Shimon unctuously suggested that these excess funds could very well be used by the king. When King Seleucus was informed about this windfall, he dispatched Heliodorus, one of his trusted officials, to confiscate the Temple treasury.

Upon arriving in Jerusalem, Heliodorus immediately disclosed to Chonyo, the *Kohen Gadol*, the purpose of his visit. Chonyo remonstrated that the richness of the treasury had been grossly exaggerated, and that most of the funds belonged to widows and orphans, and were held in the Temple treasury for safekeeping. Chonyo argued that it would be sacrilegious to despoil the Holy Temple. However, Heliodorus refused to be dissuaded and made known his intention to enter the Temple and despoil its treasury.

When the *Kohanim* heard of this they prostrated themselves before the Altar and beseeched Heaven to spare them this desecration of the Temple. The people of Jerusalem assembled in throngs to offer supplication and the women donned sackcloth. The ashen color of the *Kohen Gadol* and the pained expression on his face showed clearly the anguish he was enduring.

When Heliodorus attempted to enter the Temple, a miracle happened. A divine apparition in the form of a horse with an armed

rider rushed at him and struck him with its forefeet. Two young men appeared and flogged him mercilessly. He fell down unconscious and had to be carried away deathly sick. To the Jews it was clear that God had heeded their prayers for the honor of His Temple, but Chonyo knew full well that Seleucus would think otherwise. Chonyo hastened to offer sacrifices for Heliodorus' recovery so that Seleucus would not suspect the Jews of foul play. Upon recovering, Heliodorus hastened back to the king and attested to him about the Divine power that guarded the Temple in Jerusalem.

Shimon and his party refused to be fazed by this miracle and asserted before the king that Chonyo had influenced Heliodorus to fabricate the entire incident. The rivalry between Chonyo's people and Shimon's men rose to such a pitch that the latter did not stop even at murder. At that point Chonyo felt it was his responsibility to bring the affair to a head and call the king's attention to Shimon's machinations. Unfortunately, just at this time, Seleucus was assassinated (3586/175 B.C.E.) and succeeded by his younger brother Antiochus IV Epiphanes.

Antiochus and the Kehunah Gedolah

Antiochus IV was a man of great ambition, hoping to expand his realm as his father had done, and planning to impose Greek culture and religion as a unifying force on his polyglot empire. He was vain to the extent that his coinage carried the legend 'Antiochus Theos Epiphanes' [God Made Manifest]. His character was unstable; he was given to extremes of cruelty and generosity. He introduced the barbaric Roman custom of gladiatorial games to Syria. In his private life he indulged in hedonist excesses. He would leave his throne at banquets to dance naked with the entertainers. Because of his mad antics, the people called him Epimanes, the Mad One, instead of his illustrious official name, Epiphanes, the Divinely Manifest.

The Hellenizers, no doubt aware of the new king's leanings, now managed to usurp even the spiritual function of the Kehunah Gedolah. Yeshua, a brother of Chonyo, who had Hellenized his name to Jason, offered Antiochus a generous bribe to depose Chonyo and appoint him Kohen Gadol. He promised the king another payment of tribute if he would authorize the erection of a gymnasium for the youth of Jerusalem and if he would consider the

people of Jerusalem honorary citizens of Antioch, the Syrian capital. Having secured the king's appointment, Yeshua/Jason immediately set his program into motion. He established a gymnasium in close proximity to the Temple, and cultivated the pagan customs and mores of the Greek rulers to such an extent that even the *Kohanim* began to neglect the sacrificial service in favor of Jason's new centers of diversion.

Although the gymnasium was used primarily for athletics, it was a vehicle of paganism and licentiousness. The exercises were performed naked (Josephus informs us that the Jewish youth attending these places took pains to disguise the 'covenant of Abraham' — circumcision). Before games were held, sacrifices were offered to Heracles (Hercules). It seems that in order to qualify as Antiochenes (honorary citizens of Antioch), a privilege which no doubt carried with it many social and economic advantages, Jews had to demonstrate their total acceptance of Greek ways and culture. Surprisingly, even Jason's excesses were too mild to satisfy the more extreme Jewish Hellenists.

Three years passed and the time came for Jason to pay his tribute to Antiochus. As his emissary to the king, he sent Menelaus, Shimon's brother. Menelaus, no doubt upon the instigation of the Hellenizing party for whom even Jason's policies were too moderate, made use of this opportunity to offer the king an even greater payment to appoint him — Menelaus — *Kohen Gadol*. Having secured the king's appointment, Menelaus, who was not even a *Kohen*, proceeded ruthlessly to oppress his people and to persecute the Jewish religion. Menelaus and his brother Lysimachus, who acted as his deputy, appropriated the golden vessels of the Holy Temple and sold them to raise the money they needed for tribute. When Chonyo, the lawful *Kohen Gadol* (who had been deposed previously by Jason), protested this act, they had him murdered with the connivance of the authorities in Antioch. Jason apparently offered no resistance to his deposer, and bided his time, waiting for a propitious moment to return to power.

Alarmed at the turn of events, the people of Jerusalem began to express their dissatisfaction. Lysimachus, fearing an organized revolt, fell upon the people with an armed band of 3,000 soldiers. The people, however, fought the soldiers with stones and sticks. In the fracas Lysimachus was killed. The Sanhedrin sent three of its members to Antioch to accuse Menelaus before the king as the instigator of these troubles. Menelaus was in great danger of being found guilty, but he managed to bribe a close advisor to the king,

who characteristically saw to it not only that Menelaus was acquitted but that the three sages were condemned to death. Menelaus retained his post and persisted in his cruel ways.

Antiochus Despoils the Holy Temple

At this time Antiochus attacked and conquered Egypt (3592/169 B.C.E.), but he failed to reckon with Rome, which had become the strongest power in the region. Rome opposed an extension of Syrian power and was strong enough to intimidate Antiochus. A Roman ambassador gave him an ultimatum either to withdraw from Egypt or face attack from Rome. Antiochus retreated ignominiously. Rumors had been circulating in Jerusalem that the king had been killed in the Egyptian campaign, and Jason, taking advantage of this, attacked the city with a thousand men. He was able to penetrate the walls and Menelaus' forces had to retreat and take refuge in the citadel.

Known as the 'Acra', the citadel was a strong fortification near the Temple site. It probably corresponded to the עִיר דָּוִד, *fort of David* (*II Samuel* 5:7; see *Targum* there), of Biblical times (see *Megillas Taanis* 23 Iyar). However, some modern scholars feel it was in the northeastern corner of the upper city, i.e., near the southwestern corner of the Temple Mount enclosure.

Jason entered the city and perpetrated a massacre upon its inhabitants, although they were his own countrymen. Antiochus, not yet back from Egypt, was informed of these happenings and interpreted Jason's attack as a revolt against the throne. Enraged, he stormed up from Egypt and easily took the city which, not expecting a military action, opened its gates to him. He ordered his soldiers indiscriminately to kill men, women, and children. Forty thousand were killed and an equal number taken into captivity. Jason fled Jerusalem and died a fugitive.

Antiochus brazenly entered the Temple and despoiled it of its gold and silver. He entered the Holy and removed the holy vessels, the gold Altar, the *Menorah*, the Table for the *Panim* bread, the curtain (פָּרֹכֶת), and the gold ornamentation with which the front of the Temple was decorated. Menelaus was reinstated as *Kohen Gadol* and oppressed his people even more cruelly than did Antiochus.

After an interval of two years Antiochus sent Apollonius, the commander of the Mysians,[3] to Jerusalem, with an army of 22,000

soldiers. He gained admittance to the city without a struggle, for the people did not suspect his intention. Once inside, he attacked the people and massacred great numbers of them.

The soldiers destroyed the houses and the walls encompassing and guarding the city, plundering and murdering. Women and children were taken captive. Apollonius' men fortified the Acra and garrisoned it with Syrian soldiers and traitorous Jews. Until its fall to the Hasmoneans many years later, it remained a physical threat to the Jews and a danger to the neighboring Temple. In their fury against the Temple as the symbol of Judaism, the Syrians made thirteen breaches in the wall encompassing the Temple court.[4]

The king issued a declaration to his entire realm, but directed primarily at *Eretz Yisrael*, that it was his intention to unify the diverse ethnic and religious groups in his empire and mold them into one homogenous nation. Accordingly, all peoples must relinquish their own customs and religions and conform to the dominant Greek culture and creed. Disobedience would be punished by death.

A directive was sent expressly to Judea to cease the sacrificial service in the Temple. In its place, altars and temples should be set up everywhere for idol-worship at which hogs and other unclean animals were to be sacrificed. As if that were not enough, Antiochus commanded that the Holy Temple should be desecrated and converted into a pagan temple! The observance of the Sabbath, festivals and Rosh Chodesh, the dietary laws, the covenant of circumcision, the laws of family purity, and the use of God's Name were singled out for prohibition. All copies of the Torah and the holy writings (כִּתְבֵי הַקֹּדֶשׁ) were to be confiscated and burned. Anyone found to possess any of these books would be executed. In general all vestiges of Torah and its observance were to be obliterated; even to profess that one was a Jew was punishable by death.

No sooner was the order given than Antiochus' Jewish lackeys, headed by Menelaus and aided by the king's forces, set about to enforce its execution with extreme brutality.[5] The Temple was converted into a place of harlotry in conformance with the Greek custom in their pagan temples. On the fifteenth of Kislev (3594/168 B.C.E.) an 'abomination' — i.e., an idol — was erected upon the altar, and beginning with the twenty-fifth of this month hogs were offered upon the altar to a pagan deity.

Most of the people complied with the king's barbaric order, but many chose death rather than 'desecrate the Name.' Women who had their children circumcised were put to death, with their infants

tied to their necks; their families as well as those who had performed the circumcision were killed.

Elazar, one of the leading sages, refused to partake of the pork which everyone was expected to eat as part of the offering ritual. The Syrian officials, realizing he would not relent, but anxious to win the propaganda coup of having him *appear* to accede to their demand, took him aside and told him he would be allowed to eat kosher meat — as long as he pretended he was eating of the offering. Elazar proudly spurned this overture and replied that 'it was not becoming to his years to pretend — so that many of the young people would suppose that Elazar, at the age of ninety, had gone over to the religion of the heathen ... To the young people I will leave an example of strength to die willingly with courage for the perfect and holy Torah.'

A woman and her seven sons were captured and brought before the king himself to force them to partake of pig's meat. When they refused to do so even after being tortured, the furious Antiochus had them put to a slow, barbarously painful death. But these seven noble brothers defied the cruel king to the last and declared their faith in the true God and their determination not to transgress His Torah. Their saintly mother herself stood by and encouraged her sons 'to sanctify the Name.' Then, the distraught mother climbed up on a roof and jumped to her death. A Heavenly voice proclaimed the verse [*Psalms* 113:9] *The mother of the children is joyous (Gittin* 57b). [See below, "Chanah and Her Seven Sons" (pp. 70-77), for a full account.]

Such people served as an inspiration to their fellow Jews and played no small role in inspiring the future rebellion.

I n those trouble beset days, Mattisyahu the Hasmonean[6] son of Yochanan the *Kohen Gadol*[7] left Jerusalem (where the persecution was strongest), and settled in Modi'in — a Judean village near Jerusalem. According to the Talmud (*Pesachim* 93b) it was

Beginning of the Revolt
30,000 cubits (approx. 8.5-11.3 miles) from Jerusalem. However the terror followed him even to this little town.

One day the king's forces appeared and demanded that the townspeople offer a sacrifice in the pagan fashion. They attempted to convince the aged and venerable Mattisyahu that it would be to his material and social advantage if he would set an

example for the people. Were he to comply, he and his sons would be considered the king's 'friends', an official title carrying with it many privileges, and would receive a handsome monetary reward. Mattisyahu proudly and publicly declared his determination to remain steadfast to the religion of his forefathers. As he was declaiming his defiance, a renegade Jew neared the altar to offer the sacrifice. When Mattisyahu saw this, he, in the tradition of Phineas ben Elazar (see *Numbers* 25:1-13), was filled with indignation and rage at this blatant desecration of 'the Name', and at this traitorous desertion of the Jewish nation and its religion by one of its sons. He grabbed a sword and killed not only the Jewish renegade, but the Syrian emissaries of the king.

Mattisyahu saw the desecrations being perpetrated upon Judea and Jerusalem and exclaimed, 'Woe to me! Why was I born to witness the ruination of my people and the ruination of the Holy City, and to have lived in it while it was surrendered to its enemies and the Temple to the foreigners? Her Temple is as a man disgraced, her precious utensils have been taken into captivity, her children have been murdered in her streets, her young men slaughtered by the enemy sword. What nation has not shared, what kingdom has not appropriated, her spoils. All of her glory has been stolen — instead of a free woman she has become a slave. Our Sanctuary, our glory and beauty, has been despoiled; the heathen has desecrated it. What is our life worth?'

Mattisyahu and his sons rent their clothing and donned sackcloth and mourned greatly.

Mattisyahu published a proclamation: 'Whoever is zealous for the Torah and is steadfast in the Covenant let him follow me!' Thereupon, he and his sons left all their worldly possessions in Modi'in and fled to the mountains in the Judean desert. Many other loyal Jews followed his example and joined him to live in the mountain caves where they would be able to practice the Torah's precepts. The king's forces could not disregard this challenge to their authority and began to seek out these bands of loyal Jews in the mountains. The Jews were exhorted by Mattisyahu to resist the Greeks with force, and six thousand combat-worthy, loyal Jews gathered under his banner. They began to strike back at the Greeks in nocturnal raids and would demolish the idolatrous altars put up by the pagans. The die had been cast; the revolt had begun.

When Mattisyahu felt that his death was imminent, he said to his sons: 'Now my children, be zealous for the Torah and give up your lives for the covenant of your forefathers.' He recalled to them the

great figures of Jewish history who put their faith in God and exposed themselves to danger rather than transgress His commandments — people like Abraham, Phineas, David, Daniel; and Chananyah, Mishael, and Azaryah. 'Do not fear the threats of a sinful man, for today he is exalted and tomorrow he will turn to dust and his plans come to naught. Strengthen yourselves, my children, and be courageous for the sake of the Torah. Through it you will gain honor!'

Mattisyahu did not live to see the result of the events he had set in motion. He died in the following year (3595/166 B.C.E.), but before his death he gathered his five sons — Shimon, Yehudah the Maccabee,[8] Elazar, Yochanan and Yonasan[9] — around him and urged them to be steadfast and continue the struggle against the Greeks. He bade them to follow the advice of Shimon 'for he is a sagacious man,' but to look to Yehudah as their leader in battle.

Phillip, the official appointed by Antiochus to administer Judea and to execute the enforced obliteration of the Jewish religion, did not take Mattisyahu's revolt seriously. Even when the loyalists began to venture out of the desert and audaciously attack towns under the government's control, he felt they could be contained by troops stationed in the vicinity of Judea.

Syrian-Greek Counterattack

He called upon Apollonius, the military commander of Samaria [שׁוֹמְרוֹן], to help him. Apollonius gathered a host composed of Cutheans and others to attack Yehudah. But Yehudah was forewarned and struck first, killing Apollonius and much of his army, and routing the rest and appropriating their arms.

Then Seron, the commander of the army in Syria, heard about Yehudah's revolt. He decided he would crush Yehudah and thereby gain himself distinction and prestige: 'I will make myself a reputation by making war on Yehudah and his comrades — those who disobey the King's command!' He gathered a large and well-equipped army and marched to Judea. As he approached the pass of Beth Choron, a strategically located town that dominated the approach from the coast to Jerusalem, Yehudah and his men saw Seron's vast army.

In keeping with the ancient Jewish practice, Yehudah's men were fasting (see *Rosh, Megillah* 2a). Then Yehudah's men were frightened

and said to Yehudah: 'How can we, so few in number, combat this vast multitude? We are fatigued — not having eaten today.'

But Yehudah, remembering his father's last words, was full of confidence that God would help them. He reassured his men as he would do many times in the coming years of fierce battle for the sake of Heaven:

'It is easy for the many to be handed over to the few, for there is no difference in God's eyes between saving through a large force or through a tiny force. Triumph in battle does not depend on the size of an army — for strength comes from heaven. Our enemy opposes us full of violence and lawlessness, to destroy us, our wives and our children, and to plunder us. But we are fighting for our lives and our Torah. God will crush them before us and you must not fear them!'

Having thus exhorted his few men, Yehudah fell upon Seron and his army, killing eight hundred of their soldiers and thoroughly routing them. After this, Yehudah's fame spread and he was greatly feared by the surrounding gentiles; his fame reached even to Antiochus, himself.

Upon hearing about the ignominious defeat of his troops, Antiochus was enraged and commanded that his entire army be gathered. He opened his treasury and paid his soldiers a full year's wages and ordered them to prepare for combat. Antiochus now realized that his coffers had been depleted; his military campaigns, plus his lavish spending for grandiose buildings and games, had put a severe drain on the treasury. The unrest fomented by his violent tactics and erratic behavior had disrupted the economy of the realm and revenues had fallen off. The king was advised to go to Persia to collect tribute owed him. To head a caretaker government in his absence, he appointed Lysias, a kinsman, and also entrusted him with the care of the young heir to the throne, Antiochus (later Antiochus V Eupator). He equipped half of the army with war elephants, the ancient equivalent of tanks, and assigned it to Lysias' command with orders for him to march into Judea and crush the Jewish nation. Antiochus took the other half of his army and they marched eastward toward Persia to raise funds.

Lysias promptly appointed Ptolemy son of Dorimenes, Nikanor, and Gorgias, three of Syria's ablest generals to lead the Judean

Antiochus Attempts to Crush the Revolt

campaign, and put them at the head of an army of 40,000 footsoldiers and 7,000 cavalry. They marched into Judea as far as Emmaus, a town west of Jerusalem in the Judean hills, near today's Latrun. There they pitched camp and were augmented by reinforcements from the standing armies of southern Syria and the coastal regions (Philistia). So confident were the Syrians of victory that Nikanor summoned gentile slave dealers from the coastal cities and promised to sell them Jewish slaves at unprecedentedly low prices. With the money raised from the slaves, he planned to pay the tribute the Syrians owed Rome. (Since the Roman victory over Antiochus III twenty-five years earlier, Syria had been required to pay a yearly tribute to Rome.)

When the ominous news reached Yehudah he did not lose his trust in God. They could not go up to Jerusalem to pray, for the Holy City was still under the control of the renegade Jews and the Syrians, but Mitzpah, a city that had been a place of prayer for God's salvation in the days of Samuel, was accessible. Yehudah gathered his followers in Mitzpah for a day of prayer and fasting, sprinkling ashes on their heads and tearing their garments. Even Torah scrolls were hard to come by because the Syrian-Greeks had made it a practice to seize scrolls and desecrate them with idolatrous pictures. The Jews had managed to save some scrolls, however; they opened one and read from it.

Then they brought the priestly vestments (בִּגְדֵי כְהוּנָה),the tithes (מַעַשְׂרוֹת), the first fruit offering (בִּכּוּרִים), and the Nazirites who could not bring their required offerings to the Temple, and placed them in front of the assemblage. They all cried out to God: 'What shall we do with these and whereto shall we bring them? Your Temple has been downtrodden and defiled ... How can we withstand our enemies if You will not help us?'

Now Yehudah divided his small army into four battalions of 1,000 men each, to be commanded respectively by himself and his brothers, Yochanan, Yonasan and Shimon. Then, as set forth by *Deuteronomy* 20:1-9, Yehudah announced that those who had recently married, built houses, or planted vineyards, should leave the army; and he exhorted the remaining men to have trust in God.

'Prepare yourselves and be brave men. Be ready in the morning to fight the heathens who are gathered against us to destroy us and our Sanctuary. It is better for us to die in battle than to witness the ruin of our nation and our Temple.'

Meanwhile, Gorgias had detached a force of 5,000 men from the main body of soldiers with the strategy of surprising the Jews in

their own camp. The renegade Jews from the citadel in Jerusalem served as his guides. With daybreak, Yehudah and his 1,000 men, who had not had the resources to arm themselves properly, saw they had been surrounded by a large force of well-armed seasoned soldiers. It was probably the most critical moment for the Jews since the revolt began. Yehudah exhorted his men to pray to God and to be steadfast.

'Do not fear their numbers or their attack. Remember how our ancestors were saved at the Sea of Reeds when Pharaoh and his army pursued them. Let us now cry out to God — perhaps He will accept our prayer, remember His covenant with our ancestors and crush the enemy camp that faces us now. Then all the heathens will know that there is One Who rescues and preserves Israel!' Then Yehudah ordered them to attack. His attack broke the Syrians' orderly phalanxes and they started a disorderly retreat. The Jews decimated the entire rear, set fire to the Syrian camp, and pursued the fleeing enemy a long way, killing 3,000 soldiers during the chase. Yehudah cautioned his men that the main body of the enemy army was still in the mountains; the battle had just begun. But when the Syrians saw the fire rising from Gorgias' camp they panicked and fled the battlefield.

After a year of licking his wounds, (3597/165 B.C.E.) Lysias sent yet a stronger force, consisting of 60,000 infantry and 5,000 cavalry. Yehudah met them at Beth Tzur (בֵּית צוּר) with a vastly smaller force of only 10,000 loyal Jews. Upon seeing the vastly superior army of the enemy, Yehudah again prayed to God to give him a victory.

'Blessed are You, O, Savior of Israel, Who halted the charge of the Philistine champion, Goliath, through Your servant David and Who delivered a Philistine camp into the hands of Jonathan ben Saul and his armor bearer. Do the same to this camp — let them be ashamed of their army and their cavalry. Make them cowardly, melt their boldness, make them tremble at their imminent destruction. Strike them down with the sword of those who love You and let all Who know Your Name sing praises to You.'

Yehudah's army attacked this strong force and was able to kill 5,000 soldiers. At this, Lysias, seeing the determination of the Jews to die rather than surrender, despaired of victory over the rebels at this time and returned to his capital, Antioch.

When Yehudah saw that the Syrians had been routed and would not mount another offensive in the foreseeable future, he said to his brothers, 'Let us now go up to the Temple, cleanse and rededicate it.'

Rededication of the Temple/ Miracle of the Oil
They gathered their entire force and marched to the Temple Mount. When the brave troops saw the Temple, desolate and overgrown with vegetation, its gates burned, and the Altar desecrated, they rent their garments, spread ashes on their heads, and cried and mourned. Yehudah led his men to fight off the garrison quartered in the citadel so as to enable the *Kohanim* to cleanse and prepare the Temple. They cleansed it and removèd the idols. They would have offered the daily burnt-offering [קָרְבָּן תָּמִיד] immediately, but the invaders had defiled the Altar with myriad offerings to their abominations. The *Kohanim* were forbidden to use an altar that had been contaminated (see *Avodah Zarah* 52b), so they took it apart and hid its stones in the *Beis HaMokad*, a structure situated in the northern wall of the Temple Court (*Middos* 1:6). Quickly, they constructed a new altar in time for use the next morning.

They fashioned new utensils for Divine service and brought the Incense Altar into the Holy, where the Torah prescribed that they be, and offered incense that very afternoon.[10] They baked *Panim* bread and placed it upon the designated table in the Holy [שֻׁלְחָן לֶחֶם הַפָּנִים], and hung the *Paroches* that separated the Holy from the Holy of Holies.

The *Menorah*, however, was gone, apparently stolen during the many lootings of Temple property that had taken place during the years of Hellenist and Syrian domination (see *Rashi, Avodah Zarah* 43a). The *Kohanim* took seven iron spits, covered them with wood, and crafted them into a makeshift *Menorah* (*Avodah Zarah* 43a; *Megillas Taanis*; and *Pesikta Rabbasi* 2:1 with *Zera Ephraim*; and *Toras Moshe, Parashas Mikeitz*). [According to *I Macc.* 4:49, however, they did have the Temple *Menorah*.] But where could they find the uncontaminated oil required for the lighting of the *Menorah*?

Upon searching for oil, they found that all the oil in the Temple had been contaminated. They continued searching, however, and found a flask containing enough oil for one night's lighting, oil that had curiously been sealed with the *Kohen Gadol's* seal. This was surprising because there was never a requirement that oil flasks be

sealed nor was it even the practice to do so; certainly the personal involvement of the *Kohen Gadol* was unheard of. Not only was the flask found, its seal was unbroken, indicating that the contents had not been tampered with.

With great rejoicing the *Kohanim* filled the lamps with this oil and lit the *Menorah*. Miraculously the oil burned for the eight days that it took to prepare and bring fresh uncontaminated oil that was fit for the *Menorah* — the miracle that would be eternally celebrated with the eight-day Chanukah festival.

[See ''Chanukah Insights'' (pp. 90-110) for a detailed discussion of the miracle of the oil and many of the halachic and homiletical viewpoints concerning it.]

Early the next day, which was the twenty-fifth of Kislev[11] in the year (3597/165 B.C.E.), they offered the daily burnt offering. Three years to the day after the Temple service had been interrupted and the altar defiled with pagan sacrifices, the service was renewed with great jubilation and song and music. They celebrated the rededication of the altar for eight days and offered up peace and thanksgiving offerings. Recognizing that the miracle had eternal implications [see Overview], Yehudah and his brethren, together with the Sanhedrin, decreed that the festival of Chanukah be celebrated every year for eight days.

[*Megillas Taanis* and *Pesikta Rabbasi* (2:1) clearly assume that the Chanukah festival commemorates the rededication of the altar (and Temple), hence its name (חֲנוּכָּה=dedication; see *Numbers* 7:84). Some (*Ran to Shabbos* 21b and others) find in the name Chanukah an allusion to the Hasmoneans' victory. According to this view, חֲנוּכָּה is a fusion of two words, חָנוּ, *they rested*, כ"ה, on the *twenty-fifth* (the letters כ and ה are used in Hebrew to represent the numbers 20 and 5, respectively).]

Yehudah and his people used this opportunity to search out copies of the Torah and the Prophets, and collected them in Jerusalem to ensure the perpetuation of these holy scrolls. The Greeks, in their frenzy of persecution, had sensed that in these scrolls lay the strength of the Jewish religion and had mounted an intense campaign of scroll burning. Yehudah sent a message to all Jewish communities that scrolls were now available to all who wished to make copies of them (*II Macc.* 2:14-15).

It is apparent from the history up to this point, and even more so from the events described below, that the triumph celebrated by Chanukah was a partial one at best. Although the Temple area had been liberated and the service reinstituted, parts of Jerusalem and

nearly all of the countryside were still under Syrian-Greek and Hellenist control. Even the *Kohen Gadol* was a renegade Jew. Total independence came only many years later — but for that, no festival was proclaimed.

That a festival was proclaimed in the absence of a military or diplomatic victory in any conventional sense of the word gives us an important insight into the nature of the celebration. Mattisyahu and his sons — Yehudah and his brothers — risked their lives for spiritual freedom, the purity of the Temple, and the integrity of its service, not for freedom from foreign bondage. From the first day of renewed Jewish settlement in *Eretz Yisrael* after King Darius of Persia permitted the rebuilding of the Temple, the Holy Land had been a vassal state of Persia, Alexander, Syria or Egypt, but none of these conditions engendered revolt. The Sages and the people understood that dependence was a condition of the Second Commonwealth's diminished status. But when religious freedom was wrested from them, they rebelled. When it was regained, they celebrated. [For a further discussion of these concepts, see Overview.]

When the news of the Syrian force's crushing defeat reached the many heathen peoples living in and around *Eretz Yisrael*, they immediately rose to take up arms. Apprehensive that Yehudah would conquer the land and establish a Jewish state, these natural

Eretz Yisrael in Turmoil enemies of the Jews instinctively challenged him, and began by murdering the Jews living among them. These unfortunate Jews sent impassioned pleas to Yehudah for help. His first battle was against the Edomite descendants of Esau in the southwestern corner of Trans-Jordan. Yehudah defeated them decisively. From there he marched north and subdued the Ammonites, whose leader Timotheus had assembled a great army to challenge him. Next came an appeal for help from the Jews of Gilead (the northern part of Trans-Jordan), who were besieged in a fortress. But at the same time emissaries from the Galil (the northern province of *Eretz Yisrael)* arrived, their garments torn, with the news that the gentiles of Acco, Tyre (צוֹר) and Sidon (צִידוֹן) had raised an army to destroy the Jews in their midst. Yehudah assembled all his advisors and it was decided that Yehudah and Yonasan would go with 8,000 men to

fight in Gilead, while Shimon would take a force of 3,000 men to subdue the Galil.

Yehudah fought many battles in the Gilead against vastly superior forces, but God heard the prayers he would offer before every battle, and subdued his enemies. He arrived at the besieged Jewish fortress just as Timotheus' men were crashing into it. Yehudah cried out, 'Fight for our brothers today.' The Jewish force attacked, killing 8,000 of Timotheus' men and leaving his army in disarray. Yehudah returned to Judea and sacrificed thanksgiving offerings, for not one of his men had fallen in battle.

However, events did not let Yehudah rest. He and his brothers had to fight another battle against the Edomites, during which he wrested from them Hebron, the city of the Patriarchs.

While all this was occurring, Antiochus was far away in his eastern provinces, confident that his armies had easily put down what he perceived as a minor uprising by a few Jewish zealots. He was informed that a temple in the city Elymais, in Persia, **Antiochus' End** contained fabulous riches that had been stored there by Alexander the Great. He promptly went to this city and tried to rob the temple through trickery. The townspeople, however, apprised of his intentions, resisted him and forced him to flee. Antiochus sought to march to Babylon, but his spirit had been broken and he was greatly depressed by the reversal in his fortunes. Then, a messenger brought him the news that his forces in Judea had been shamefully routed and that the entire country was in turmoil.

Realizing that his entire empire was crumbling, the king fell into a deep depression and his nerves were further shattered. As his mental capacities declined, so he also deteriorated physically and contracted a mysterious disease. According to one account *(II Macc. 9:5-12)* the disease was precipitated by a fall from a speeding chariot. He gradually lost the use of his limbs and began to smell so foully that no one wanted to come near him. Feeling that his end was near, he called his close advisors and expressed his regrets that he had oppressed the Jews needlessly and had despoiled the Holy Temple: 'I remember the wrongs I committed in Jerusalem ... it is because of this that misfortune has overtaken me. Now I am dying in a strange land.'

He bade Phillip, his closest confidante, to supervise the education

of his son the crown prince Antiochus V Eupator, and to raise him to be king. Antiochus died friendless and deserted in Ecbatana (Hamadan), Persia, in the year 3598/163 B.C.E. When the news of the king's death reached Lysias, he crowned the prince and named him King Antiochus V Eupator.

Antiochus V

Although Yehudah had scored many glorious victories and subdued the nations in and around *Eretz Yisrael*, he was by no means in control of the country. He had succeeded in breaking the military might of his enemies only to the extent that they could not strike at him and the Jews in their midst, but even in Jerusalem where the *Kohanim* held the Temple and performed the daily service, the Jews were not yet dominant. The Accra, the Hellenist fortress near the Temple, held a strong garrison of Syrian soldiers and Jewish renegades. They caused continuous trouble, trying to surround the Temple and bring about the cessation of the service. In the year 3599/162 B.C.E., two years after the rededication of the Temple, Yehudah assembled a force and besieged the Acra. The people of the citadel, hard pressed, sent an urgent message to Antiochus V pointing out that Yehudah's action was a move not only against the citadel, but a revolt against the authority of the king. If Yehudah were not checked now, they argued, he would be so strengthened that it would be impossible to dislodge him later.

The message impressed the seriousness of the situation upon the young king (or his advisors) and he proceeded to mobilize to the maximum. Taking his commander Lysias with him, Antiochus moved against Yehudah with 100,000 footsoldiers, 20,000 cavalry and many battle elephants, the huge animals that were the ultimate weapon in ancient warfare. That Antiochus committed battle elephants in such numbers to the battle is indicative of the zeal with which he wanted to subdue the Jews. Many years before, in 3571/190 B.C.E., his grandfather Antiochus III had been defeated by Rome at Magnesia, in one of the pivotal wars of the period. As part of the peace treaty imposed upon him, Antiochus was forced to agree never to employ elephants in a military campaign. For Antiochus V to do so now meant that he was willing to risk retaliation by Rome in order to subdue the Jews.

They entered Judea from the south passing through Edom. Yehudah met them at Beth Zecharyah, a few miles south of

Jerusalem. The king's host covered the mountains and terrified anyone hearing its noise. But Yehudah, undaunted in his reliance upon God, attacked and managed to kill 600 Syrian soldiers. His brother, Elazar, seeing one of the elephants decorated with the royal emblem, thought, erroneously, that the king was in its turret. He fought his way through the battalion of soldiers surrounding this elephant and plunged his lance into its entrails. Falling dead, the animal crushed Elazar beneath it. After gallantly battling the king's forces, Yehudah was forced to retreat to Gophna (in Samaria, north of Judea; *Josephus, Wars* 1:1:5).

The Syrian army now proceeded to beleaguer Jerusalem. As the siege dragged on, the loyal Jews in the city held off Antiochus' vastly superior force. However, soon another enemy endangered them — hunger. It was a *Shemittah* [Sabbatical] year and provisions had been low to start with.

But here Divine Providence intervened.

Phillip, Antiochus IV's confidante, returned to Antioch from Persia at the head of the dead king's army. Finding the young Antiochus and all the major officials away from the capital, Phillip attempted to set himself up as regent. Lysias learned of this traitorous act and promptly conferred with the king and his generals, and convinced them that it was counterproductive to keep up the siege, pointing out that provisions were low and that Jerusalem had proven very difficult to take.

He hastened to add that the trouble with the Jews had started only because their religion had been restricted. He urged the king to 'give these people his right hand' in peace and to pledge that they could practice their religion freely. A truce was hastily arranged and the appropriate oaths were given. However Antiochus did not keep his word totally. Upon seeing the fortifications the Jews had erected around the Temple, he commanded his soldiers to demolish them. Then he and his host marched back to Antioch, took it without much difficulty and executed Phillip.

The lifting of the siege against Jerusalem was celebrated as a miraculous salvation, as related in *Megillas Taanis:*

> On the twenty-eighth (of Shvat) King Antiochus was removed from Jerusalem; for he tyrannized Israel and came to destroy Jerusalem and to exterminate all the Jews. Jews were able to come and go (in and out of Jerusalem) only at night. But he heard bad tidings, left and fell in his place. That day on which they eliminated him from there (i.e. Jerusalem) they (the Sages) designated a festival.

When Antiochus III was defeated by the Romans at Magnesia some 27 years before the lifting of the siege against Jerusalem, the terms of the armistice forced him to leave members of his household in Rome as hostages to guarantee that Syria would not

Demetrius I — the Reaction

again attack Rome. The hostages could be rotated as long as someone was always held by Rome, and this arrangement continued for many years. One such rotation of hostages took place just before the assassination of Seleucus, the eldest son and successor of the defeated Antiochus III. In 175 B.C.E. Seleucus' younger brother Antiochus IV, who was to become the arch oppressor of Israel in the Chanukah era, was released by Rome and replaced by Demetrius, son of the soon-to-be slain Seleucus. As crown prince, Demetrius was the lawful heir to the crown, but Antiochus IV took advantage of his absence to hurry to Syria and usurp the throne.

In the year 3600/161 B.C.E., three years after the Chanukah miracle, Demetrius I, now a mature man, managed to escape from Rome. No sooner had he landed on Syrian soil than he proclaimed himself king. In a short while he managed to win over the influential people in the country and establish himself as ruler; Lysias and Antiochus V were summarily executed. This turn of events had a profound effect on Judea.

With Demetrius' accession to the throne, the peace agreement reached just months earlier between Yehudah and Antiochus was now null and void. Shortly thereafter, the present leader of the Hellenizers, Alcimus,[12] a *Kohen* who aspired to the post of *Kohen Gadol*, came to the new king and convinced him to attack Yehudah the Maccabean. The king appointed Bacchides, one of his most trusted officials, to lead the fight and gave the *Kehunah* Gedolah to Alcimus. Bacchides and Alcimus now marched with a great force to Judea. Upon arriving they sent messages of peace to Yehudah and his people, giving them assurances under oath that they would not be harmed. The Jews, not suspecting that a fellow *Kohen* would betray them, sent a party of sixty sages and devout people to meet them. No sooner had they arrived in the Syrian camp than they were executed.[13] Bacchides also rounded up many Jews who were suspected or accused of having fought against the Syrians in the uprising and executed them.

Believing he had reestablished the Syrian domination in the land,

Bacchides left Alcimus with an armed force and returned to Antioch. Alcimus, now with the help of his fellow renegades, proceeded to take over Judea and oppress the loyal Jews even more barbarically than the gentiles had done. Apparently, Yehudah's force had disbanded after the successful conclusion of his peace with Antiochus. Thinking that Bacchides had come on a peaceful expedition, Yehudah would have no reason to recall his men to arms; perhaps he was not even in Jerusalem at the time. Now, however, Yehudah realized that he could not rest on his laurels, but had to take up the fight again.

When Alcimus realized he had as his opponent the implacable Yehudah, he hastened to Antioch and requested the king's help. Demetrius now sent Nikanor — an old foe of Yehudah who had taken part in the campaign of Lysias during the rule of Antiochus IV — with a great army to wage war with Yehudah, and to obliterate the Jewish resistance to Hellenism. In his first engagement with Yehudah, five hundred Syrians fell and Nikanor retreated hurriedly to Jerusalem. In Jerusalem, the *Kohanim* came out of the Temple to greet him and to show him the sacrifices they were offering for the king. But Nikanor rebuffed them haughtily and swore that if he succeeded now in conquering Yehudah he would return and burn the Temple.

Nikanor marched his force to Beis Choron (a few miles north of Jerusalem) where he rendezvoused with an additional Syrian army. Yehudah encamped nearby with an insignificant force of 3,000 devout Jews. Never before, in all his wars, had Yehudah's cause seemed more hopeless, but his faith in God never weakened.

Yehudah encouraged his troops by telling them of an inspiring dream, a vision that assured him — and them — of victory. In his dream, he saw old Onias, the former righteous *Kohen Gadol*, standing with his hands outstretched in prayer for the Jewish people. Then another man appeared in Yehudah's dream, gray-haired and dignified and wrapped in sublime majesty.

Onias introduced the second man as the prophet Jeremiah 'who loves his brothers and prays devotedly for Israel and Jerusalem!'

Then Jeremiah gave Yehudah a golden sword and said, 'Take this sacred sword as a gift from God — and with it, strike down your foes.'

Then, as always before battle, Yehudah prayed:

'It was You, God, Who sent an angel in the time of King Hezekiah of Judah, and he destroyed 185,500 in the blaspheming camp of Sennacherib. Now, too, Master of the Heavens — send an angel

before us carrying fear and terror. May Your strong right arm strike down those who blaspheme against Your holy people.'

After offering his short prayer, Yehudah fell upon the Syrian forces. Nikanor was the first to fall. His troops, seeing their leader die, panicked. They threw down their arms and began a disorderly flight. Many loyal Jews in the surrounding towns of Judea, seeing the enemy's rout, poured out of their homes and joined the fight. Nikanor's once proud army was wiped out on that day; none of his 35,000 soldiers survived. Yehudah and his men went up to Jerusalem and offered thanks to God Who had again delivered them. Yehudah and the Sages designated the day of victory, the thirteenth of Adar, as a festival.

> On the thirteenth (of Adar) is the day of Nikanor. They (the Sages) said, Nikanor was one of the nobles of the Greek kings; every day he would wave his hand toward Jerusalem and the Holy Temple and blaspheme, accuse, abuse, and say, 'When will they fall into my hands so that I will demolish this tower?' When the noble house of the Hasmoneans gained power and defeated them [the Greeks], they penetrated his armies and killed until they reached his chariot. They cut off his head and the fingers of his hands and feet and hung them up opposite [the gates of (see *Taanis* 18b)] Jerusalem and wrote beneath them; 'The mouth that spoke haughtily and the hands that waved at Jerusalem and the Holy Temple — this is the vengeance inflicted on them!'
>
> That day on which they [the Hasmonean warriors] did thus to him, they [the Sages] designated a festival (*Megillas Taanis*; see *Taanis* 18b. *Yer. Taanis* 2:12 gives an account differing in a few details).

A fter a few months, Demetrius sent yet another army, an even larger one, under Bacchides and Alcimus. They confronted Yehudah's camp near Elasah (אֶלָעֲשָׂה), west of Jerusalem. Most of Yehudah's men, upon seeing the mighty army of the enemy, lost

After Yehudah heart and deserted him; he was left with only 800 men. Yehudah refused to flee, however, and gave battle. In the ensuing contest many fell from both sides, but when Yehudah himself was killed the remnants of his force fled the

fray. Yonasan and Shimon carried their brother to Modi'in for burial. All of Israel mourned for him a long time (3601/160 B.C. E.).

After Yehudah's death the Hellenist party was greatly strengthened. Just then there was a great famine and most of the devout, out of necessity, chose to make peace with the Hellenizers. Bacchides appointed Alcimus and others of his party to administer the country. These renegades used the opportunity to avenge themselves upon those loyal to Yehudah; they were brought to Bacchides to be tortured and executed. The surviving devout Jews assembled and entreated Yonasan to reorganize and lead the resistance against the Hellenizers and the Syrians. Bacchides was informed of these entreaties and sent a force to capture Yonasan.

Yonasan, together with his brothers Yochanan and Shimon and their loyal followers, fled to the Judean desert near the southern extremity of the Jordan. While on a mission, Yochanan was captured and killed by one of the Trans-Jordanian tribes. Bacchides was advised of the location of Yonasan's hideout and marched there with a considerable force. Yonasan was surrounded and forced to fight his way out of the trap in order to flee across the Jordan. Bacchides lost 1,000 men in this battle and Yonasan made his way to safety. The Syrians returned to Judea and refortified the fortresses of the land. Alcimus was now in full control of the country. He began to demolish one of the walls surrounding the Temple Court[14], but he was suddenly stricken with paralysis and lost his speech (probably he had a stroke) and died shortly thereafter (3602/159 B.C.E.). With his death the persecutions against the devout Jews ceased; Bacchides returned to Syria and the land enjoyed a well deserved peace of two years' duration.

However the Hellenists refused to rest as long as Yonasan was alive and posed a threat. They again prevailed upon King Demetrius I to send Bacchides with a force to destroy Yonasan (3604/157 B.C.E.). The loyal Jews had gained control of one of the towers near Bethlehem and fortified themselves. Bacchides besieged them but could not gain a victory. The Maccabees began to press his army strongly and Bacchides, deciding he could not prevail, retreated, with the intention of returning to Syria. Just then Yonasan sent messengers with offers of peace and assurances that the Syrian captives would be returned if the wars would end. Since Bacchides had lost heart for his mission to *Eretz Yisrael*, Yonason's offer came at a perfect time. The Syrian accepted the terms and returned to his land, never again to molest *Eretz Yisrael*. Yonasan went to Michmash [מִכְמָשׁ], north of Jerusalem, and established a base there.

This would be the nucleus around which the Hasmoneans would soon forge their kingdom.

A short while after this (3609/152 B.C.E.), Divine Providence brought about a new development that brought long-lasting benefits to the Jews; the political situation in the region changed dramatically. Alexander Balas appeared on the scene, claiming to be the son of Antiochus IV and the legitimate claimant to **Yonasan's** the throne. Well-informed people knew he was an **Fortunes** impostor, but his marked resemblance to Kings **Rise** Antiochus IV and V lent credence to his claim. The hoax was abetted by the neighboring kings of Pergamum, Egypt, and Cappadocia, all of whom wanted to topple Demetrius. Alexander won backing and proclaimed himself in Acre [עַכּוֹ] with the connivance of his backers, the kings who opposed Demetrius.

Finding himself isolated, Demetrius reached out for support. Afraid that Yonasan would use his forces to back the usurper, he quickly sent him a message inviting him to be his ally. He gave Yonasan permission to raise an army and to gather arms. Yonasan left his stronghold in Michmash immediately, went up to Jerusalem and began to refortify the city. The Syrians, who garrisoned the fortresses built almost ten years before by Bacchides, were now faced with a Yonasan who was acting as Demetrius' ally, so they left their posts and the country.

When Alexander heard of these developments, he would not be outdone in bidding for Yonason's friendship. He sent Yonasan a gold crown and a purple mantle (a gesture equivalent to formal recognition in our days) and appointed him *Kohen Gadol*.

Finally, Judea had ceased to be the oppressed victim of its more powerful neighbors and enjoyed the opportunity to consolidate its Jewishness while the rival Syrian monarchs vied for its favor. Having experienced Demetrius' cruelty and sure that he could not be trusted, Yonasan cast his lot with Alexander. On that Succos (3609/152 B.C.E.), Yonasan donned the vestments of the *Kohen Gadol* and performed the service in the Temple. At the festivities in honor of Alexander's marriage to Cleopatra, the daughter of the King Ptolemy VI of Egypt (3611/150 B.C.E.), Alexander ordered Yonasan dressed in the royal purple and rebuffed the Hellenists who

had come to complain about Yonasan's growing power. Thus, through shrewd diplomacy, Yonasan achieved a stature for his people and himself that had eluded them through all their miraculous victories in battle.

On the Road to Total Victory

During the next few years the Seleucid Empire was considerably weakened and thrown into turmoil through the incessant struggle for the throne occasioned by the claims and counterclaims of a half dozen usurpers. Alexander had defeated Demetrius in battle and killed him, but Alexander proved to be a despotic and unpopular king. His own father-in-law, Ptolemy of Egypt, turned against him. Against this background, Demetrius II, a son of the dead king, came upon the scene and led a successful rebellion against Alexander. Ptolemy took his daughter away from Alexander and married her to Demetrius II. Having lost both his kingdom and his wife, Alexander fled to the king of Arabia, who killed him.

Yonasan used this opportunity to wrest further concessions from the new king. Three provinces of Samaria were annexed to Judea, and a relaxation of tribute and taxes was granted. But Syria was still not tranquil. Triphon, one of Alexander's erstwhile officials, capitalizing on Demetrius II's unpopularity, brought the dead Alexander's baby son Antiochus out of hiding, toppled the king, and set himself up as regent for the baby king Antiochus VI. An epistle was sent to Yonasan in the name of the new king recognizing all the privileges granted Yonasan by Demetrius. Yonasan used the general unrest to further expand his realm to the southern coast (Gaza, Ashdod) and the Galil.

Triphon, having usurped the throne for all practical purposes, now set his sights on greater things. He dreamed of restoring the Seleucid kingdom to its former glory and boundaries. A primary object in his plans was to crush the growing power of Judea. He marched forthwith into Judea with a sizable force and was met in Beth She'an by Yonasan at the head of an army of 40,000 men. Realizing that he would be defeated in battle, Triphon resolved to gain by treachery what he could not win in war. He convinced Yonasan that his intentions were peaceful, and that Yonasan should come to Acre, with a token force, where he and Triphon would

confer. Triphon promptly arrested Yonasan and demanded an exorbitant ransom for him. After collecting the ransom, Triphon treacherously kept Yonasan and put him to death.

The people now looked to Shimon, the last surviving son of Mattisyahu, to lead them. He led an army against Triphon and forced him to return to Syria. From the year 3619/142 B.C.E. on, 'the yoke of the gentiles' was removed from Israel (I *Macc.* 13:41). In

Shimon Becomes An Independent Ruler

their books and documents, Jews designated this as 'the year one of Shimon the *Kohen Gadol,* commander-in-chief, and prince of the Jews.'

The Acra, the citadel near the Temple, which had not been dislodged in all these years, was now cut off from its base of support. Being unable to leave their fortress and replenish their provisions, the gentiles and renegade Jews in the garrison suffered hunger, and cried out for peace. Shimon granted them clemency and expelled them from their stronghold in 3620/141 B.C.E. The Jews entered the Acra on the twenty-third of Iyar with great jubilation and festivity and designated that day a festival.

> On the twenty-third (of Iyar) the people of [the] Acra left Jerusalem ... for [until then] they had oppressed the people of Jerusalem, who could not go or come (in and out the Temple) during day — only at night. When the house of the Hasmoneans grew strong they expelled them from [the] Acra ... (*Megillas Taanis*).

On the Eighteenth of Elul, in the year 3621/140 B.C.E., the people of Judea, the *Kohanim* and the Sanhedrin convoked a general assembly and acknowledged Shimon as their prince.[15] The revolt begun by the venerable Mattisyahu had run its course; *Eretz Yisrael* was free!

NOTES

1. The reference to 'books of the Hasmoneans' [הַחַשְׁמוֹנָאִים] in R' Yosef ben Shmuel of Fez's preface to *Sefer HaYashar* (concerning the translation of the Torah into Greek) is not drawn from any source known today, nor does the story fit the time frame dealt with in these books. R' Ch. D. Friedberg (*Beth Eked Sefarim, s.v.* המעשיות) reports the existence of a Yiddish translation of the books of *Maccabees*, published in

Prague 5385 (1625). Perhaps R' Eliyah Shapiro *(Eliyah Rabbah)* made use of this Yiddish translation.

2. As R' Isaac HaLevi *(Doros HaRishonim,* vol. 1 ed. Israel, pp. 169-170; vol. 2, pp. 358-364, 391-407) points out, the necessity for supplying a Torah-oriented philosophy to legitimize transgression of the Torah arose only after the victory of the Hasmoneans.

Until then, it was much more expedient to be an out-and-out Hellenist. Only after the establishment of a Jewish state did Sadduceeism fill a real need for those erstwhile Hellenists who now needed to cloak themselves in the respectable garb of a 'Jewish' philosophy. But no doubt the Sadducean heresy strengthened the Hellenistic trend, just as it can be assured that the Hellenists resorted to Sadduceeism during the Hasmonian period.

3. Mysia was an ancient country in the northeastern corner of Asia Minor that contributed a division of soldiers to Antiochus' army. The version in our text is based on *II Macc.* 5:24. The Greek version of *Macc.* 1:29 describes the officer sent on this mission as Antiochus' collector of taxes. But why would a tax collector be sent on a military mission? *A. Kahanah* (see his edition of the Apocrypha, הַסְּפָרִים הַחִיצוֹנִים, *loc. cit.*) and others surmise that the original Greek translator (*I Macc.* was originally written in Hebrew) erred and read שַׂר הַמִּיסִים, lit., *official over taxes,* instead of שַׂר הַמּוּסִים, *commander of the Mysians.*

4. The Mishnah *(Middos 2:3)* relates that thirteen breaches were made in the *soreg* (סוֹרֵג), the low wall of lattice work that encompassed the Temple Court at a ten-cubit distance from the Court walls. *Tosefos Yom Tov (loc. cit)* surmises that the Greeks vented their fury against the *soreg* wall because it demarked the place beyond which gentiles were not permitted to enter the courtyard (see *Keilim* 1:8).

It is logical to assume that these breaches were made when the Greeks were in control of the Temple prior to its rededication by the Hasmoneans. However it is also possible that this occurred at a later date, during Alcimus' tenure as *Kohen Gadol* (see page 60 and footnote 12, page 69). *Megillas Taanis* (see H. Lichtenstein's edition; the version in prevalent editions evidently has been corrupted) relates: On the twenty-third of Cheshvan, the *soreg* (סוֹרִיגָא) in the Temple Court was demolished (סוֹרִיגָא מִן עֲזַרְתָּא אִיסְתַּתָּר). For there the Greeks built a place and stationed harlots in it. When the Hasmoneans overpowered them, they [the Hasmoneans] took it from them and destroyed it ... The day on which they destroyed it they designated a festival.

Thus *Megillas Taanis* adds yet another dimension to the report in the Mishnah. Perhaps the Syrians made the thirteen breaches to facilitate the use of the area between the *soreg* and the Temple Court wall

for the immoral purpose described by *Megillas Taanis.* Out of respect for the holiness of the Temple, the Mishnah may have refrained from specifying the purpose of the breaches. Because of the indecent use to which the walls of the *soreg* had been subjected, the Sages felt it would not suffice merely to repair the breaches. The entire structure was viewed as an abomination and demolished, to be newly erected in a consecrated manner. The day of its demolition (not its rebuilding) was celebrated as a festival, because the Jews rejoiced at removing an abomination from the Holy Temple's environs. It seems that during the initial rededication of the Temple (25 Kislev), when the miracle of the lights took place, the Hasmoneans had been too busy readying the Temple itself to be able to purify the *soreg* area, which was on the Temple Mount outside of the Temple Court wall (see *Middos* 2:3). This was left for a later date, perhaps when Yonasan and Shimon were in full control of Judea. Significantly, in describing the strength of the Hasmoneans that enabled them to replace the *soreg*, *Megillas Taanis* uses the strong verb כְּשֶׁתָּקְפָה, *overpowered,* in contrast to the milder term כְּשֶׁגָּבְרָה, *became stronger,* that it and *Shabbos* 21b use to describe the conquest which led to the Chanukah celebration. The Sages also initiated that one prostrate himself at the site of these breaches in the *soreg* in gratitude to God for Israel's deliverance from Syrian domination. (See *Middos* 2:3; *Shekalim* 6:3 with ArtScroll comm.)

5. *Tosefta (Succah* 4:13; cited in the Talmud *Succah* 56b) relates that Miriam the daughter of Bilgah (i.e., the daughter of a member of the 'watch' of Bilgah) adopted pagan beliefs and married an officer in the service of the Syrian-Greek kings. When the Syrians entered the Temple in the days of Antiochus Epiphanes she pounded the altar with her sandal, saying 'Lokos, Lokos! (Lykos=wolf in Greek; Aruch's version here is לְקוֹס) — How much longer will you devour Israel's money while you do not deliver them in their time of need?'

When the Sages heard of this, they punished the entire watch in three ways that would demean it in the eyes of all onlookers (see Artscroll *Succah* 5:8). To explain the fairness of punishing the entire watch for the outrageous behavior of Miriam, the *Gemara* (ad loc) explains that it was clear to the Sages that her blasphemous exclamation and revolting conduct resulted from the contemptuous attitude she absorbed from her

entire family; thus her behavior was symptomatic of the corruption of them all.

6. Many interpretations have been suggested for the word חַשְׁמוֹנָאִים, *Hasmoneans*. The author of the famous liturgical poem *Maoz Tzur* calls them חַשְׁמַנִּים, from the Hebrew word חַשְׁמַנִּים, *nobles* (*Psalms* 68:32). However the Talmud uses the term חַשְׁמוֹנָאִים with the prefix בֵּית (בֵּית חַשְׁמוֹנָאִים, *the family of Hasmoneans*, *Shabbos* 21b, *Bava Basra* 3b), suggesting that this is a family name. Others (see *Siddur Avodas Yisrael* p. 101) suggest that one of Mattisyahu's ancestors was born in a town called *Cheshmon* (see *Joshua* 15:27), whereupon all his descendants were denominated Chesmonites [Hasmoneans]. According to *Josephus* (*Ant.* 12:6:1), Asmoneus was the name of Mattisyahu's great-grandfather. The term בְּנֵי חַשְׁמוֹנָאִים, lit. *the children of Chashmon*, used in the Mishnah (*Middos* 1:6) and in *Megillas Taanis* (25 Kislev, 27 Iyar, 15 Sivan), supports Josephus' interpretation that Chashmonai was the proper name of a person (see also *Rambam Hil. Chanukah* 3:1, *Pesikta Rabbasi* 2:1).

However the identification of Hasmoneus as Mattisyahu's great-grandfather is not certain. Josephus contradicts himself: in his 'Wars of the Jews' (1:1:3) he names Hasmoneus as the father of Mattisyahu, while in 'The Life of Joseph' (sec. 1) Hasmoneus is described as Mattisyahu himself. If we are not to accept the unlikely supposition that Josephus was unsure of Hasmoneus' identity — unlikely because Josephus prided himself on his own descent from the Hasmoneans — we must assume that Hasmoneus, in addition to being the proper name of the founder-ancestor of a clan, was also used as a surname by many of his descendants and by some even as their proper name. This explains the assignment of this name to Mattisyahu himself, as well as to his father and great-grandfather. There is also much evidence that Hasmoneus and Mattisyahu are two different people, both of whom were instrumental in the revolt. The Talmud (*Megillah* 11a), referring to the central figures of the revolt, lists Hasmoneus and his sons, and also Mattisyahu the *Kohen Gadol* (חַשְׁמוֹנַאי וּבָנָיו וּמַתִּתְיָה כֹּהֵן גָּדוֹל). The version of the *Al HaNissim* liturgy given in *Soferim* 20:8 reads: בִּימֵי מַתִּתְיָהוּ בֶּן יוֹחָנָן כֹּהֵן גָּדוֹל וְחַשְׁמוֹנַאי וּבָנָיו, *In the days of Mattisyahu son of Yochanan Kohen Gadol and Hasmoneus and his sons.* The prevalent version of *Al HaNissim* can also be interpreted in this vein. See also *Midrash*

Ma'aseh Chanukah versions 1 and 2 and *Midrash LeChanukah* in *Otzar Midrashim v.* 1 pp. 189-193.

7. There is much speculation as to whom the title *Kohen Gadol* refers (see *Siddur Avodas Yisrael* p. 101). According to Josephus, the post of *Kohen Gadol* was hereditary in the family of Shimon HaTzaddik until the persecutions under Yochanan. In the century before these events, this honor was held by Chonyo II (son of Shimon HaTzaddik), his son Shimon II, and finally by Chonyo III, who was deposed by Antiochus Epiphanes. In the remaining eight years before the revolt, the *Kehunah Gedolah* was held by Yeshua/Jason and then by Menelaus. Mattisyahu died in the first year of the revolt and did not see the conquest of the Temple by his sons. Consequently, the difficulty arises: when could either Mattisyahu or his father Yochanan have been *Kohanim Gedolim*? Perhaps Chonyo is a diminutive form of Yochanan, so that Mattisyahu could be the son of the *Kohen Gadol* Chonyo III. Indeed, according to Josephus (*Ant.* 12:6:1; see also *I Macc.* 2:1), Shimon was the name of Yochanan's father — and Chonyo III was the son of Shimon II (cf. *Otzar HaTefillos v.* 1 p. 163 and R' Sh. Rottenberg, *Toldos Am Olam* vol. 2, p. 405). If so, the title *Kohen Gadol* refers only to Yochanan, not Mattisyahu. However the absence of any evidence positively linking the Hasmoneans to Shimon HaTzaddik's family makes this a doubtful conjecture. Moreover, Josephus (*Life of Josephus* sec. 1) says that Hasmoneus and Matisyahu *Kohen Gadol* were one and the same person. (See also R' Werdiger, *Siddur Tz'losa D'Avraham.*)

8. *Yossipon* 1(ch. 20) adds that this surname was given Yehudah because of his heroism and strength (מַקֶּבֶת is a hammer). Others (R' Yochanan Treves in his commentary *Kimcha D'Avishuna to Machzor Roma*) maintains that מַכַּבִּי, *Maccabee*, is an acronym for מִי כָמוֹךָ בָּאֵלִים, *Who is like You among the mighty, O HASHEM.* This legend was emblazoned on Judah's shield. *Chasam Sofer* (*Derashos Chasam Sofer v.* 1, p. 138) suggests that מכבי is an acronym for מַתִּתְיָהוּ כֹּהֵן בֶּן יוֹחָנָן, *Mattisyahu Kohen, son of Yochanan.*

9. *I Macc* 2:2-6, *Josephus* (*Ant.* 12:6:1), *Yossipon* (ch. 20) and *Megillas Antiochus* (v. 41, 51-6) speak about only five sons. However *Rashi* (*comm.* to *Deut.* 33:11) refers to the 'twelve' sons of Chashmonai (בְּנֵי חַשְׁמוֹנַאי). The Midrashim *Ma'aseh Chanukah* and *Midrash Chanukah* (see

Otzar Midrashim v. 1 pp. 190-194) also speak about twelve leaders of the revolt; however, those twelve are from *two* families, Mattisyahu and Chashmonai (חַשְׁמוֹנָאִי). The author of a commentary to the liturgy for the first Sabbath of Chanukah (s.v. אֵין צוּר חֶלֶף; see *Seder HaDoros* 3621) also refers to this tradition. See above note 6.

10. The narrative in *I Maccabees* (4:50-53), that incense was burned in conjunction with kindling the *Menorah*, is corroborated by the Halachah as given in the Talmud and *Rambam*. The inner golden altar may be dedicated only by the burning of the afternoon incense, but the outer altar, upon which the blood of the offerings was sprinkled and their sacrificial parts burnt, can be dedicated only with the sacrifice of the morning daily offering *(Menachos* 50a; *Hil. T'midin UMussafin* 1:12, 3:1). Therefore the Maccabees commenced with the incense service immediately in the afternoon, but were not permitted to offer the daily afternoon offering before having offered the morning offering. Therefore they waited until the next morning and commenced the sacrificial service upon the new altar with the morning daily offering as prescribed by Halachah. The sequence followed in *Maccabees'* narrative is also that set forth in the Talmud *(Pesachim* 59a), which mandates that first the afternoon incense be burned, to be followed by the kindling of the *Menorah* (see *Hil. T'midin U'Mussafin* 6:11 with *Lechem Mishneh* and comm.; cf. *Hil Korban Pesach* 1:4).

11. *Rambam (Hil. Chanukah* 3:2) assumes that the victorious Maccabees entered the Temple on the twenty-fifth and only on the eve before the twenty-sixth did they light the lamps. See *Binyan Shlomo* in *Rambam* ed. Vilna, *Maaseh Rokeach* loc. cit., and *Pri Chadash* to *Orach Chaim* 670, *Derashos Chasam Sofer v.* 1 p. 135.

12. Josephus renders this name Jakimus. Some scholars (see *Doros HaRishonim* ed. Israel v. 1 p. 173) identify Alcimus/Jakimus with Yakim Ish Tzroros, the renegade nephew of Yose ben Yoezer (see *Bereishis Rabba* 65; fn. 13 below).

13. Some scholars see in this event the basis of the story related in *Bereishis Rabbah* (65:22) about Yakim Ish Tzroros, the nephew of Yose ben Yoezer, who rode in front of his illustrious uncle as the latter was being led to his execution as a martyr. Yakim taunted Yose saying: 'Behold the horse upon which my master mounts me and see the horse upon which your Lord mounts you!' Yose responded: 'If this fate is accorded to those who perform His will then surely it will be so to those who anger Him!' Yose's words had such a profound impact upon the renegade — 'the matter penetrated him like the poison of a snake' — that he went and committed suicide out of remorse for his sinful ways. As Yose neared his place of execution he saw the angels transporting Yakim's bier to heaven. He exclaimed, 'This one has preceded me by a short while to Gan Eden'.

The supposition is that Yose was among the sixty scholars killed by Alcimus. This identification is clearly spurious because the main point of the story — Alcimus' death — could not have occurred now. However it is possible that Yose was martyred at the time of Alcimus' death two years later (3601/160 B.C.E.), although *I Macc.* (9:54-7) makes no mention of this and reports that Alcimus' death occurred naturally.

14. Perhaps the breaking of the *soreg* recorded in the Mishnah *(Midos* 2:3) refers to this occurrence.

15. *I Macc.* 14:27-45 preserves for posterity the formula which the people had inscribed on a bronze tablet put up on a pillar upon the Temple Mount. Among other things a declaration is made (v. 41) ... *that the Jews and the Kohanim agreed that Shimon be for them a prince* (נָשִׂיא) *and Kohen Gadol until a true prophet arises.* The provision limiting Shimon's tenure only until a true prophet arises appears incongruous at first glance. See "Duration of the Hasmonean Monarchy" (p. 87) for an explanation.

Chanah and her Seven Sons

ᵉᵍ Preface

The martyrdom of a heroic mother and her seven sons occupies a prominent place in the Chanukah story, and has inspired generations of Jews. Although a brief version of this story is presented in the Talmud (Gittin 57b) and Midrash (Eichah Rabbah 1:50; Pesikta Rabbasi 44:4; Seder Eliyahu Rabbah chap. 30; see also Chibbur Yaffe MeHaYeshuah by R' Nissim Gaon, Jerusalem, 5730, pp. 15-17), the books of Maccabees (II chap. 7; IV chapts. 8-12) and Yossipon (ch. 19, with (significant variations) give a much lengthier and more detailed account. The story is briefly summarized in the liturgy for the first Sabbath of Chanukah, by R' Yosef bar Shlomo, found in Ashkenazic Siddurim (Otzar HaTefillos, s.v. אזרח and Avodas Yisrael, p. 637) and Machzor Roma.[1] This liturgy is quoted by Rashi (Yechezkel 21:18; see Amudei HaAvodah p. 96). The following is adapted from Yossipon (ed. Huminer) chapter 18-19.

Before leaving Jerusalem to return to Antioch, his capital in Syria, Antiochus appointed Phillip governor of Judea and ordered him to execute a harsh program of anti-Jewish decrees. Among them was: 'Whoever will acquiesce to my command, bow to my image, eat pig's meat, and reject the religion of Moses' Torah will live; whoever refuses shall be killed without pity.' Phillip decided to initiate his campaign with a dramatic public example of Jewish submissiveness, one that would break the back of Jewish stubbornness. He arrested an aged and respected sage, Elazar the *Kohen*, and ordered him, on pain of death, to prostrate himself before the king's image and eat from the pig that had been sacrificed in Antiochus' honor. But Elazar steadfastly clung to his convictions and chose a martyr's death instead.

The Arrest

Thwarted and frustrated, Phillip struck again. He arrested Chanah[2] and her seven sons. Although Antiochus was on the way to Antioch, he was still not far from Jerusalem. Learning of the events in Jerusalem, he decided to participate personally in the execution of his decree. Now, Chanah and her children were brought to him.

One of Chanah's seven sons — the oldest — was brought before Antiochus. Apparently the king thought it wiser to achieve his end

through conciliatory means, especially since he was dealing with youngsters whom he thought he could win over through flattery and bribes. Antiochus conversed with him at length to entice him to break God's covenant and to abandon the Torah of his nation.

The youth responded, 'Why do you trouble yourself with long conversations, to speak of and to teach us the religions of your abominations? Our forefathers have already taught us God's Torah. We stand ready to ascend to God, for we welcome death for the sake of God and his Torah. So we have promised our forefathers! Why need you speak more? Dispatch us speedily to HASHEM our God — kill us!'

Hearing his words, the king flew into a rage. He commanded that an iron frying-pan be brought and put on the fire. He ordered his servant to cut off the boy's tongue, hands, and feet, flay the skin of his head, and place everything upon the frying pan over the fire, while his brothers and mother were forced to watch. Then, the victim — still alive — was put in a copper pot over burning coals. As he was about to die, the king commanded Phillip to remove the fire from under the pot so that he would not die rapidly. In this manner he hoped to intimidate the mother and the brothers so that they would obey him.

They, watching their brother die, said to one another, 'Moses the servant of God declared in his song (*Deut.* 32:36), *When HASHEM will judge His people, He will relent toward his servants.* Now, as a result of our suffering, God will relent from the harm He has decreed upon His people and will have compassion on them.'

And the first brother died.

Then they brought the second brother. The king's nobles and servants exhorted him saying: 'We beseech you — obey the king's directive! Why must you die with great suffering as your brother died?'

Martyrdom Proudly, he answered them: 'Hurry with your fire and sword and do your will with me — do not omit anything that you inflicted upon my brother! I am not inferior to him in devotion, pureness of soul, and fear of God.'

Thereupon, Antiochus bade his men to cut off all the boy's limbs, to put them in the frying pan over the fire, and to do to him as had been done to his brother.

He told the king, 'Woe upon you, you pitiless tyrant. Do you think you can take our souls and wrap them in your cloak to do with them as you wish? They go to the God Who bestowed them, to the

place of the great light that is with God. When God will awaken the dead of His people and His martyred servants, we will yet live endless, boundless lives. But you? — your soul will be consigned to everlasting abhorrence!'

Then they brought in the third brother and the king turned to look at him. He faced Antiochus and said, 'Woe to you, wicked foe! Why do you seek to intimidate me? It is to no avail; we fear not, nor are our hearts anxious, for we know that God's will is to atone through us for His nation, Israel. From Heaven this has come upon us, from there this punishment has reached us; we accept it all with love. But as for you, you are disgraced and despicable in our eyes, and all your tortures and punishment are nought to us. From our God we look forward to honor and kindness; He will reward us for our deeds, but you will be wretched!'

The king and his nobles were flabbergasted at the lofty spirit of this young man. Then he, too, was murdered.

The fourth brother was brought before the king. He said, 'Do not say anything to me, you vicious person. Your plans will not avail you, O lawless one. Do not bore me with your conversation, but do as you wish with my body. My soul will ascend to God my Savior; we shall die for God's Torah. God will return to resurrect us and we shall arise before Him. But for you there will be no resurrection or life.'

Then Antiochus killed the fourth brother.

The fifth brother was brought, and he said to Antiochus: 'Do not suppose that God has handed us over to you to exalt you, or that you are deserving of honor. Nor is it because He hates us that He wants us to stand in judgment before you on this day. Rather it is because He loves us that He has granted us this honor. As for you — in vain do you think that through your cruelty you can make us believe in your pagan deity. To the contrary, your name and your progeny will be wiped off the earth, for God's wrath and his vengeance will be kindled against you and your household. It is true that God is angry with us and has incited you to do whatever you are about to do to us, but He will wreak vengeance upon you and your progeny.'

They killed him as cruelly as the others.

Then the sixth brother was brought. He spoke up, saying, 'We are aware of our wickedness and of the sins of our forefathers, for we have sinned against God. Now, since God is content to let our death atone for the nation, we go to our death. But you, who dare to perpetrate such punishment upon the servants of our God and to

wage war against Him — He will wage war upon you and uproot you from the land of the living!'

And Antiochus killed the sixth brother.

Then the seventh brother — a mere child — was brought. The saintly mother of these children, the pious Chanah, all of whose sons were sentenced to a gruesome death in one day, felt no fear nor did she lose her composure. She recited psalms and exclaimed, '*The* **Chanah's** *mother of the children is joyous, Halleluyah (Psalms* **Pride —** 113:9)!'

The She stood courageously over her slain children — **Youngest** over their limbs which lay strewn about on the ground **Son** and said, 'My children, O my children! I do not know how you entered my innards. I did not fashion your bodies in my womb, nor did I bequeath life and soul to you. I did not raise or exalt you. Rather HASHEM, the God of Israel, created you. He built up your frame, He wove your veins, He grew flesh over you, covered it with skin, sprouted hair over it, breathed the breath of life into you, and brought you out into the light of this world and its air. Now! since you chose to give up your lives for His holy Torah, to die a quick death and to depart from a short life, He will return your souls to you, will return breath to you and you shall live. You shall be saved from the eternal death and will inherit the eternal life, my children, and He will reward you for your deeds. You are fortunate, and fortunate are your parents! May God's providence be with you as He has been with your forefathers.'

The king marveled at her courage, and Phillip, too, was crestfallen that a woman had triumphed over them.

Said Antiochus: 'Bring the seventh brother, who is yet a young lad; perhaps I can persuade him to do my will. Let not a woman boast that she has defeated King Antiochus and inspired her young son to die for the Torah of her God.'

So they brought the seventh brother — a mere child — before the king. Antiochus implored him saying: 'Do my will and I swear to you I will appoint you as my viceroy; you will reign over my entire kingdom. You will be wealthy, with gold and silver and many possessions.'

The lad, contemptuous of the king's proposal, answered him: 'O you old, foolish king! How can you boast of a false gift? You do not even know what today will bring. How can you propose to foretell the morrow?'

Upon hearing this, the king answered harshly, threatening the

boy with the various tortures he would inflict upon him if he persevered in his refusal to do the royal will.

The lad retorted again: *'Why do you pride yourself with evil, O mighty warrior? The kindness of God is all day long (Psalm 52:3).* Hurry — do as you have said. Do not delay. God has made my journey successful, so let me embark upon it.'

Hearing the youngster's words, the king was amazed. He summoned the lad's mother. She stood before him with her hands tied. Antiochus said to her, 'Good woman! Have compassion upon this child; have pity upon the fruit of your womb! Persuade him to do my will so that you will have at least one surviving child and you too will live and not be destroyed.'

She answered, 'Give him to me, I will take him aside at a distance from you. Perhaps I will be able to convince him.'

So they gave him to his mother and she took him a short distance away. She kissed him and smiled contemptuously at the king's humiliation. Said she to her child: 'My son! Meditate upon my words and understand them. I carried you nine months in my belly, for two years I nursed you with my milk, and I have nurtured you with food and drink to this day. I also taught you about the fear of God and His Torah as your ability and years allowed. Now my son! Open your eyes and see heaven and earth, sea and land, fire, water, wind, and all the other creations. Contemplate them and be aware that *With the word of HASHEM were the heavens made (Psalms 33:6).* Afterwards God created man so that he serve Him perfectly, to cleave to Him, and to imbue the fear of God in his heart, and God will reward him for his deeds. The assurances of man are vain and empty — they will not avail nor give success. It is all nothing compared to the everlasting world to come.

A Mother's Pleading

'Now my son! Let not this merciless tyrant reassure you with deceitful promises, do not rely upon his pronouncements — for what can he give you? What can a human give, who has no control over his own body, over his own life? Because the king sees that he is condemned before God for killing your brothers, therefore he persists in vindicating himself, hoping God will forgive him. He thinks that if he convinces you and you do not die, his compassion on you will save him from God's judgment.

'Now my son! If you submit to him, you may be saved temporarily from *his* judgment, but how will you escape *God's* judgment if you exchange His Torah for the king's folly? God

controls your life's breath and can take your soul to Him if He so desires, and He can destroy you and all creatures on earth in one second. It would be sacrilege for you to do this! Listen to me and die for God. Go as your brothers did!

'Would that I could — my son — see now the greatness of your glorious place where we would be illuminated with God's light and rejoice and exult together. As for me, my son, I will come to you there with joy and rejoice with you as if I had participated in your wedding; let me have a share in your holiness and righteousness.'

As she spoke to him thus at length, the lad responded to her and said: 'Why do you delay me from going to my martyred brothers? I do not intend to obey the king; I will not listen to him. His words and promises are nothing to me. Rather I will listen and submit only to the Torah of our God, which was given through Moses our teacher, peace be upon him, to Israel the Holy nation.'

Thereupon the woman returned her son to the king and said: 'He is in your hands; I could not convince him.'

Again the king said to the lad: 'Woe, O you silly child! Why do you not take my advice and do my will and not die?'

A Child Defeats the King

Said the lad to him: 'Woe, O old and foolish king, tyrant and foe of God! Over whom do you seek to aggrandize yourself, saying you have triumphed with your arguments and your foolish enticements? Over me, a boy of seven years, while you are seventy years old? I scoff at your foolishness, but you have refused to be humiliated. I believe in the Torah of HASHEM, our God, Whom you have blasphemed and profaned by word and deed, and I do not take heed of your delusion and folly.

'As for you, O you foolish king, woe to you! Where will you hide from our God's spirit? Where will you flee from before Him? O wicked foe! O lawless man! Lo, He will exalt and elevate *us*, but as for *you* — who conspired to lay hands upon His servants — it would have been better had you never left the womb of your vile mother who gave birth to an ignoramus and fool such as you. You have harmed yourself, but you have benefited us. Though here, in this world, we suffer the pain of your judgments, we go to an everlasting life, to the place of light where there is no darkness, to the place of life where death does not exist. But you will remain an abomination upon all mankind, loathsome and far removed from God. He will wreak vengeance upon you, you will die an unnatural death, suffering many afflictions and excruciating pain. To the nethermost

abyss will you sink, to a place where there is no light or life, — it is the place of darkness and overshadowed by death. There you will find neither rest nor solace, rather calamity and distress will embrace you, fire and brimstone will surround you; this is your lot from my God, as befits a bloodthirsty and lawless man.

'HASHEM our God will have compassion upon His people, and bestow mercy upon His devout ones. Until now His wrath was upon us, but from now on He will not be angry with us any longer and will reconsider all that He has done to us. For He has acted with truth and justice and we have sinned before Him — but He will once again have compassion upon us and repress our iniquities for the sake of His Name. He will accept our punishment as atonement for all of Israel, and will make our souls live an eternal life.'

The king — enraged that his will had not been done — commanded that they beat this last son more brutally and severely than his brothers, and they killed him too.

According to the version of this story in the Talmud (Gittin 57a), Antiochus offered the youngest child a chance to save himself, 'I will throw my signet ring in front of you so that you can bend down to pick it up. Then people, thinking you bowed to me, will say that you have accepted my authority.'

But the little boy mocked the monarch, 'Woe to you, O King, woe to you, O King! If your own self-respect is so important to you, how much more so the respect due the Holy One, Blessed is He!'

As they removed him to be killed his mother pleaded, 'Give him to me so that I can kiss him briefly!'

She said to him, as if she were speaking to all her seven sons, 'My children, go and tell your ancestor Abraham, "You bound only one [son upon an] altar, but I bound [seven sons upon] altars." '

Then their mother, the holy Chanah, the pious and pure, who was unique in her devotion, stood over the seven bodies that lay strewn about upon the earth, and lifted her hands skyward.

And Chanah prayed[3] saying, 'My heart exults in HASHEM. My

The Mother is Joyous pride is uplifted through my God, for through my sons He has chosen to reconsider His wrath against His people, that may they again be His servants.

'My mouth opens wide against my enemies, for they were unable to entice even one of my sons to turn to the service of their delusions (i.e. idols) which are of no avail and save not, for they are as nought. There is none as holy as HASHEM, and none but He is the savior of the souls trusting in Him. Do not increase your

haughty bombast, you foes of HASHEM and enemies of Yehudah and Israel! Let not haughty talk escape your mouths, saying that you have triumphed with your might, that your gods have power.

'HASHEM is the God Who knows all, and by Him are deeds counted, and just as He has punished us for our and our forefathers' sins, so will the God of our Salvation return and have compassion upon us, while the enemies of Yehudah will be destroyed.'

To this she added, 'God Who is above all powers, exalted and awesome, God of the world, HASHEM! Please, HASHEM, grant success now to Your maidservant Chanah, gather in my soul and let not the foe smite me, let not the infidel mock me, let him not defile me. Show me the place You have designated for Your servants, my sons who died for the holiness of Your Torah, and bestow upon me a small portion together with them. All Your creatures shall laud You, Your devout ones shall bless You, and so will I together with them'.

When she finished praying and pouring out her supplication to God, her soul departed her and her spirit left her. She fell over the bodies of her sons and lay upon the earth together with them.[4]

NOTES

1. Although in the passage in the Talmud and the Midrash the king is given the title Caesar (קיסר), suggesting that this story took place under one of the Roman emperors, the striking similarity to the story in *Maccabees* and *Yossipon* leads one to the assumption that all the sources deal with one occurrence. *R' Yaakov Emden* in his glosses to the Talmud remarks tersely: This story occurred in the presence of Antiochus. However *Seder Eliyahu Rabbah* (ch. 30) reports that the name of the 'Caesar' figuring in this story is the Roman emperor Hadrian (אדריינוס) who reigned from 117-138, thus placing this occurrence within the time frame of the religious persecution (שעת השמד) which followed the suppression of the Bar Koziva uprising. Thus one is led to the conjecture that there were two almost identical events in different centuries — the first during Antiochus' tenure as reported in the books of *Maccabees, Yossipon* and the liturgy to Shabbos Chanukah; and the second which occured more than 250 years later and is recorded in the Talmud and Midrashim.

2. Yossipon is the only source that gives her name as Chanah. The books of *Maccabees* are silent about her name as is the Talmud. The Midrashim (*Eichah Rabbah* and *Pesikta Rabbasi*) give her name variously as Miriam bas Tanchum or Nachtum. Indeed some versions of *Yossipon* (see ed. Flusser p. 70) omit her name.

3. The prayer recited here by Chanah is interspersed with segments of a prayer by an earlier Chanah, the mother of the prophet Samuel (*I Samuel* 2:1-10).

4. The sources disagree about the circumstances of her death. Our version, found in *Yossipon*, agrees with that of *II Macc.* (7:41) which reports tersely that 'After the sons, the mother died'. The Talmud (*Gittin* 57b) relates that the mother ascended a roof and threw herself off it. A Heavenly voice was then heard saying, '*The mother of the children is joyous*' (*Psalms* 113:9). [Yossipon has the mother reciting this same verse at the death of each of her sons.] A similar account is given in *IV Macc.* (17:1). The Midrash (*Eichah Rabbah*) says she lost her sanity and committed suicide.

The Daughter of the Kohen Gadol

One of the important motifs in the Chanukah story is the heroism of Jewish women in preserving their modesty. The Sages have been reluctant to give many details about the ordeals and indignities inflicted by the Syrian-Greeks, no doubt out of respect for the dignity of the Jewish woman. Nevertheless, here and there we find veiled references to it in the Talmud,[1] and more explicit ones in Midrashic sources.[2]

Megillas Taanis (17 Elul) relates that the Syrian-Greek kings would appoint officers in the towns of *Eretz Yisrael* to ravish all Jewish brides. Only after submitting to the officers would the women be permitted to marry their intended husbands. Consequently, Jewish people refused to marry or they would marry clandestinely. Mattisyahu ben Yochanan the *Kohen Gadol* (the father of the Hasmonean brothers) had a daughter who was engaged to be married.[3] When her wedding date arrived and the Syrian-Greek official came to defile her, Mattisyahu and his sons prevented him from doing so. They did battle against the offending officials and their troops and, miraculously, were able to defeat and kill them. The day of this victory was designated as a festival.

A sequel to this story is given in the Midrash for Chanukah (*Beis HaMidrash* part 1 p. 132, *Otzar Midrashim* p. 192). Upon hearing about the execution of his officials, the Syrian king gathered his entire army and besieged Jerusalem. A widow named Yehudis volunteered to go to the king and rescue the city. She gained an audience with him and succeeded in seducing him. He made a lavish feast in her honor during which much wine was consumed. He became drunk and fell into a deep sleep. That night as he slept, she took his sword and decapitated him. She put his head in her pouch and brought it back to the city with her, whereupon the Jews hung it on the city walls. When the Greeks realized they had lost their leader they panicked and fled.[4]

From the information given in the various versions found in different sources, it is difficult to pinpoint with certainty the time frame during which this story took place. However the *Midrashim Ma'aseh Chanukah* (version 1; *Otzar Midrashim* p. 189) and *Midrash LaChanukah (op. cit.* p. 192) and the liturgy for the first

Sabbath of Chanukah concur that the decree against Jewish brides was in force for three years and eight months. If we can assume that the first three years of the decree coincide with the three years of persecution under Antiochus Epiphanes, which commenced in Kislev 3594 and ended in Kislev 3597[5] with the rededication of the Temple on Chanukah, we can assume that even after the Temple was rededicated, *some* of the immoral legislation of Antiochus remained in force for the next eight months.

NOTES

1. The Talmud *(Kesubos 3b)* cites a ruling in *Tosefta* (op. cit 1:1) that: 'from the era of danger (סַכָּנָה) and afterward' the people are accustomed to get married on the third [day of the week]. The *Gemara* explains that this refers to the edict commanding, 'every Jewish maiden (בְּתוּלָה) who married to consort first with the [king's] officer.' A ruling in the Mishnah *(Kesubos* 12a הָאוֹכֵל אֵצֶל חָמִיו) is based on a custom current in Judea as a consequence of such an immoral decree. Although *Yerushalmi's* elaboration on this custom indicates that the Mishnah refers to persecution by the Romans, this does not preclude an identical occurrence much earlier during the Syrian period. *Yerushalmi* refers to the Romans because they were much closer historically to the period of the Mishnah. *Rashi* explains the Talmud's statement *(Shabbos* 23a): 'They (women) too participated in the miracle,' as referring to the story of a woman's heroism in defiance of the immoral edict (cf. *Chiddushei HaRitva HaChadashim, loc. cit.).* Other commentators (see *Ran* and others) follow *Rashi's* interpretation.

2. *Midrash Ma'aseh Chanukah* (both versions) in *Beis HaMidrash* part 5; *Otzar Midrashim* p. 189-92; *Midrash LaChanukah, Otzar Midrashim,* p. 192; *Beis HaMidrash,* part 1, p. 132. Some versions of *Megillas Antiochus* (see *Batei Midrashos,* v. 1, p. 325) report that the incident involved 'Chashmonai's' daughter. The liturgies in the Ashkenazic machzor for the first and second Sabbaths of Chanukah (authored by *R' Yosef bar Shlomo* and cited by *Rashi* in his comm. to *Yechezkel* 21:18, and *R' Menachem ben Machir,* a disciple of *Rashi)* add a few particulars unknown from other sources (see further note).

Some communities observe a custom to eat cheese on Chanukah based on one version of this occurrence (see *Shulchan Aruch Orach*

Chaim 670:2). According to this version, a daughter of Yochanan *Kohen Gadol* was forced to come to the Syrian-Greek commander on her wedding day, but she outwitted him. By inducing him to eat cheese and dairy products, she made him drowsy. When he fell asleep she decapitated him. (I have not found this particular in any of the extant historical narratives of this story.)

Rambam (Hil. Chanukah 3:1) states: During the Second Temple era, when the Greeks ruled, they instituted (oppressive) decrees upon Israel, banned their religion, and did not let them engage in Torah and *mitzvos* (לעסוק בתורה ומצות). They availed themselves of their money and daughters.

3. *Midrash Ma'aseh Chanukah* (both versions) concurs with *Megillas Ta'anis* that she was a daughter of Mattisyahu. This Midrash even reports that she was betrothed to one of Chashmonai's sons (see also liturgy for the first Shabbos of Chanukah). Version 1 adds that his name was Elazar, a detail mentioned in the liturgy for the second Sabbath of Chanukah, which adds that her name was 'Chanah.' However, other sources *(Midrash LaChanukah; Ran; Kol Bo;* the liturgy for the first Sabbath of Chanukah) report she was a daughter of Yochanan *Kohen Gadol.* However *Midrash LaChanukah* makes it clear that she was a sister of Yehudah, thus contradicting itself. In *Megillas Antiochus* she is styled 'the daughter of Chashmonai'.

4. The story as told in *Ran, Kol Bo,* and *Rama (Orach Chaim* 670:2), merges both of the above stories: Yochanan's daughter herself causes the Greek to fall into a deep sleep and slays him. The source for this version is not known.

The story of the widow Yehudis strongly resembles the tale of Yehudis in the apocryphal book *Judith.* However, the latter

has as its time framework the reign of Nebuchadnezzar. The version given by *Chemdas Yamim (see Otzar Midrashim,* p. 204-209) is clearly a different version of *Judith* differing in only one detail: In both sources, the enemy leader is named Holofernes [אֲלְפוֹרְנִי], but in *Chemdas Yamim* he is a Syrian-Greek king, while in *Judith* he is one of Nebuchadnezzar's generals. The liturgy in the Ashkenazi *machzor* for the first Sabbath of Chanukah (s.v., אוֹדְךָ כִּי אָנַפְתָּ) mentions Holofernes in the context of the war with the Hasmoneans and the story of Yehudis. The scant details given in this liturgy also agree essentially with the apocryphal story except that here Holofernes is a Greek and wars with the Hasmoneans.

Clearly the story of Yehudis was traditionally associated with the Chanukah miracle. Although the apocryphal account agrees with the tradition in most of even the minute details, it was somehow perverted and transported into another time frame, that of Nebuchadnezzar. Historically, the time frame of the apocryphal account is untenable, for under Nebuchadnezzar there was no Jewish community in *Eretz Yisrael.*

5. These Midrashim indeed relate that this decree was accompanied by other anti-religious enactments, including some traditionally assumed to have been enacted by Antiochus. This is a plausible assumption if we bear in mind that Yehudah and his followers were not in control of the country even after the Chanukah miracle. The decree lasted for another eight months, which brings us to Tammuz, whereas *Megillas Taanis* reports this event in Elul, two months later. Perhaps the struggle to eradicate the evil decree lasted for some time, or alternatively this specific decree was enacted after the other anti-Jewish legislation (as indicated in *Midrash Ma'aseh Chanukah*), in which case the three-year eight-month duration of the decree ended in Elul. The story of Yehudis could have occurred during Antiochus V's siege of Jerusalem (3598) and would thus constitute another factor in the hasty peace agreement reached with the Syrians, or alternatively, happened later during the siege of Jerusalem by Demetrius I (3601). See also *Tzemach David* (3622) and *Mor UKetzia (R' Yaakov Emden)* to *Orach Chaim* 670.

The Dating of Chanukah

The exact date of the rededication of the Temple by the Hasmoneans and the simultaneous occurrence of the miracle of the oil celebrated by the lighting of Chanukah candles is not given by the Talmud or other authoritative Torah sources. Indeed, it has become the subject of controversy. The books of *Maccabees* (followed by Josephus Flavius) give exact dates for the events they report, and according to them the rededication occurred on 25 Kislev 3597[1] (165 B.C.E. see; *I Macc. 4:52*).

It is clear from the account in *Maccabees* (and Josephus Flavius) that the rededication of the Temple — the 'Chanukah' — was just that and nothing more: not a total victory, that gained control over the country, but a triumph that gave the loyal Jews free access to and control over the Temple. Yehudah and his followers were far from having conquered the country, or even Jerusalem. As our History of Chanukah relates, it took over twenty years — and the death of four out of five Hasmonean brothers — for the Hasmonean revolt to gain sovereignty over *Eretz Yisrael*. However, from the Chanukah miracle on, the Syrian authorities made no attempt to interrupt the Temple service, and on 15 Adar or Nissan in the year following the Chanukah miracle[2] Antiochus V Eupator officially confirmed the abrogation of his father's anti-Jewish legislation. Although the successful Hasmonean revolt made impossible the enforcement of many such decrees, they all remained *legally* in force, and some were *actually* enforced. With the formal abrogation, the Jews would be allowed to live 'undisturbed,' 'their Temple would be returned to them,' and they were to live as citizens according to their ancestral customs' *(II Macc. 11:25; see there v. 27-33)*.

The fortunes of Yehudah and his followers waxed and waned with the events of the next few years, reaching a nadir with the death in combat of Yehudah four years later (3601 — 160 B.C.E.; *I Macc. 9:1-22*), when the surviving Hasmonean brothers were forced to flee and hide in the caves of Trans-Jordan. But never did Yehudah presume to be the ruler of Judea. Yonasan, who succeeded Yehudah as leader of the revolt, established a beachhead in Michmash some time after the year 3602 (159 B.C.E.) and took advantage of the civil

war between Alexander and Demetrius I in the year 3609 (152 B.C.E.) to establish himself in Jerusalem. On Succos of that year Yonasan officiated as *Kohen Gadol* for the first time *(I Macc. 10:21)*. The warring contenders to the Syrian throne vied with each other for Yonasan's support and promised him concessions. Clearly at this point, however, he was merely a local overlord still legally subordinate to the central government in Antioch. Indeed some of the concessions took the form of release from certain taxes.

Two years later the Syrian king Alexander acknowledged Yonasan as the governor of a province. Only in the year 3619 (142 B.C.E.) did the Hasmonean Shimon, the last surviving son of Mattisyahu, consider himself strong enough to be entitled 'Prince of the Jews' *(I Macc. 13:41-2)*. However formal recognition of his princeship by the people and the Sages (Sanhedrin) came only two years later on 18 Elul 3621 as related in the document reproduced verbatim in *I Macc.* (14:27-47). This date corresponds to that given by the Sages for the establishment of 'the kingdom of the Hasmoneans.' The *kingdom* of the Hasmoneans, in the sense that they were sovereign monarchs with the *title* of king, did not materialize until twenty-four years had passed after the initial conquest of the Temple and the miracle of Chanukah.

This is corroborated by the tradition given in *Seder Olam Rabbah* (ch. 30) and the Talmud *(Avodah Zarah 9a)*, which records that the 'kingdom of the Hasmonean house' commenced 206 years before the Destruction. The Destruction occurred in the year 3828[3] (see *Tos.*, s.v. האי *ad loc.*) so that the 'kingdom of the Hasmoneans' is designated to have commenced in the year 3622 (3828—206=3622), less than two weeks after the date (18 Elul 3621) given in *Maccabees*[4]. This time frame for the occurrence of the Chanukah miracle was evidently followed by the anonymous author of the ancient (from the Geonic era) chronicle *Seder Olam Zuta*[5] and *R' Yitzchak Abarbanel (Mayenei HaYeshuah 2:3)*,[6] as pointed out by *Tzemach David* (3590)[7].

Rambam (Hil. Chanukah 3:1-2) states: '... and when the Hasmoneans, (בְּנֵי חַשְׁמֹנָאִי) the *Kohanim Gedolim* prevailed, killed them (i.e. the Syrian-Greeks), and saved Israel from their hands, they set up a king from among the *Kohanim* and kingship reverted to Israel for more than two hundred years until the second Destruction. When Israel prevailed over its enemies and annihilated them it was the twenty-fifth of Kislev.'

On the surface, *Rambam* seems to say that the beginning of the monarchy, the Hasmonean victory, and the Chanukah miracle, all

occurred at the same time — if so, *Rambam* contradicts the time frame cited above. This is not so, however. Obviously, *Rambam* did not intend to telescope the entire history of the period into a few lines. His vague phrase 'more than two hundred years' (evidently based on the 206 year total given in *Seder Olam* and the Talmud) refers only to the last event he mentions, the establishment of the kingdom. Surely, according to all the sources, all the events did not occur in one year; the beginning of the revolt preceded the miracle of the oil by at least a year (according to *Maccabees* by three years). *Rambam* does not give a date for the occurrence of the Chanukah miracle in accordance with his expressed principle (see the preface to his *Mishneh Torah)* to summarize only the words of the Sages in the Talmud and other Rabbinic literature. Even if he had access to the books of *Maccabees* — and there is no evidence that he had — he would not have included such information in his Code.

As pointed out previously, the time frame assigned here to the Chanukah events is the one accepted by most contemporary Orthodox historians[8] and is the basis of most history texts used in Orthodox schools. The father of modern historical research as seen from the traditional perspective, the eminent Gaon *R' Isaac HaLevi,* also accepts this date without reservation in his monumental work *Doros HaRishonim*[9].

However many of the early chroniclers, notably *Ravad HaLevi in Sefer HaKaballah,*[10] *R' Yitzchak HaYisraeli (Yesod Olam* 4:18), *Tzemach David,* and others, assume the year 3621 or 3622[11] to be the year of the Chanukah miracle. Many of the occurrences reported in *Maccabees* are telescoped by these chroniclers into a much shorter period. With the exception of *Tzemach David,* none of these chroniclers had access to the books of *Maccabees* and presumably had no knowledge of many of the events related there. *Tzemach David* (with the above named chroniclers) assumes that the term 'the kingdom of the Hasmoneans' used in *Seder Olam Rabbah* and the Talmud should be applied to the period immediately following the Chanukah miracle. In his view, these sources contradict the dates found in *Seder Olam Zuta* and *Maccabees.* However, as demonstrated above, these sources *do* conform with the statement in *Seder Olam Rabbah* and the Talmud.

The ancient document popularly known as *Megillas Antiochus*[12] also assigns the Chanukah miracle to the time slot accorded it by *Tzemach David* and the old chronicles. However there are other major discrepancies between the narrative in *Megillas Antiochus* and that given in all the other chronicles. The two most notable are:

A) According to the *Megillah*, the initiator of the revolt is not Mattisyahu but his son Yochanan; B) Yehudah 'the Maccabee' plays a minor role in the Chanukah event according to *Megillas Antiochus*; in fact, he is killed in the first engagement with the enemy.

NOTES

1. *Maccabees* calls this the 'year 148.' The era in use at that time for counting years was the Seleucid Era — or, as the Talmud calls it, the Greek Era — as set forth in *Seder Olam Rabbah* (Ch. 30) and the Talmud *(Avodah Zarah* 10a). This era begins with the year 3449 as the year zero, and with the year 3450 as the year 1, according to the comparative dates given by *Rambam (Hil. Shemittah VeYovel* 10:4). That our method of counting years from Creation agrees with that of *Rambam* is evidenced by the agreement of our year of *Shemittah* [Sabbatical Year] with that which *Rambam* gives as the one traditionally used in *Eretz Yisrael* according to the Geonim. Since *Shemittah* is observed every seventh year without exception, it is impossible for an error to have crept into the calculations, just as it is inconceivable that the Sabbath is not in its rightful place — every succeeding seventh day is Shabbos. *Ravad HaLevi (Sefer HaKabbalah),* who gives the year 3450 as the starting point of the Greek Era, probably refers to the year 1. The Talmud *(Avodah Zarah* 9a), which seems to start the Greek Era in the year 3448, is explained by *R' Avraham bar Chiyu HaNussi (Sefer Halbbur, Ma'amar* 3 sec. 8) as having a calendar counting the Creation from the creation of Adam, and does not count the days preceding Adam as a year. But the halachically accepted system is defined by *Rambam* as beginning a new year with the life of Adam; that we accept *Ramham's* view is proven by the simple fact that three elements of our calendar are in accord with his thesis: the *Shmittah* year universally in use; the calculations used to extablish the time of the New Moon; and the year in which *Birkas HaChammah* [Blessing of the Sun] is recited. Using the year 3449 as the starting date and adding to it 148 years we get the year 3597. If we are to assume (as argued by some scholars) that the Greek Era used by the books of *Maccabees* starts a year earlier than that in use in North Africa in *Rambam's* time, then all of the dates used in this book should have to have one year subtracted from them.

2. II *Macc.* 11:33 gives the date Nissan of the year 148 (Seleucid era) in the context of a letter from Antiochus V to the assembly of the people (Sanhedrin). However this is improbable, for a preceding letter from Antiochus V to his general Lysias mentions the death of Antiochus IV, arch villain of the Chanukah story. According to I *Macc.* 6:16, Antiochus IV's death occured in the year *after* the Chanukah event (149 Seleucid era). Even if we are to assume that the reference to the king's death in the letter to Lysias was based on erroneous information (Antiochus' death during a foreign military campaign had been rumored long before the actual event), it is difficult to telescope all the events in *I Macc.* 5-6 and *I Macc.* 8-11 into the short period of four months Antiochus V's letter is dated in Xanthipus (Nissan) and the earlier letter to Lysias is dated 24 Dios (Cheshvan; see A. Kahanah's notes to *II Macc.)* in the year 148, and would antedate the Chanukah event, a hypothesis contradicted by the tenor of the letters. Two resolutions present themselves. Either *II Macc.* should read *149 (3598)* or *II Macc.* employed a Seleucid era starting one year before that used in *I Macc.* — an unlikely assumption, although it is accepted by some scholars. At any rate this would be the year 3598 which corresponds to the year 149 in the system used by *I Macc.*

3. This is the date arrived at when one adds the sum of the years assigned to the Second Temple era by the Sages — 420 — to the year of its building — 3408 — as calculated in *Seder Olam Rabbah* (ch. 30) and the Talmud *(Avodah Zarah* 9a). The controversy between *Rashi* and *Tosafos* (op. cit. 9b s.v. האי) whether the Destruction actually occurred in this year or on the succeeding year — 3829 — is not pertinent here. Those accepting the later date believed that the Destruction occurred in the 421st year from the erection of the Temple. If so the Talmud's figures for the four periods in the Second Temple era, which total only 420 years, obviously does not include the year of the destruction.

4. Although halachically the year 3622

would be the second year of Shimon's rule – because the remaining fraction of the year 3621 was considered as a year in ancient times for the purpose of numbering years (see *Rosh Hashanah* 1:1) — this is so only insofar as assigning a number to a given year is concerned. When a sum of elapsed years is given, however, only *actual* years are counted, i.e., the time elapsing between 18 Elul 3621 to 18 Tishrei would still be only one month, although, in the calendar used for dating contracts, the period would have begun in one year and continued into a second year. However, if R' Avraham ben Chiya's assertion (see fn. 1) that our Creation-based calendar antedates that of the Talmud by one year is true, the result is that the Destruction occurred in the year 3829 (or 3830 according to *Tos.* interpretation) of our calendar, with the consequence that the 'kingdom of the Hasmoneans' (206 years earlier) began on the year 3623. Even so, the discrepancy of a year (or even two) is too minor a divergence to be considered a contradiction. The years given in the tradition must contain fractions of years not included in the total sum (these eras surely did not all commence at the same day of the year), i.e. the 103 years of the Herodian era could be 103½ and those of the Hasmonean era 103½ so that the aggregate years of these two eras add up to 207 years. Since the total sum of years allotted to the Second Temple era is not more than 420 years, the year(s) which accrue(s) through the addiction of the fractions must be subtracted from other components of the sum, e.g. the 180 years allotted to the rule of the Greeks. Similar lines of reasoning are found in the Talmud (*Megillah* 11b; אמר רבא שנים מקוטעות היו).

5. Although *Seder Olam Zuta* surprisingly omits any mention of the Chanukah miracle, it gives the death of Mattisyahu as the year 140 of the Seleucid era (3589 from creation), six years earlier than the date given by *Maccabees*. The year of Mattisyahu's death antedated the start of the revolt (which clearly occurred 'in the days of Mattisyahu ben Yochanan *Kohen Gadol*' as attested to in the *Al HaNissim* prayer). *Seder Olam Zuta* also reports that Mattisyahu's last surviving son, Shimon, died in 170 (3619) shortly before the date assigned to Chanukah by the old chroniclers. *I Maccabees* (16:14-16) reports that he died in Shevat 177 (3626). Perhaps the number 170 in *Seder Olam Zuta* is a scribe's error and should read 177; the context of *Maccabees* rules out the possibility of such an emendation there.

6. *Abarbanel* allows for only 145 years of Greek domination before the Chanukah revolt, but as pointed out by *R' Azaryah min HaAdumim* (*Meor Einayim, Imrei Binah* ch. 36) this should be emended to read 148 to accord with *Maccabees*.

7. *Tzemach David* arrived at the figure 3590 (probably) by assuming that the Seleucid era used in *Maccabees* was that used by some very punctilious scribes (סָפְרֵי דַוְקָנָא) who used the year 3442 as the starting point for their calendar as reported by the Talmud (*Avodah Zarah* 10a). Adding 148 — the year in the Seleucid era year assigned to Chanukah — to 3442 you arrive at the year 3590.

8. R' Ch. D. Rabinowitz (author of the commentary *Daas Sofrim* on *Tanach*), in *Hadrachah BeLimud Toldos Yisrael* (Israel, 1979), in a note to ch. 39 arrives at a solution differing only slightly from the one put forth here.

A notable exception among modern historians is R' S. Rottenberg who (*Toldos Am Olam*, vol. 2, pp. 139-224 and 403) adheres to the timetable drawn by *Tzemach David*.

9. R' I. HaLevi does not deal directly with the Chanukah miracle, but his references to other events of that period indicate unmistakably that he accepts the dating of *Maccabees*, e.g., he places the death of Yose ben Yoezer in the Seleucid year 151 (3600) on the basis of the dates given in *Maccabees* for the tenure of Alcimus, the Hellenist *Kohen Gadol* who assumed office after the Chanukah miracle occurred (see *Doros HaRishonim*, vol. 1, pp. 168, 177, ed. Israel).

10. *Ravad* places this event in the year 3681 — an obvious error, which should read 3621 (A. Neubauer in *Seder HaChachmim*, vol. 1, p. 52, gives variant readings from manuscripts, all of them erroneous).

11. *Tzemach David* places the revolt in the year 3621, and the ultimate victory over the Greeks and the ensuing rededication of the Temple and the miracle of Chanukah in the year 3622.

12. Although unknown to most of the Diaspora in recent times, this ancient scroll was widely known in earlier times. R' Saadiah Gaon's Arabic translation of Megillas Antiochus is extant in many Yemenite manuscripts and has been printed in *Batei Midrashim* (R' S.A. Wertheimer, v. 1 pp. 311-330). In his preface to the Megillah, R' Saadiah writes that the Megillah is read

'by most of the nation,' a practice alluded to by the early Italian authorities *Tosefos Rid (Succah* 446) and *Shibolei HaLeket* (174). In later times the Megillah was popular in Italy, as indicated by its inclusion in almost all editions of the *Machzor Roma* and in some editions of the Italo-Ashkenazic machzor (Sabionetta-Cremona 5317-21). *R' Yosef Kafich (Halichos Teiman* p. 38) reports that in Yemen the Megillah was read by many with R' Saadiah's Arabic translation. In the Crimea, it was read publicly after *Minchah* on the Sabbath of Chanukah *(Siddur Otzar HaTefillos).* In modern times this Megillah has become well-known among Ashkenazic Jews because of its inclusion in the popular Siddurim *Avodas Yisrael* and *Otzar HaTefillos.*

The Megillah's authorship and time of composition are debatable. *R' Saadiah Gaon (Sefer HaGaluy* in *Zikaron LaRishonim* v. 5 p. 150, see there pp. 162, 180) ascribes its authorship to Yehudah, Shimon, Yochanan and Elazar, the sons of Mattisyahu. If so, we must assume that additions and revisions were made later since the narrative summarizes the 206 years subsequent to the Hasmonean victory and mentions the Destruction (v. 72), describes the death of Yehudah and Elazar, two of its purported authors, and is written in third person. The author of *Halachos Gedolos* states *(Hil. Soferim,* ed. Warsaw p. 282; see also R' Nissim Gaon's preface to *Chibur Yaffeh MeHaYeshuah) that the 'sages of Bais Hillel and Bais Shamai' wrote 'the scroll of the Hasmonean House'* (מְגִילַת בֵּית חַשְׁמוֹנָאִי). However this passage is not found in the Hildesheimer edition (see notes there).

Duration of the Hasmonean Monarchy

The History and the previous essay, 'The Dating of Chanukah,' have suggested that the tenure of the Hasmoneans as the rulers of *Eretz Yisrael* can be seen on different levels: Yehudah's liberation of the Temple, Yonason's success in gaining major concessions from the competitors for the Syrian throne, and Shimon's accession as 'Prince' or 'Ruler' of the Jews. In addition, two later events should be considered. Shimon's successor, Yochanan Hyrkanos, revolted against the last vestige of Seleucid control over *Eretz Yisrael* and made the land *fully* independent for the first time since the days of the first Temple. The next Hasmonean ruler, Yehudah Aristobulos, who no longer followed the glorious spiritual tradition of his ancestors, had the temerity to give himself the official title of king, something that neither Shimon or Yochanan Hyrkanos had done. These differing forms of Hasmonean power and status help us understand seemingly contradictory statements of the Sages.

Let us begin with the text of the official acceptance by the people of Shimon as their leader:

> ... they engraved on brass pillars and set on pillars on Mount Zion the following: [there appears a long list of Shimon's achievements on behalf of the nation.] And when the people saw Shimon's faithfulness and the prestige he brought his people, they made him their prince and *Kohen Gadol* ... And the Jews and their *Kohanim* resolved that Shimon should remain their prince and *Kohen Gadol* until a true prophet will appear (*I Macc.* 14:27-45).

Maran Hagaon R' Yaakov Kaminetzky, שליט״א, finds a key to a proper understanding of the period in two key phrases: they accepted Shimon as a **prince,** [נָשִׂיא], not a *king;* and they limited his tenure until a *true prophet will appear.*

Ramban (Gen. 49:10) categorizes the Hasmonean monarchy as illegal, since it contravened Jacob's blessing to Judah that kingship would remain with his tribe. So serious was this unsanctioned assumption of the crown that it caused the Hasmoneans to suffer a total, murderous extermination at the hands of Herod in 3725. However, this impropriety could not have been ascribed to Shimon and his brothers, the first Hasmonean rulers who were totally

righteous and God-fearing. They never presumed to call themselves 'kings' — only *Kohanim Gedolim* and *'princes'*, or rulers, of the people. That they assumed power at all was only because there was no qualified member of the Davidic dynasty; only the Hasmoneans were capable of exercising leadership at that juncture.

To accentuate this principle the people's pledge of allegiance included the proviso that Shimon was nothing more than a 'prince' and that he would lead until the emergence of a prophet — presumably to herald the longed-for Messianic age when a scion of David would reign.

Harav Kaminetzky finds in another practice of the Second Temple era an attempt by the Sages to preserve Jewish allegiance to the goal of the Messianic era. The Sages teach that the presently used names for the Hebrew months are of Babylonian origin and were brought to *Eretz Yisrael* with the returnees from exile (*Yerushalmi Rosh Hashanah* 1:2; see *Tos. Rosh Hashanah* 7a s.v. מדברי and *Ramban Exod.* 12:1). Since some of these months, such as Tammuz (*Yechezkel* 8:14), were the names of idols, it seems strange that the Sages authorized their use as part of Jewish observance. In this case, too, the Sages wished to establish constant reminders for a principle of Jewish belief. There was a danger that the returnees from Babylon, having built the Second Temple, might have deluded themselves into thinking that the period of גְּאוּלָה שְׁלֵמָה, *Complete Redemption*, had arrived. To dispel this notion, the Sages of the period decreed that the Babylon names of months — including the blatantly pagan ones — should be used. This would emphasize to the Jews that even though they were back in *Eretz Yisrael*, Israel was not yet considered to be free from its exile status.

As we have shown above (the Date of Chanukah), the Talmud's description of the Hasmonean dynasty as enduring for 103 years should be understood as beginning *not* from the time of the Chanukah miracle in 3597, but from Israel's acknowledgment of Shimon as its prince, in 3621.

However, in a seemingly conflicting passage (*Sanhedrin* 97b) the Talmud describes the dynasty as having endured for only *seventy* years. As *Rashi* explains, during seventy of the 103 years of Hasmonean rule the Jewish rulers enjoyed a greater degree of sovereignty — and those were the years of which the Talmud speaks in *Sanhedrin*. Which seventy years were they?

Part of the answer can be found at the end of the 103 years. Although the Hasmoneans ruled until 3725/36 B.C.E., Jerusalem was conquered by the Roman consul Pompei in 3698/63 B.C.E.

Consequently, for the last twenty-seven years of their reign, the Hasmoneans were subject to the whims of Rome; those twenty-seven years are clearly not part of their seventy-year golden era. Now let us return to the beginning of the period.

After the death of Antichus VII (Pius), the power of the Seleucid kings was weakened by internecine strife and Yochanan Hyrkanos revolted and succeeded in removing the Seleucid yoke from Israel forever (*Josephus, Ant.* 8:10:1). Presumably, the seventy finest years of the Hasmoneans could be said to begin from that point. History puts the death of Antiochus VII at 3632/129 B.C.E., leaving an interval of only *sixty-six* years until Pompei's conquest. It may be that the 'seventy' is a round number, but the period was truly sixty-six years; or it is possible that the generally accepted year of Antiochus' death is inaccurate by a few years.

We suggest another alternative: it may be that the seventy years began *during* the life of Antiochus.

Josephus relates that after his successful siege of Jerusalem in the first year of Hyrkanos' reign (3627/134 B.C.E.), Antiochus formed an alliance with Hyrkanos, and the latter actually accompanied Antiochus' as his ally in his fatal campaign to Parthia. Hyrkanos' acceptance as an ally and equal by his erstwhile ruler can be considered as a beginning of the new era beginning in the year 133 B.C.E. (3628) and ending with Pompei's conquest in the year 63 B.C.E. (3698).

◁§ Table of Important Dates During Second Temple Era*

3338/423 B.C.E.	Destruction of First Temple and beginning of Babylonian Exile
3389/372 B.C.E.	Babylon falls to Medes and Persians under Darius the Mede and Cyrus the Great of Persia
3391/370 B.C.E.	Cyrus reigns; permits Jews to return to *Eretz Yisrael*
3408/353 B.C.E.	Darius the Persian permits Jews to rebuild Temple
3442/319 B.C.E.	Beginning of Greek era
3448/313 B.C.E.	Egyptian Ptolemaic dynasty rules *Eretz Yisrael*
3562/199 B.C.E.	Antiochus III the Great, scion of the Seleucid dynasty and ruler of Syria wrests *Eretz Yisrael* from Egypt
3571/190 B.C.E.	Rome defeats Antiochus III at Magnesia
3586/175 B.C.E.	Antiochus IV reigns
3594/168 B.C.E.	Desecration of Temple by Antiochus
3597/165 B.C.E.	**Conquest of Temple by Hasmoneans; the miracle of Chanukah**
3598/163 B.C.E.	Antiochus IV dies
3599/162 B.C.E.	His son, Antiochus V besieges Jerusalem
3600/161 B.C.E.	Demetrius I (son of Seleucus IV) rules; Alcimus appointed *Kohen Gadol;* defeat and death of Syrian general Nikanor (13 Adar)
3601/160 B.C.E.	Yehudah killed in battle; Yonasan elected leader of the Jewish rebellion
3602/159 B.C.E.	Alcimus dies
3609/152 B.C.E.	Alexander (Balas) I, alleged son of Antiochus IV, contests Demetrius' I rule; both recognize Yonasan as *Kohen Gadol*
3610/151 B.C.E.	Alexander I rules
3614/147 B.C.E.	Alexander I deposed (by Ptolemy IV king of Egypt); Demetrius II (son of Demetrius I) rules
3617/144 B.C.E. (approx.)	Tryphon deposes Demetrius II (who escapes), and rules on behalf of the infant Antiochus VI (son of Alexander I)
3619/142 B.C.E.	Tryphon tricks Yonasan and kills him; Shimon takes over *Kehunah Gedolah;* proclaims himself 'Prince of the Jews' (נְשִׂיא הַיְהוּדִים)
3619/142 B.C.E.	Tryphon kills Antiochus VI and proclaims himself king
3621/140 B.C.E.	Sanhedrin and the People proclaim Shimon 'Prince of the Jews' (18 Elul).
3621-3725/ 140-36 B.C.E.	**Rule of the Hasmonean dynasty (Shimon, Yochanan Hyrkanos, Yehudah Aristobulus, Alexander Yannai, Queen Alexandra [שְׁלְצִיּוֹן], Hyrkanos and Aristobulus)**
3630/131 B.C.E.	Yochanan Hyrkanos forms an alliance with Antiochus VII
3632/129 B.C.E.	Antiochus VII dies
3698/63 B.C.E.	Roman consul Pompei conquers Jerusalem
3725-3828/ 36 B.C.E.-68 C.E.	Rule of Herodian dynasty and Roman governors (Herod, Archelaus, Roman governors, Agrippa I, Roman governors)
3828/68 C.E.	**Destruction of Second Temple by Romans** (according to some, the year was 3829)

*The dates in this table pertaining to the events of Chanukah (3585-3621) have been taken from *I Maccabees* and converted into Creation and Common Era dates, using the formula described in note 1 of page 84.

Insights

The Miracle

◆§ The miracle of oil which we commemorate by lighting the Menorah is
recorded in the Talmud, *Shabbos* 21b:

מאי חנוכה? דת"ר ... כשנכנסו יוונים להיכל טמאו כל השמנים
שבהיכל, וכשגברה מלכות בית חשמונאי ונצחום בדקו ולא מצאו אלא
פך אחד של שמן שהיה מונח בחותמו של כהן גדול (בהצנע וחתום
בטבעתו והכיר שלא נגעו בו — רש"י) ולא היה בו אלא להדליק יום אחד.
נעשה בו נס והדליקו ממנו שמונה ימים. לשנה אחרת קבעום ועשאום
ימים טובים בהלל והודאה.

What is Chanukah [i.e., which miracle does Chanukah
commemorate]? The Rabbis learned [in a baraisa from *Megillas
Taanis*]: ' ... When the Greeks entered the Temple they defiled
all the oils that were in it; and when the Hasmonean dynasty
triumphed and defeated the Syrian-Greeks, [the victorious
Kohanim] searched, but found only one container of oil, which
had been laid aside [in some hidden place *(Rashi)*], with the seal
of the High Priest [in such a manner that it had obviously been
untouched, and hence undefiled, by the Syrians *(Rashi)*]; but
there was only enough oil in it to light the [Temple Menorah]
for one day. A miracle occurred with it, and they lit with it for
eight days. The following year, they fixed and established these
[days] as festivals of praise and thanksgiving.'

◆§ The Talmudic expression, 'They ... established these days as festivals of
praise and thanksgiving,' refers to the recital of *Hallel* [praise], and
therefore, the complete *Hallel* is said during morning services all
eight days of Chanukah. The expression 'thanksgiving' refers to *Al
HaNissim* which is added to the *Shemoneh Esrei/Amidah* prayers and to
Grace After Meals *(Rashi; Tur)*.

☐ Why did the Sages wait until the following year before proclaiming it
a holiday?

In the Torah concept, a 'festival' represents the annual return of the
same kind of spiritual force that resulted in the original miracle that is
being commemorated. Only God, speaking through a prophet, can
assure us that a particular miracle is of a sufficient spiritual dimension
that it should be celebrated every year — but prophecy no longer
existed at the time of the Chanukah miracle. Originally, the Sages of the
time thought it was probably an isolated miracle like countless others in

Jewish history, but the following year they sensed that its spiritual effect was still present. Then they realized that the miracle of the lights would shine forever with a message of hope, because it was a part of the light which will glow with the coming of Messiah *(Bnai Yisas'char)*.

Why Not a Feast?

✥§ The days of Chanukah were established as a time of 'praise and thanksgiving' (הַלֵּל וְהוֹדָאָה) only, but not 'feasting and joy' (מִשְׁתֶּה וְשִׂמְחָה) as was Purim. As the legal codifiers note, 'though it is customary to indulge in some feasting on Chanukah, this is not obligatory' *(Tur).* Now why should Chanukah be different in this way from Purim, when a similarly miraculous salvation of Israel is commemorated by feasting and other physical expressions of joy and thanksgiving?

□ The author of *Levush* explains that at the time commemorated by Chanukah, Israel did not fall under the control of a ruler who intended to exterminate them as did Haman. Rather, the enemy demanded only that Israel submit to foreign rule and give up their religion, as is seen in the story of Antiochus. He did not decree death and annihilation upon them, but only oppression and measures to convert them from their religion ... And if Israel had submitted to the Greeks, behaving like a conquered people and paying tribute, and had (God forbid) converted to the conqueror's faith, the Greeks would have made no further demands. (This is reflected in the wording of *Al HaNissim,* the Chanukah prayer of thanksgiving that appears in the *Siddur:* 'to make them forget Your Torah and forsake the statutes of Your will.') But the Holy One, Blessed is He, granted that Israel's hand should prevail and defeat the enemy. And that is why these days were fixed only for praise and thanksgiving, but not for feasting and joy. For since it was precisely praise of, and thanksgiving to, God that the Greeks wanted to prevent, and they wanted us to deny (God forbid) the Blessed One, and since we overcame the enemy with His help and their schemes failed, therefore the Sages established these days for us to spiritually reaffirm our praise and thanksgiving to Him — for being our God, for not abandoning us, and for letting us continue to serve Him. But in the time of Haman, the decree was to kill and annihilate us bodily, which is a negation of feasting and joy ... When we were saved, therefore, it was decreed that we should praise and extol Him with feasting and joy as well (cited by R' S. Y. Zevin, *The Festivals in Halachah* II:58; See *Orach Chaim* 670:5).

□ Though festive meals are not prescribed for the days of Chanukah, it is customary to honor the Chanukah meals with special rejoicing, by discoursing on Torah themes, and by recounting the miracles performed for Israel. The meals are thereby accorded the status of סְעוּדוֹת מִצְוָה, *mitzvah meals (ibid; 670:3).*

Why Eight Days?

◆§ Why was it necessary for the oil to burn miraculously for a period of exactly eight days?

☐ The place where pure olive oil was available for the Temple was an eight-day round trip from Jerusalem (Meiri, Shabbos 21b).

☐ According to another opinion, the eight-day waiting period was necessitated by the halachic condition of the *people* rather than the oil. The Jews had become contaminated by contact with the dead during the war [טָמֵא מֵת]. The purification process from such contamination requires seven days (Leviticus 19:12-12). Therefore, the Jews had to wait seven days before they could press new pure oil. On the eighth day they pressed pure olive oil, and had it ready for use in the Temple on the ninth day (Bais Yosef 670; Mizrachi, glosses to Semag).

☐ But, it is an established principle in the Halachah that 'defilement is repealed for the community' (i.e., the entire community may perform the service of the Sanctuary if its majority is in a state of contamination). Why then was it necessary for the Jews to wait seven days for their purification?

One answer is: Although they were permitted to light the Menorah even with defiled oil, they were unwilling to do so. Since this was to be the first lighting after an interruption, it was an act of dedication; and an act of dedication should be done in accord with the most stringent requirements of purity (Ner LaMeah citing Avnei Nezer).

Why Not a Ninth Day?

◆§ Why do we in the Diaspora not observe a ninth day of Chanukah, just as we add an additional day to other festivals of the Jewish calendar outside of *Eretz Yisrael?* In the case of other festivals, the extra day is based on the principle of סְפֵקָא דְּיוֹמָא, *doubt concerning the day,* because communities far away from Jerusalem did not know which day had been proclaimed by Beis Din as Rosh Chodesh. Even now, when the Calendar is predetermined and not based on witnesses testifying to their sighting of the new moon, the extra day is still observed; why does Chanukah not have this extra day? In considering the question, the Rishonim give the basic reason: we are not strict in this respect because Chanukah is a *mitzvah* of Rabbinic rather than Scriptural origin. During an era when our festivals are based on the predetermined calendar and no doubt exists as to which is the right day, the Rabbis retained the extra day for Scriptural festivals, but did not impose for Rabbinic festivals (Abudraham; Baal Halttim).

☐ Minchas Chinuch (§301) points out that in the era when the beginning of the month was determined by eye-witness reports of the

new moon, and messengers were sent out from Jerusalem to announce on what day the festivals would fall, we know that messengers were sent for Chanukah as well (see ArtScroll *Rosh Hashanah* ch. 2]. *Minchas Chinuch* claims that in that era, in places too distant to be reached in time by the messengers, Chanukah was indeed celebrated for nine days. And in conclusion he adds these words: 'When the Temple is rebuilt — may it be swiftly and in our time — and we shall again determine the beginning of the month according to eye-witnesses, then the far-flung communities will certainly again celebrate nine days of Chanukah.'

Why Not a Seven-Day Festival?

As noted above (see p. 89), Chanukah is celebrated for eight days to commemorate the miracle of the oil. All that was left of the pure oil after the Syrian-Greek desecrations was a one-day supply of oil, but it burned miraculously for eight days until a fresh supply became available. In one of the most famous questions in Rabbinic literature, *Bais Yosef (Tur Orach Chaim §670)* raises a basic difficulty with this reason:

☐ Since the untainted jug contained enough oil to burn naturally for one night, nothing miraculous happened on the *first* night that the *Kohanim* kindled the *Menorah*. Since the miraculous nature of the burning was only on the *following* seven days, why should not Chanukah be observed for only *seven* days?

This question has engaged some of Judaism's most brilliant minds since it was first raised over four centuries ago.

Bais Yosef himself offered three possible answers, and countless scholars have offered an endless stream of answers down through the years. We shall offer a sampling of such answers, beginning with the three of *Bais Yosef*:

1. Had the *Kohanim* used all the oil on the first night, they would have been forced to leave the *Menorah* unlit for the following week. Instead, they decided to use one eighth of the oil each night until they could obtain a new supply. But instead of the flames going out during the night, the Menorah remained lit until morning, as if its cups had been filled with oil. Thus, a miracle occurred every night *(Bais Yosef)*.

2. After they *filled* all the cups of the Menorah, the *Kohanim* found that a miracle had happened — the jug of oil had remained brimful *(ibid.)*.

3. In a variation of the previous answer, *Bais Yosef* suggests that each morning the *Kohanim* found that the cups of the Menorah were still full of oil, even after having burned all night *(ibid.)*

4. *Zohar* states a principle that God performs a miracle only on something that already exists in some measure; thus, for example, a

partially filled jar can become full miraculously but God does not fill a jar that is totally empty. According to this rule, we must assume that after the first night's burning, some oil had to be left, despite the fact that it had burned for the full duration. The first day's miracle was that this remnant remained. On the succeeding days, this remnant burned for a full night *(Turei Zahav)*.

5. True, the miracle of the oil did not begin until the *second* day, and lasted for only seven days. But the Sages designated the first day of Chanukah as a festival in commemoration of the miraculous military victory over the massive Syrian-Greek legions *(Pri Chadash)*.

6. According to one version found in *She'iltos d'R' Achai Gaon,* the jug of oil contained *less* than a one-day supply. If that is correct, even the first full night of burning was miraculous.

7. The purity of the hidden jug was verified by the fact that it was closed with the still unbroken seal of the *Kohen Gadol.* But it was never the Temple practice — before or since — for jugs to be sealed by the *Kohen Gadol* or anyone else. Instead, a responsible *Kohen* was put in charge of the manufacture of the oil and its safekeeping. The very fact that God had inspired an earlier *Kohen Gadol* to seal a jug of oil so that it should be available when needed by the Hasmoneans was in itself a miracle *(Bnai Yisas'char)*.

8. One of the commandments whose observance was forbidden by the Syrian-Greeks was circumcision. Accordingly the Sages added an eighth day to Chanukah to allude to circumcision, which is performed on an infant's eighth day *(Shiltei HaGibborim)*.

9. *Megillas Taanis* teaches that the *Kohanim* dismantled the Altar that had been contaminated by the Syrian-Greeks, and replaced it with a newly built Altar, which they then dedicated in an eight-day celebration. The extra day of Chanukah commemorates its dedication *(Birkei Yosef)*.

10. Since the Temple building had been desecrated by pagan sacrifices and the emplacement of idols, the Hasmoneans lit their *Menorah* in the Courtyard, out in the open. Normally, a flame exposed to breezes and open air will burn more quickly than one that is sheltered indoors. Nevertheless, the single-day supply burned as long on the first night outdoors as it would have inside the Temple *(Derasho Chasam Sofer)*.

11. *R' Chaim Soloveitchick* of Brisk argues that oil produced through miraculous means would be unfit for the *mitzvah,* for the Torah calls for שֶׁמֶן זַיִת, *olive oil,* not שֶׁמֶן נֵס, *miracle oil.* According to this line of reasoning, the miracle could not have involved an

increase in the quantity of oil through the filling of a nearly empty jug or cup but an intensification of its ability to burn. Instead of using up a cupful of oil each night, each cup of the *Menorah* consumed only an eighth of its usual need, while burning all night. Since only an eighth of the normal quota was consumed each night, the miracle occurred on each of the eight days.

12. Having returned to the Temple and found its purity and sacred materials in shambles, the Hasmoneans had no logical reason to think they would find any pure oil. They could have been expected to give up all hope of finding pure oil, and planned ahead for the time when they could obtain a new quantity of oil. Instead, they refused to surrender to the 'obvious'. So powerful was their will to begin the *mitzvah* of lighting the *Menorah* immediately that they began what seemed like a hopeless search for pure oil — and they succeeded! This powerful desire to battle all odds for the sake of a *mitzvah* represents the miracle of Jewish survival. To commemorate it, the Sages ordained the first day of Chanukah *(Harav Yosef Dov Soloveitchick)*.

13. The Sages chose Chanukah, a festival that revolves around oil's ability to burn, as the time to teach the fundamental truth that even so-called 'natural' events take place only because God wants them to. When seen in the perspective of God's will, the burning of oil is no less miraculous than would be the burning of water. The Talmudic Sage R' Chanina ben Dosa pithily expressed this truth in explaining a miracle that occurred in his own home. Once, his daughter realized that she had poured vinegar instead of oil into the Sabbath menorah. R' Chanina calmed her, saying, 'מַאי אִיכְפַּת לָךְ? מִי שֶׁאָמַר לַשֶּׁמֶן וְיִדְלַק, יֹאמַר לַחֹמֶץ וְיִדְלַק, *Why are you concerned? The One Who commanded oil to burn can command vinegar — and it will burn.'* The Talmud goes on to relate that those Sabbath lights remained aflame until after the Sabbath ended *(Taanis* 25a). To hammer home this truth, the Sages decreed that Chanukah be observed for eight days: The last seven to commemorate the miracle of the *Menorah,* and the first to remind us that even the 'normal' burning of oil is only in obedience to God's wish *(Harav David Feinstein)*.

Omission of Chanukah in Mishnah

⥤ Why does the Mishnah fail to mention the festival of Chanukah as a major Rabbinic commandment?

□ There are only two Rabbinically ordained festivals, Chanukah and Purim. Whereas an entire tractate, *Megillah,* is devoted to the Purim miracle, not even one Mishnah is dedicated to the Chanukah festival.

An explanation attributed to *Chasam Sofer* notes *Ramban's* discourse in *Genesis* 49:10 that although the Hasmoneans were great and righteous people, and were it not for them the Torah would ו״ח have been forgotten, the entire family was murdered by Herod more than a century after the Chanukah miracle. Why should no remnants have remained of this great family? Because they appropriated not only the *Kehunah Gedolah* [High Priesthood], but even kingship. By retaining the monarchy for themselves on a permanent basis, they violated Jacob's testament that the dynasty should remain with Judah. As a consequence, God did not intervene to save them from Herod.

The redactor of the Mishnah, R' Yehudah the Prince, was a scion of the Davidic dynasty. Because the Hasmoneans flouted the honor due to his family, R' Yehudah omitted mention of their miracle from the Mishnah.

Both *R' Reuven Margulies* and *Ziv HaMinhagim* protest that R' Yehudah could not have omitted mention of a festival for so apparently petty a reason; they question whether the *Chasam Sofer* could have given such an explanation. They give a historical reason:

Until R' Yehudah's time, the Roman overlords of *Eretz Yisrael* had made it a crime — often a capital offense — to teach Torah. Such Sages as R' Akiva were brutally murdered for maintaining their academies. Furthermore, the Romans always feared rebellions in their empire and ruthlessly retaliated if they even *suspected* disobedience. R' Yehudah the Prince was the first Sage in many decades who had succeeded in establishing friendly relations with Rome. Were he to include in the Mishnah that the Jewish people celebrate a festival commemorating the overthrow of an oppressive, foreign kingdom, the Romans could have taken that as a call to insurrection, and retaliated with brutal repression.

The Name Chanukah

◆§ The name Chanukah was given in commemoration of the historical fact that the Jewish fighters *rested* [=חָנוּ] from their battles against the Syrian-Greeks on the *twenty-fifth* [כ״ה=25] of Kislev (*Kol Bo; Abudraham; Tur; Ran*).

□ The Hebrew חֵן, *chein*, denotes grace. Thus '*Chanukah*' could be meant to allude that the Jewish warriors found Divine 'grace' on the 25th of Kislev (*Noam Elimelech*).

□ One of the most direct explanations of the name Chanukah is that it is related to the Dedication [*chanukah*] of the Altar. As *Or Zarua* observes: 'The name Chanukah derives from the consecration of the Altar, for the Altar had been destroyed and the Hasmoneans rebuilt it.' We learn similarly in *Avodah Zarah* 52b that the Hasmoneans removed and stored

away the Altar-stones which the Greeks had polluted with idolatry, and had to build a new Altar. That is why the festival is called 'Chanukah' which means 'dedication' (*Maharsha* to *Shabbos* 21b).

☐ In *I Maccabees* [4:44-9] and *II Maccabees* [10:2-4], we also find that the Hasmoneans cleansed the Temple and built a new Altar, which they completed on the 25th of Kislev. *Megillas Taanis* also records that when the Hasmoneans regained possession of the Temple, they 'built the Altar, smoothed it with plaster, and provided it with the implements of the Temple service — and they were occupied with these tasks for eight days.'

☐ *Rav Yaakov Emden* [*Mor U'Ketziah* §670] suggests that the name refers also to the dedication of the Second Temple, which occurred on almost the same date in the time of the prophet Chaggai [see *Chaggai* 2:18]. It is because of this consecration of the Second Temple that the miracle of the lights that happened in that season — generations later — is called Chanukah.

☐ The name also commemorates another Chanukah [dedication] that nearly occurred on a 25th of Kislev, for it was on that date that work was completed on the Tabernacle [*Mishkan*] in the desert. Although the work was finished in Kislev, the Tabernacle was not dedicated then, for, as the Midrash [*Yalkut Shimoni Melachim* §184] records, God wished to combine the joy of the Tabernacle with Nissan, the month in which the Patriarch Isaac was born. Thus God repaid the loss to Kislev, in which the labor was actually completed, with the Chanukah of the Hasmoneans. Furthermore, it is for this reason that the chapter of the *Nesiim*, dealing with the sacrificial offerings brought by the Tribal princes at the dedication of the Tabernacle [*Numbers* ch. 7], forms the Synagogue Torah readings during Chanukah. (*Shibbolei HaLeket*; see *The Festivals in Halachah* II:67.)

☐ Homiletically there is an allusion in the Hebrew name *Chanukah* to the fact that we conduct ourselves on Chanukah in the manner advocated by the School of Hillel, who hold that we begin on the first night with one light and add additional lights on each of the subsequent nights, as opposed to the practice of the School of Shammai who begin with eight lights and subtract one light on each of the subsequent nights. The initials of Chanukah spell: ח' נֵרוֹת וְהֲלָכָה כְּבֵית הִלֵּל, *Eight Lights and the Halachah follows the School of Hillel* (Abudraham; Ateres Zekeinim; Pri Megadim).

☐ Kabbalistically, at the time of the lighting of the Chanukah lights there is a revelation of part of the *or haganuz*, the great light hidden away since the beginning of Creation — the light of Messiah. And that is why the festival is called 'Chanukah' — because it is a spiritual preparation [*chinuch*] for our destined Redemption (Bnai Yisas'char).

Biblical Allusions to Chanukah

☞§ It is axiomatic in Rabbinic perspective that לֵיכָּא מִידִי דְּלֹא רְמִיזֵי בְּאוֹרַיְיתָא, *there is nothing that is not alluded to in the Torah.*

The Midrashic Sages and later Kabbalists and Rabbinic thinkers have dwelt extensively upon deriving such allusions from sometimes obscure references, word and letter associations, and *gematrias* [the study of the numerical equivalents — since every letter in the Hebrew alphabet represents a number as well as a letter].

Such investigations have also focused upon finding a hint to the post-Biblical Chanukah miracle in the Torah.

A small selection of such allusions as recorded in the Rabbinic literature follows:

□ In *Parshas Emor* [*Levit.* ch. 21-24; the Torah mentions all the festivals of the year: Sabbath, Pesach, Shavuos, Rosh Hashanah, Yom Kippur and Succos. This section concludes: [*ibid* 23:44]: וַיְדַבֵּר מֹשֶׁה אֶת מֹעֲדֵי ה' אֶל בְּנֵי יִשְׂרָאֵל, *Thus Moses declared to the children of Israel the set times of HASHEM.* The very next verse [24:1] gives the *mitzvah* of maintaining an Eternal Light in the Temple with pure olive oil. Since no sequence in the Torah is haphazard, the Sages draw an inference from the proximity of the passages — the *mitzvah* of Succos is followed by the *mitzvah* of kindling the Menorah with pure olive oil. The inference is that the Torah was anticipating a future time when the kindling of the Menorah would become an annual festival — Chanukah — directly following Succos *(Sefer Roke'ach).*

Additionally just as Succos is eight days, so would Chanukah be observed eight days (ibid.). [In the Diaspora we do not observe Chanukah for an extra day because, as *Abudraham* explains, the Festival itself is of Rabbinic ordinance, and the Rabbis did not wish to add to it.]

□ Furthermore, in *Parshas Emor* [*Leviticus* 24:4] we encounter the phrase לְהַעֲלֹת נֵר, *to cause the light to burn,* followed in the next verse by יַעֲרֹךְ אֶת הַנֵּרֹת, *he shall prepare the lights.* This singular [נֵר, *light*] followed by the plural [נֵרֹת, *lights*], is perceived as alluding to the Chanukah practice of first kindling one light, and on subsequent nights many *(Roke'ach).*

□ The Chanukah festival commemorates the rededication of the Temple in the days of the Hasmoneans. As such, it is perceived as relating in many ways to the original dedication of the Tabernacle in the time of Moses. Indeed, the Torah section relating the offerings that the Tribal Princes — *Nesi'im* — brought to dedicate the Tabernacle

[*Numbers* ch. 7] forms the Synagogue Torah reading during the mornings of Chanukah.

This association between the Princely offerings and Chanukah is strengthened by the proximity of the passages dealing with their dedication and the next passage in the Torah [*ibid.* 8:1], which deals with the Menorah that was to be kindled by Aaron and his descendants. The Sages perceive that 'kindling' as alluding to the Rededication of the Second Temple in the time of the Hasmoneans, and the *mitzvah* of the Menorah as part of the Chanukah observance, for those events were brought about by the priestly family of Mattisyahu.[1]

☐ At the end of every *Sidrah* [weekly portion] in the Torah there is a Masoretic note printed in large Chumashim noting the amount of verses in that *Sidrah*.

At the end of *Sidrah Mikeitz* [*Genesis* 41-44] which is the portion almost always read in the synagogue on the Shabbos of Chanukah, there is an additional note not found in any other *Sidrah:* mention of how many *words* the *Sidrah* contains — in this case 2025.

Bnai Yisas'char notes that this is the only portion where such information is provided. He finds in this unique note an allusion to Chanukah, which usually falls in the week of *Mikeitz*. On Chanukah we light a new נֵר, light, for each of the eight lights. The numerical value of the letters of נֵר, is 250; accordingly, the 8 lights of Chanukah yield a *total*

1. In expounding upon the significance inherent in the proximity of these passages, *Ramban* writes in his commentary to *Numbers* 8:1:

"Why does the section dealing with the *Menorah* [in which Aaron and his descendants were charged with the *mitzvah* of kindling the *Menorah*] follow the section dealing with the dedication offering of the Tribal Princes? ...

"The proximity teaches not only that the Menorah in the Tabernacle was lit by Aaron, but also that the Chanukah [Dedication] of lights which occurred in the period of the Second Temple would come about through the descendants of Aaron — Mattisyahu the Hasmonean, and his sons.

"*Megillas Sesarim of R' Nissim,* expounds similarly: 'I saw in the Midrash that when the twelve tribes had each brought their offerings to the dedication of the Altar, and the tribe of Levi had not been included in the Altar offerings, God said to Moses: Speak to Aaron and tell him that one day there will be another inauguration [Chanukah] with kindling of lights, and through your offspring I will perform miracles and salvation for Israel. I will give them another Dedication to be called by their name — Chanukah of the Hasmoneans. For this reason the present passage of kindling the Menorah was placed in proximity with that of the altar dedication.' Thus far, is R' Nissim's words."

Ramban also cites *Midrash Yelamdeinu,* and *Midrash Rabbah:* "God said to Moses: 'Go and say to Aaron: Have no fear. You are designated for something of greater importance than this. The Altar offerings are brought only while the Sanctuary is in existence. The lights however will burn forever ... and all the blessings which I gave you, whereby you will in turn bless My children, will never cease.' It is obvious, however, that in the absence of the Temple, and after the cessation of the sacrifical offerings, the *Menorah* would likewise no longer be lit. [What then, is the intent of the Midrash in stating that the lighting of the *Menorah* will never cease?] Obviously, therefore, the reference of the Sages must be to the lamps of the Hasmonean Chanukah, whose lighting remains binding even after the destruction of the Temple."

of 2000 [250x8]. And Chanukah begins on the 25th of Kislev. Thus, 2025 is an allusion to the lights and the date of Chanukah (*ArtScroll Bereishis* p. 1902).

□ Since it is prohibited to enjoy the illumination of the Chanukah lights for any purpose, it has become a custom to kindle a *shammash* ['attendant'], i.e., an additional light on the *Menorah,* so that any benefit from the illumination of the *Menorah* will not be enjoyed from the Chanukah lights themselves, but from this *shammash.*

[That the Sages were so stringent concerning personal benefit from this light is because the Chanukah light is a memorial to the light which burned in the Holy Temple whose light also was not to be used for any personal benefit or pleasure *(Bnai Yisas'char).*]

The law is that this *shammash* must be on a different plane than the Chanukah candles in order to distinguish it from them *(Rama 673:1; Roke'ach).*

A Biblical allusion to this is derived from *Isaiah* 6:2: שְׂרָפִים עוֹמְדִים מִמַּעַל לוֹ, *Seraphim* [lit. *those which burn* — in this case the *shammash*] *stand above it* [the Hebrew word לוֹ, *it,* is numerically equivalent to 36 — alluding to the total of 36 Chanukah lights kindled during Chanukah] *(Ateres Zekeinim §646; Maharil).*

□ A further allusion in the Torah to the fact that we utilize the light of the *shammash* on Chanukah is derived from a homiletical reading of *Genesis* 32:32: instead of וַיִּזְרַח לוֹ הַשֶּׁמֶשׁ, *the sun shone for him,* read וַיִּזְרַח לוֹ הַשַּׁמָּשׁ, *the shammash illuminated for him;* or the *shammash illuminated* לוֹ, *the thirty-six* lights kindled throughout Chanukah *(Maharil).*

□ Although Chanukah was ordained as a primarily spiritual festival for reciting praise and thanksgiving [*Hallel,* and *Al HaNissim*] and not for physical pleasures such as festive meals [see p. 92], nevertheless, as *Shiltei HaGiborim* on *Hagahos Mordechai* notes, there is some degree of *mitzvah* in the manner of festive meals that are accompanied by song, thanksgiving and praise. Some allusion to this may be elicited from the words [*Genesis* 43:16]: וּטְבֹחַ טֶבַח וְהָכֵן, *have meat slaughtered and prepare it,* the last five letters of this phrase, ח והכן are the letters of חנוכה, *Chanukah.* Furthermore, the *gematria* [numerical values of the letters] of וּטְבֹחַ טֶבַח equal 44 — the total number of lights kindled throughout Chanukah [36 plus the 8 *shammashim*].

□ The passage in *Genesis* 1:2, *And darkness upon the face of the Deep* refers to Greece which darkened the face of Israel. Accordingly, God commanded [*ibid.* v. 4]: *Let there be light!* — the Light of Messianic Redemption *(Zohar).*

◆§ Other allusions to Chanukah in the Torah are:

□ The twenty-fifth word in the Torah is אוֹר, *light* [*Genesis* 1:3];

□ The twenty-fifth place of the Israelites' encampment in the desert was *Chashmonah* [*Numbers* 33:29].

Chashmonai [Hasmonean] and Maccabee

◆§ The origin of the name Chashmonai as a family name is uncertain. Some maintain that the word means *distinguished,* which is the meaning it has in *Psalms* 68:32. Thus, it is a title of honor conferred upon the family to denote its high standing *(Bais Yosef)*.

□ Others postulate that the family originally hailed from the town of Cheshmon in Judah [see *Joshua* 15:27], or that Cheshmon was the name of some ancient ancestor, and the name was adopted by the family.

□ The name Chashmonai is also mentioned several times in the Mishnah and in *Targum Yonasan* to I *Samuel* 2:4.

◆§ The Hasmoneans were also known as Maccabees. Originally only the third son, Yehudah, was designated by this surname, but eventually the entire family came to be so called.

□ The exact etymology of the word is obscure. According to one Hebrew spelling of the word, מֵקַבִּי, it means *hammer,* and refers to the heroism of Yehudah and Mattisyahu's family. Some suggest *MaCaB* is an acrostic of the final letters of the Patriarchal names AbrahaM, IsaaC and JacoB.

□ The preferred Hebrew spelling, however, is מַכַּבִּי, and its etymology is even more obscure.

Some explain it as being composed of the Initial letters of the verse [*Exodus* 15:11]: מִי כָמֹכָה בָּאֵלִים יי, *who is like You among the heavenly powers, HASHEM,* which was inscribed on the banners of the Hasmonean family; or מַתִּתְיָהוּ כֹּהֵן בֶּן יוֹחָנָן, *Mattisyahu the Kohen, son of Yochanan.* [See also note 6 to *History,* p. 68.]

Thoughts

The Precious Mitzvah

◆§ The *mitzvah* of the Chanukah light is very precious. One must be very scrupulous about it in order to popularize the miracle and to offer additional praise and thanksgiving to God for the wonders that He performed on our behalf *(Rambam, Hil. Chanukah* 4:12).

◆§ Even if one has no food to eat except what he receives from charity, he should beg — or sell his clothing — to buy oil and lamps, and light them *(ibid.)*.

☐ Why is Chanukah unique in this respect; other *mitzvos* do not require one to sell his garments in order to comply with their performance?

In the case of other *mitzvos,* if one intended to perform a *mitzvah* but was prevented from doing so, the Torah accounts it to him as if he fulfilled it. The commentators explain that this is not the case, however, in observances that involve פַּרְסוּמֵי נִיסָא, *popularizing miracles.* In such cases, mere *intentions* are valueless, since one's neighbor cannot know what he intended to popularize. Therefore, one must even sell his garment to popularize the Chanukah miracle by kindling, for he has no other way of receiving credit for the *mitzvah.* The same law applies to the requirement of Four Cups of Wine at the Passover *seder* as well, which also has an aspect of publicizing the miracle of freedom *(Avnei Nezer, Orach Chaim 101; cf. Maggid Mishneh, Hil. Chanukah 4:12; Be'ur HaGra).*

Israel Compared with the Olive

ৰ্ড The *halachah* specifies that the oil used for the Chanukah light should be שֶׁמֶן זַיִת, *olive oil.*

☐ The Midrash [*Sh'mos Rabbah* 36:1] mentions that Israel may be compared with the olive. All liquids co-mingle with one another, while oil does not, but keeps separate. When Jews perform God's will, they too, stand separate from every group. Kindling the Menorah with olive oil commemorates the separateness that has kept Israel immortal *(Bnai Yisas'char).*

Longest Grace After Meals

ৰ্ড The longest Grace After Meals recited during the year is when *Rosh Chodesh* Teves [the sixth and/or seventh day of Chanukah] falls on the Sabbath. On such occasions, three passages are added to the regular Grace: *Al HaNissim* for Chanukah, *Retzei V'Hachalitzeinu* for the Sabbath, and *Ya'aleh V'Yavo* for Rosh Chodesh.

☐ Similarly, in the Synagogue when such an occasion happens, three Torah Scrolls are taken out. In the first Torah, six people are called up for the reading of the weekly *Sidrah*; in the second, a seventh person is called for the *Rosh Chodesh* reading; in the third, the reading of the *Nassi* of the respective day is read as the *maftir (Shulchan Aruch).*

Daytime Lighting of the Synagogue Menorah

ৰ্ড There is a widespread custom to also re-light the Synagogue Menorah each Chanukah morning without a blessing. The purpose is to publicize the miracle. It is a beautiful custom since during the day it is more obvious that the lights are being kindled for that express purpose. It also

serves as a reminder to one who might have been unable, or had forgotten, to kindle his own *Menorah* at night *(N'har Mitzraim)*.

□ *Shaarei Teshuvah §679* cautions that on the Sabbath, however, the synagogue *Menorah* may not be kindled by a gentile — since we find nowhere that kindling Chanukah lights in the morning is a *mitzvah*.

The Light of Mashiach

◄§ The *Rosh* [*Shabbos* 21b] comments: 'מצותה משתשקע החמה עד שתכלה רגל מן השוק ... מכאן ואילך עבר הזמן, *The* [*time of the*] mitzvah *is from sunset till the last person has left the market, thereafter since the miracle can no longer be publicized, one should no longer light the Menorah.'*

We are also told in the Talmud: 'נר חנוכה מצוה להניחה על פתח ביתו מבחוץ ובשעת הסכנה מניחה על שלחנו, *The mitzvah of the Menorah is to place it at the door of one's home, but in time of danger one may put it on his table'* [ibid.].

The *Maharal* points out a contradiction. In the first case, the *Rosh* records that we may not light the *Menorah* after the last person is gone from the market. In the second case, however, the danger makes it impossible to publicize the miracle, but we light inside the home instead. Reason would dictate the opposite. In the case of danger, the Sages should dismiss the *mitzvah* entirely, but in a case where most people would no longer see the *Menorah,* because of the lateness of the hour, it should still be required to light because some stragglers may yet see it.

The answer lies in a deeper understanding of the *mitzvah's* purpose. It is twofold. One, to publicize the miracle, and secondly, to re-kindle hope in the heart of every Jew. When the hour is late, the time for touting the miracle has passed, and this purpose can no longer be served; therefore the light is not kindled. But in time of danger, hope must be given to every Jew. He must never forget that the long exile will not last forever. Then, the light is kindled to give inspiration, for the light of Messiah must burn brightly in our hearts, even if others can no longer see it. Therefore we must light the *Menorah* on the table to provide inspiration for every member of the household. The Chanukah flames must reignite the inner flame of our people and provide them with strength and hope that the end of our long exile will yet come.

The Light of the World

◄§ Israel said to the Holy One, Blessed is He: 'You are the light of the world and You ask us to kindle a light before You?'

God answered, 'Not because I require your light but in order to elevate you before the nations who will then exclaim, 'Israel is lighting before Him Who provides light for all!' *(Yalkut to Exod. §378; Shmos Rabbah 36:2; Cf. Shabbos 22b).*

Children Who Are Torah Scholars

◆§ The Talmud teaches הָרָגִיל בְּנֵר חֲנֻכָּה הַוְיָן לֵיה בָּנִים תַּלְמִידֵי חֲכָמִים, *One who scrupulously observes the kindling of the Chanukah light will have children who are Torah scholars (Shabbos 23b).*

□ As it is written [*Proverbs* 6:23]: כִּי נֵר מִצְוָה וְתוֹרָה אוֹר, *for the lamp is a mitzvah and Torah is light.* As a result of the *mitzvah* of the lamp, the light of Torah follows *(Rashi).*

□ This *mitzvah* is a Rabbinic ordinance. Therefore one who is scrupulous in its performance merits children who are Rabbinic scholars *(Menoras HaMa'or).*

□ Citing the above Talmudic statement, *Chiddushei HaRim* notes the relationship between הָרָגִיל, *one who customarily observes,* and הֶרְגֵּל, *habit.* The Rabbis are teaching us that one who wants his children to be Torah scholars should be careful to bring spiritual light into his habitual mode of living. If his observance of *mitzvos* is not treated as a mere habit, but is suffused with a spiritual glow, he can expect it to be reflected in his family.

Surrounded By Mitzvos

◆§ The primary mitzvah [as it used to be practiced] is to place the *Menorah* at the doorway near the public domain in such a way that the *mezuzah* is to his right and the Chanukah flames to his left [with the master of household adorned, with his *tzitzis,* between them *(She'iltos)*] to fulfill the verse [*Song of Songs* 7:7]: *How beautiful you are, and how pleasant you are — How beautiful,* with your mezuzah; *how pleasant,* with the Chanukah light *(Soferim 20:5; cf. Shabbos 22a).*

□ Thus, one should be 'surrounded with *mitzvos.*' The Sages have declared that the walls and stones of man's house give testimony about him on the Day of Judgment [*Chagigah* 16a]. Accordingly, when the walls and stones appear to bear witness against him, the two doorposts, representing the *mezuzah* and *Menorah,* will testify on his behalf. Thus, there will be two witnesses in his favor and two against him, accordingly he must be given the benefit of the doubt *(Sifsei Tzaddik).*

The 'Door' of Redemption

◆§ Chanukah signals the ultimate salvation and rededication of the entire world. Lighting the *Menorah* at the doorway demonstrates how the days of Chanukah are symbolically the 'door', the beginning, of the ultimate redemption *(Sfas Emes).*

Gazing at the Flames

◄§ If one will not have the opportunity to kindle his own Chanukah lights or to participate in another's kindling, he may recite the latter two of the three blessings if he merely *sees* someone else's Chanukah flames (see *Shabbos* 23a and *Orach Chaim* 676:3). From this, the Kabbalistic authors have derived that spiritual enrichment is to be derived from the very act of *gazing* at the Chanukah lights. Many Chassidic masters made it a practice to look at the flames for the full thirty-minute period that they were required to burn.

Sabbath, Rosh Chodesh, Circumcision

◄§ The Syrian-Greeks forbade the observance of the Sabbath, Rosh Chodesh, and circumcision (see Overview). The observance of Chanukah recalls all three of these *mitzvos*. Rosh Chodesh Teves always occurs during Chanukah, every Chanukah has at least one Sabbath, and Chanukah is eight days long, to allude to circumcision which is done on the eighth day (cited by *Harav David Cohen*).

Women and the Mitzvah

◄§ R' Yehoshua ben Levi said, 'Women are obligated in regard to the [*mitzvah* of the] Chanukah light for they, too, were part of that miracle' *(Shabbos* 23a).

□ That is, because the Greeks had decreed that all Jewish maidens about to be married first submit themselves for violation to the Greek prince. And the miracle [of the Hasmonean victory] was brought about through the agency of a woman [a reference to the daughter of Yochanan the High Priest who intoxicated the tyrant King and beheaded him (see p. 78); an act which, in effect, rescued Jewish women from this decree] *(Rashi ibid.).*

□ The *Shulchan Aruch* rules that because of their great role in the Chanukah victory, women should abide by the custom of not doing work as long as the candles burn, and they should not be lenient in the matter [*Orach Chaim* 67; see Laws of Chanukah].

How Many Chanukahs?

◄§ How many 'Chanukahs' — events celebrated by 'dedications' — are there?

The Midrash *(Pesikta Rabbasi* 2:2) lists seven, as follows:

1. The *chanukah* [dedication] of Heaven and Earth [*Gen.* 2:1], which was commemorated by the setting of the two great

luminaries in the heavens to light up the earth [*ibid.* 1:17];

2. the *chanukah* of the Tabernacle celebrated by the Tribal Princes [*Numbers* chap. 7];

3. the *chanukah* of the First Temple [*I Kings* chap. 8];

4. the *chanukah* of the city wall [*Nechemiah* 12:27];

5. the *chanukah* of the Second Temple [*Ezra* 6:17];

6. the *chanukah* of the Hasmonean *Kohanim,* the one for which we kindle the Menorah;

7. the *chanukah* of the World to Come [*Zephaniah* 1:12].

Chanukah — The Messianic Sabbath

◄§ The Patriarch Jacob had longed to institute that every day of the week be like the Sabbath of Messianic times — totally saturated with the holiness of that Sabbath — but he was unsuccessful, for it *was* premature. He was successful, however, in that his descendants would be able to experience some taste of this Messianic Sabbath even during the week, at such times as Chanukah and Purim *(Sfas Emes).*

Seventeen Shehecheyanus

◄§ The *Shehecheyanu* blessing is recited seventeen times a year in the Diaspora. The Hebrew word טוב, *good,* also equals seventeen. This mnemonic alludes to the fact that *Shehecheyanu* is recited only on joyous occasions, as is demonstrated, for example, in the law that it is not recited at the counting of the Omer.

The seventeen occasions are: (1-2) the first two nights of Passover; (3-4) the two nights of Shavuous; (5-6) the two nights of Rosh Hashanah; (7-8) the two mornings of Rosh Hashanah prior to Shofar-blowing; (9) the night of Yom Kippur; (10-11) the two nights of Succos; (12) the first day of Succos prior to performing the *mitzvah* of Esrog and Lulav; (13-14) the two nights of *Shemini Atzeres-Simchas Torah;* (15) the first night of Chanukah; (16-17) the night and morning of Purim before reading the Megillah *(Bnai Yisas'char).*

Torah Study and Chanukah Gelt

◄§ Since the revolt of the Hasmoneans was undertaken in defense of the Torah and its commandments, and since the miracle of the oil symbolized the 'light' of Torah study (see Overview and History), it was natural that Torah academies and their students receive special attention during the festival.

□ In many communities, the leaders would meet during Chanukah to discuss ways and means to improve the state of Torah education.

□ Parents customarily distribute *Chanukah gelt* [money] to their young children, as a reward for their past diligence in their studies and as an incentive for them to resume their studies with even more intensity in the future.

□ Many rabbis would travel to outlying peasant communities during Chanukah to teach, preach, and exhort the people to greater study and observance.

Dreidel

⋽ There is a virtually universal custom that children — and even adults — play *dreidel* during Chanukah. Apparently this was a natural outcome of the fact that the children had the coins given them as Chanukah gifts and they had more free time than usual. This, too, had an educational purpose, however. The children were encouraged to enjoy their Chanukah evenings so that they could return to their Torah studies refreshed after Chanukah.

□ There was a further educational *motif* in the *dreidel* play. The four sides of the *dreidel* are inscribed with the letters נ, ג, ה, ש, standing for נֵס גָּדוֹל הָיָה שָׁם, a great *miracle occurred there.* In Israel, the letters are נ, ג, ה, פ for נֵס גָּדוֹל הָיָה פֹּה, a great miracle occurred *here.* Thus, even the Chanukah toy contains a reminder of God's providence.

□ According to folk tradition, the *dreidel* and similar games were devised in ancient times by Jews who were imprisoned for the 'crime' of studying Torah. They would congregate in their jails under the guise of playing games, but in reality they carried on their discussions of Torah.

Yom Tov of Torah

⋽ Because it is a *mitzvah* to rejoice during Chanukah, it is called a *Yom Tov.* ... It is only proper, however, that this joy be one of Torah, and its regular study should not be interrupted thereon (*Teshuvos Maharshal* cited in *Be'ur Halachah* 670).

The Few Will Vanquish the Many

⋽ *Not because you are more numerous than all the nations has HASHEM favored and chosen you, for you are the smallest of all nations* [Deut. 7:7].

With these words God showed His people its role among the nations. Not without reason did God chose the weak Jewish people, so inferior in numbers, to be the bearers of His eternal truths. With its weakness and numerical smallness, it is to open the eyes of the world, and to convince it that life-giving strength flows from Divine Truth, not from physical power.

Chanukah serves as a reminder that in the future too, the few are destined to vanquish the many *(R' Shlomo Breuer: Chochmah Umussar).*

Jacob's Small Jugs

❧ We learn in *Genesis* 32:25, וַיִּוָּתֵר יַעֲקֹב לְבַדּוֹ, *Jacob was left alone,* which *Rashi,* citing the Talmud, explains to imply that Jacob had returned to fetch some small earthenware jugs that he had forgotten [לְבַדּוֹ=לְכַדּוֹ].

The Holy One, Blessed is He, said to him: 'You endangered yourself to return for some small jugs so that you could use them, like all your possessions, for My sake. I will personally repay your descendants in the time of the Hasmoneans when a miracle will be performed with a small jug' *(Tzeidah LaDerech).*

Kindling is the Duty.

❧ Though we Jews are only a small minority of the world's population, we have been assigned the formidable, seemingly impossible, task of enlightening the entire world. But the Sages have given us a hint as to how this can be accomplished. The Sages taught [*Shabbos* 23a] הַדְלָקָה עוֹשָׂה מִצְוָה, *the kindling* [of the Chanukah lights] *is the essence of the mitzvah;* כָּבְתָה אֵין זָקוּק לָהּ, *if* [the light] *becomes extinguished, we are not obligated* [to rekindle it]. This symbolizes to us that we are charged with the responsibility to *start* the task of enlightening the world; God will see to its successful conclusion.

By ruling that the kindling is the key to the *mitzvah,* our Sages taught us a profound lesson. While the preservation of the Torah springs from its inherent Divine potency, we must remain active and do our share despite all difficulties. But although the 'kindling' is *our* duty, we may calmly leave the continued burning to God. He does not expect us to guarantee success, only to do what He asks of us. The same is true of all measures we must take when called upon to fulfill our Jewish duty. Let us go through life as an example to our children. Let us fight for God and His Torah. For in the same measure in which we fight for God, God also fights for us *(R' Shlomo Breuer, Chochmah Umussar).*

'Zos' Chanukah — The Final Seal

❧ It is Kabbalistically known that Chanukah marks the period of the final seal from Yom Kippur *(Likkutei Mahariach).*

□ From Rosh Chodesh Elul until Chanukah, a spiritual 'Hand', so to speak, illuminates the Heavens, waiting to receive those who were unable to repent fully before Yom Kippur. A Biblical allusion to this is in *Isaiah* 27:9: בְּזֹאת יְכֻפַּר עֲו‍ֹן יַעֲקֹב, *through this* [zos] *will Jacob's sin be atoned.* The word זֹאת *zos* is homiletically understood as an allusion to

'zos Chanukah' — the name by which the eighth day of Chanukah is known in Rabbinic literature [because of the closing portion of the Torah-reading of that day זֹאת חֲנֻכַּת הַמִּזְבֵּחַ, *this (zos) was the dedication offering (chanukas) of the altar* ...]. *Thus, the verse in Isaiah suggests that there is still time for Jacob's sin to be forgiven until 'zos', the last day of Chanukah* (B'nei Binyamin *citing* Bnai Yisas'char *in the name of* "tzaddikim").

✑ Observance:

The Laws

The Ritual

The Laws

The following halachos are culled, in the main, from the authorities having the widest acceptance, the *Shulchan Aruch Orach Chaim* [here abbreviated OC] and *Mishnah Berurah* [MB]. We have restricted ourselves to the most important halachos, and have also included some decisions from the Halachah literature of our generation where we feel that this is warranted.

◆§ The Eight Days of Chanukah

1. The Chanukah festival starts on the 25th of Kislev and continues for eight consecutive days. Eulogies, except in the presence of a Torah scholar's bier, may not be delivered on these days. Fasting is prohibited on them (OC 670:1,3).

2. These eight days were denominated *Yamim Tovim* [festivals] by the Sages (*Shabbos* 21b) and *Hallel* is recited every day (OC 683).

3. A segment starting with the words עַל הַנִּסִּים, *Al HaNissim*, is inserted in the benediction of the *Shemoneh Esrei* beginning with the word מוֹדִים, *modim*, and in the second benediction of *Bircas HaMazon* [Grace after Meals] (OC 682).

4. If *Al HaNissim* was omitted, the *Shemoneh Esrei* or *Bircas HaMazon* need not be repeated. However even if one had forgotten to recite *Al HaNissim* in the place indicated in the prayerbook, he must still recite it if he had not yet recited the words, בָּרוּךְ אַתָּה ה', at the end of the blessing. Moreover, even if he had already said the words בָּרוּךְ

אַתָּה but had not yet said the word ה', he must recite *Al HaNissim* (OC 682). [He should go back to *Al HaNissim* and conclude the rest of the text from the end of the segment of *Al HaNissim*.]

5. If one forgot *Al HaNissim* in *Bircas HaMazon* and had already concluded the benediction (as above §4), he should nevertheless give praise for the Chanukah miracle among the short prayer segments beginning with הָרַחֲמָן, as follows: At the conclusion of the segment beginning בַּמָּרוֹם, He says הָרַחֲמָן הוּא יַעֲשֶׂה לָנוּ נִסִּים וְנִפְלָאוֹת כְּשֵׁם שֶׁעָשִׂיתָ לַאֲבוֹתֵינוּ בַּיָּמִים הָהֵם בַּזְּמַן הַזֶּה, *The Compassionate One! May he work for us miracles and wonders as He did for our forefathers in those days at this time.* Then he says בִּימֵי מַתִּתְיָהוּ, *In the days of Mattisyahu …*

6. Although Chanukah is considered a *Yom Tov*, there is no obligation to feast on these days. Therefore the customary Chanukah banquets *per se* are not to be considered סְעוּדוֹת מִצְוָה, *mitzvah banquets.*[1] However, it is customary to recite psalms or songs of thanksgiving to God for His miracles at these meals, and these recitations elevate the meals to the status of *mitz-*

---

1. The *Poskim* (*Maharam of Rothenburg* cited by *Tur, Orach Chaim* 670) point out that the Talmud (*Shabbos* 21b) states only that the Sages 'made it a Yom Tov with regard to [recital of] Hallel and thanksgiving' [i.e. the recital of *Al HaNissim* (*Rashi*)], omitting any mention of feasting.

Levush (*Orach Chaim* 670 cited by *Mishnah Berurah* §6) explains that Chanukah differs in this from Purim (where feasting is an integral part of the festival) because of the nature of the event commemorated. The festival of Purim celebrates the deliverance of the Jewish nation from *physical* annihilation, therefore the celebration takes a physical form. By contrast, the Syrian-Greeks did not seek the *physical* destruction of the Jews, but their *spiritual* obliteration. King Antiochus demanded only that they reject the Torah and their beliefs. Appropriately, therefore, the celebration of their deliverance expresses itself in spiritual ways — the lighting of lamps, recital of *Hallel* and *Al HaNissim* (cf. *Bach* and *Turei Zahav ad loc.*).

vah banquets[2] *(OC 670:1)*. However some authorities maintain that there is a degree of merit to celebrating Chanukah with feasts *(Rama ad loc.)*.[3]

7. Women[4] have a custom not do work as long as the Chanukah lamps burn *(OC 670:1)*, i.e., for the half an hour period that they must burn *(MB)*. Some authorities explain that only *hard* work is avoided *(Orchos Chaim ad loc.)*.

❧ The Chanukah Lights: Who is required to light them.

8. The basic obligation is that each household kindle at least one light every night of Chanukah *(Shabbos 21b)*.[5] However it is a commonly ac-cepted custom that every male in the household kindles his own lights *(OC 671:2)*. Women generally do not kindle their own lights, but they should be present when the male members kindle the lights and should listen to the recitation of the benedictions.[6] Nevertheless, if they were not present during the kindling their obligation is discharged as long as someone in the household kindles with them in mind (see *OC 676:3*).

9. Although women customarily do not light when adult males are present,[7] they are obligated in this *mitzvah*, and may act as agents to discharge the males of their obligation. Therefore if there is no adult male

2. Any banquet convened to praise God, or to publicize a miracle or *mitzvah* (e.g., the *bris milah* meal), is to be considered a *mitzvah* meal *(Maharshal* cited by *Mishnah Berurah 670:9; Maharam of Rothenburg, Teshuvos, ed. Prague 205)*.

3. This view holds that Chanukah is celebrated on two levels: (a) To mark the rededication of the Temple, the Sages instituted eight days of 'feasting and rejoicing' (מִשְׁתֶּה וְשִׂמְחָה); (b) to mark the miracle of the oil, the lighting of the lamps was instituted *(Darkei Moshe)*. Rambam *(Hil. Chanukah 3:3)* states: 'Therefore the Sages in that generation instituted that these eight days ... be days of rejoicing ...' Some *(R' Shlomo HaKohen* and *R' Aryeh Leib Yevnin* in their glosses on *Rambam*, ed. Vilna) understand that by 'rejoicing' Rambam refers to feasting. However *Tzafnas Pa'ane'ach* understands that he means the joyous recital of Hallel.

4. Women have adopted this custom distinctive to them because of the important role they played in the victory over the Greeks *(MB loc. cit;* see p. 78). Some *(Beur HaGra 670:3* and *Mor UKetzia ad loc.)* feel that this custom was instituted to stress the prohibition against making use of the burning lamps. Others *(Maharil* cited by *Ba'er Heitev 670:2)* advocate abstention from work even for men.

5. There is debate among the commentators whether the provision that all the members of a household may fulfill their obligation with the kindling of one of its members is a case of relegating the performance of an action to an agent (שָׁלִיחַ), and is based on the principle that 'one's agent is as oneself' (שְׁלוּחוֹ שֶׁל אָדָם כְּמוֹתוֹ), or whether the obligation to kindle was placed on each domicile and not on the individual; i.e., perhaps the Sages did not obligate each individual to kindle lights, but rather stipulated that lights be kindled and exhibited in each household. See *Pnei Yehoshua* and *Sfas Emes, Shabbas 21b,* s.v. תַּ"ר, and *Hararei Kodesh,* notes to R' Z.P. Frank's *Mikra'ei Kodesh,* p. 33.

6. See *MB 672:10*. The reason to require their presence during the kindling lies at the core of the *mitzvah* of kindling — to publicize the miracle. Furthermore in our days the function of kindling is primarily to proclaim the miracle to the household members (see *Rama 671:7,8; 672:2; 671:1)*. Consequently, someone who arrives home after the household members are already asleep may not recite the blessings unless he awakens them; otherwise he may not recite the benedictions *(MB 672:11;* see *Sha'ar HaTziyun)*. Additionally there is specific merit in hearing the recitation of the benedictions, for according to many authorities one who has fulfilled the *mitzvah* by proxy, must nevertheless recite the benedictions *She'assa nissim* and *Shehecheyanu* upon seeing the lights (see *MB 676:6)*. By listening to the benedictions it is considered as if one had recited the benedictions himself (שׁוֹמֵעַ כְּעוֹנֶה) and one is spared the dilemma of whether or not to recite *She'assa* and *Shehecheyanu* (see further §30).

7. The reason for this custom is not clear. Some authorities explain it with the well-known dictum, אִשְׁתּוֹ כְּגוּפוֹ, *one's wife is as oneself,* i.e. they are considered as one person concerning

(above the age of 13) in the household, the woman of the house must kindle (OC 675:3, MB there).

10. A minor male, who is old enough to understand the significance of Chanukah, should kindle the lights, but adults (men or women) may not discharge their obligation through him *(ibid.)*.

◆§ The Time

11. Ideally one should kindle immediately upon nightfall, i.e. צֵאת הַכּוֹכָבִים, *the emergence of stars,*[8] or within the half hour following nightfall[9]. However since in our days kindling is performed within the house (in contrast to Talmudic times when it was performed at the outer doorway), one may kindle and say the benedictions even after this time. In Talmudic times, the lights were lit to publicize the miracle to passersby, therefore, they had to be lit while people were still up and about outdoors. Nowadays, they are lit primarily for the family, however (OC 672:1-2).

12. One should not kindle before the designated time (OC 672:1; see *Be'ur Halachah*, s.v. וְלֹא מקדימין). However if it will be impossible for him to kindle later one may kindle up to approximately one hour before this time (OC 672:1 with MB).[10] If one must kindle earlier than this he should consult a halachic authority.

13. The lights should burn for at least half an hour. If one kindles an oil lamp one must be sure that there is sufficient oil to burn until the end of this period before reciting the benedictions. Where one kindled before the indicated time (see §12), he must make sure that there is sufficient oil for the light to burn a half hour past nightfall, in addition to the time it burns in the period between kindling and nightfall. Likewise, if one uses candles, they must be of sufficient length to burn the required time *(ibid)*.

◆§ Sabbath

14. On Sabbath eve one kindles the Chanukah lights prior to the kindling of the Sabbath candles. A woman who forgot and kindled the Sabbath candles first may not kindle the Chanukah lights. She must ask another adult to kindle for her. In this case the person who kindles on her behalf must recite the first benediction, but she may say the next two benedictions (MB 679:1).

15. On the Sabbath eve one must make sure that at least one of the lights will burn through the entire half hour period following nightfall (as in §13; see MB 679:2). It is not sufficient that they burn for half an hour after kindling (as usual) because the *mitzvah* is performed prior even to sun-down, and at least an hour before nightfall.

the *mitzvah* of kindling (see *Sha'alos UTeshuvos Sha'ar Ephraim* 42, *Machatzis HaShekel* 675:4, *Eliyah Rabbah* 671, and *MB* 671:9; *Chidushei Chasam Sofer, Shabbos* 21b).

8. There is much controversy as to exactly when this takes place halachically; opinions range from approximately 40-72 minutes after sunset.

9. The above is the view expressed in *Shulchan Aruch*, and the one generally followed in practice. However some (see *Beur HaGra* 672:2) advocate that the lamps be lit immediately after sundown. This view is especially followed in Jerusalem's old community (see *Moadim Uz'manim* 1:72, 2:154). See *Rabbi R' S. Eider, Halachos of Chanukah* p. 20 for other views.

10. The period after *plag haminchah* is considered night for some halachic requirements, e.g., the *Maariv* prayer may be recited then (see OC 233:1 for a discussion of *plag haminchah*). Although technically the length of this period is 1¼ hours, this does *not* mean 75 minutes. These hours are not sixty-minute periods, but are reckoned as ¹/₁₂th of the daylight hours of that particular day. During the short 9 hour winter days of Chanukah, 1¼ hours would be approximately 60 minutes. In general there is a question if the Mishnaic hours are counted from dawn to nightfall (i.e., emergence of the stars) or from sunup to sundown. *Mishnah Berurah* (672:3) rules (concerning the above halachah) that *plag haminchah* occurs 1¼ halachic hours before the emergence of the stars.

16. At the conclusion of the Sabbath in the synagogue, the Chanukah lights are kindled after the *Shemoneh Esrei* prayer and before the *Havdalah* is recited *(OC 681)*. There are conflicting opinions and customs as to the sequence to be followed in the home. Some recite the *Havdalah* first and then kindle the lights, while others reverse the procedure. Both views have validity *(MB 671:2)*.

⋇§The Place

17. In Talmudic times the lights were placed at or near the outer part of the doorway facing the street, i.e., in the space between the door and the outside or on the street near the doorway *(Shabbos 21b, OC 671:5)*. Furthermore, according to the halachically accepted view *(Tos. Shabbos 21b, s.v.* מצוה; *OC 671:5)*, if the domicile entrance faced a courtyard, the lights may not be placed in that doorway, but rather they are put in the courtyard doorway leading to the street. The reason for this is obvious — to publicize the miracle. The lights are placed on the left side of the doorway, opposite the *mezuzah (ibid.)*. However in the Diaspora it has become accepted custom to kindle the lights indoors[11] (see *Tur O.C. 671* and *673* with *Bach; Shulchan Aruch OC 671:7)*. Nonetheless one should kindle the lights near an interior doorway (at its left side). (See next paragraph about kindling by a window.) Nowadays many observant Jews in *Eretz Yisrael* perform the *mitzvah* as it was done in Talmudic times.

18. If one lives above the ground floor and has no door leading to the street [his entrance is through the ground floor apartment *(MB 671:23)*], he kindles at a window facing the street *(M.B. 671:5)*. However if the window is more than twenty cubits above street level (and thus the light will be inconspicuous from the street) there is no advantage in putting the light there and it should be placed near a door *(Sha'ar HaTziyun 671:42)*.

[The above applies to the *mitzvah* as practiced in Talmudic times. It follows logically that in our times when the lights are not kindled on the outside, one should at least light at a window facing the street, if possible. However many people kindle in the house near a doorway, preferring to enhance the *mitzvah* by lighting opposite the *mezuzah*, and relying on the view that in our day publicizing the miracle is directed primarily at the household.

19. Ideally one should elevate the lights at least three handbreadths (טְפָחִים) above the ground (of the street or apartment) and below ten handbreadths. However one has discharged his duty if these directions were not adhered to *(OC 671:6 with MB)*.

20. The essence of the *mitzvah* is the act of *kindling* and not the *placing* of the candles or lamps in the proper spot. For example, if one had already kindled the lights in the house, he does not discharge his duty with merely placing the burning lights in the doorway or window facing the street, but must extinguish the flames and relight them after placing the candles or lamp in its proper place. Therefore, one must place the candles or lamp in the correct place before kindling *(OC 675:1)*. Even when kindling is performed in the house, one may not kindle the lights in one place and then move them to a more appropriate spot because it would seem as if he had lit them for his own use, and *post facto* (בְּדִיעֲבָד) he has not discharged his duty *(MB 676:5)*. Similarly one who holds the light in his

---

11. The Talmud *(Shabbos 21b)* rules: 'In time of danger one places it (the Chanukah lamp) on his table and this is sufficient.' To this *Ba'al Halttur (Asseres HaDibros, Hil. Chanukah)* remarks, 'Since they have already adopted this usage (to kindle indoors) because of the danger, it has acquired the status of a valid custom, and remains valid even after the danger has passed.' *Aruch HaShulchan (671:24)* reasons that the present custom is due to the inclement weather prevailing in Europe at the time of Chanukah which all but renders outdoor kindling impossible (cf. *Chidushei HaRitva HaChadashim, Shabbos 21b s.v.* ראי לא אדליק).

hand while kindling does not discharge his duty (OC 675:1).

21. Lamps are also kindled in the synagogue before the *Maariv* prayer and the appropriate benedictions are said. However one does not discharge his obligation by kindling in the synagogue; he must kindle the lights in his home as well. The *menorah* is placed near the southern wall (as it was in the Holy Temple) and the lamps arranged from east to west (OC 671:7). However some have a custom to arrange the lamps from north to south; this, too, is a valid custom (MB 671:42). Both customs are based on conflicting opinions among the *Tannaim* as to how the *Menorah* in the Temple was arranged (ibid). In many communities the lamps are also lit during the *Shacharis* prayer, albeit without the *benedictions*.

◄§ The Number of Lights

22. Basically the *mitzvah* can be performed by kindling one light for an entire household every night (Shabbos 21b). However the Talmud (ibid.) notes that it is desirable to 'enhance' (מְהַדֵּר) the *mitzvah* by lighting more than the minimum of a light per night in each household. There are two possible 'enhancements' to this *mitzvah*. Those who enhance their performance of *mitzvos* (הַמְהַדְרִין) kindle one light for each member of the household (e.g., if the household consists of five members, five lights are kindled every night). Those who enhance their *mitzvos* even more (מְהַדְרִין מִן הַמְהַדְרִין) begin with one light on the first night and add one additional light on each succeeding night until eight lights are kindled on the eighth night. The custom in Ashkenazic communities is to incorporate both 'enhancements', that is: each male member of the household kindles one light on the first night, and adds an additional light on each night (OC, Rama

671:2). Most Sephardim, however, conduct themselves according to the custom described in *Rambam*[12] (Hil. Chanukah 4:3) as 'the prevalent custom in all our cities in Sepharad (Spain)' and that given by R' Yosef Karo in the *Shulchan Aruch* (OC 671:2). This custom calls for one *menorah* to be used for an entire household, and for one lamp to be lit on the first night and an additional light on each of the succeeding nights.

23. According to the custom most widely followed, on the first night one kindles the lamp at the extreme right of the *menorah*; on the second night one adds a light to the left of

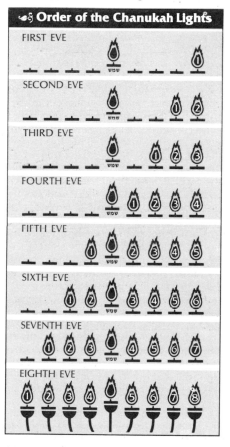

◄§ Order of the Chanukah Lights

FIRST EVE

SECOND EVE

THIRD EVE

FOURTH EVE

FIFTH EVE

SIXTH EVE

SEVENTH EVE

EIGHTH EVE

---

12. *Rambam* himself is of the opinion that a set of lamps should be kindled for each member of the household. *Turei Zahav* (OC 671:1) points out the anomaly that the Ashkenazim conduct themselves according to *Rambam* while the Sephardim adopt the view of *Tosafos (Shab-*

the first one, kindles the added light first and then, moving to his right, lights the one at the extreme right. This procedure is repeated every night; first one kindles the added light and then kindles the rest, moving from left to right (OC 675:5). See accompanying illustration.

◆§ The Fuel

24. Any fuel may be used for the lights and all materials are suitable to serve as wicks. However in order to perform the *mitzvah* in a most meritorious manner one should use olive oil[13]. If olive oil is not readily available one should use an oil which gives a steady and clear flame, or wax (or paraffin) candles (OC 673:1). However oil is preferable to candles (MB 673:4).[14]

25. Electric or gas lights may not be used to perform the *mitzvah*.[15]

◆§ Activity Before Performing the Mitzvah

26. One may not eat, perform work, or even study Torah once the time for kindling has arrived (MB 672:2).

◆§ The Berachos
Performance of the Mitzvah

27. Before kindling the lights the appropriate benedictions must be recited. On the first night three benedictions are said: (a) אֲשֶׁר ... בָּרוּךְ קִדְּשָׁנוּ בְּמִצְוֹתָיו וְצִוָּנוּ לְהַדְלִיק נֵר שֶׁל חֲנֻכָּה, *Blessed ... who has sanctified us with His commandments and commanded us to kindle the Chanukah light;* (b) ... שֶׁעָשָׂה נִסִּים לַאֲבוֹתֵינוּ בַּיָּמִים הָהֵם בַּזְּמַן הַזֶּה— ... *who has performed miracles for our forefathers in the those days at this season;* c) שֶׁהֶחֱיָנוּ וְקִיְּמָנוּ ... וְהִגִּיעָנוּ לַזְּמַן הַזֶּה, ... *who has kept us alive ... and brought us to this season.* On the second night only the first two benedictions are said and *Shehecheyanu* is omitted. However if one had forgotten to recite *Shehecheyanu* the first night, he should recite it prior to kindling on the second night, or on whatever night he recalls his oversight (OC 676:1; see MB 82 with Sha'ar HaTziyun).

28. All three benedictions must be recited prior to kindling the first light. If one forgot to recite the benedictions and already kindled some lights he may say them prior to kindling one of

bos 21b, s.v. וְהמדרין). However it should be noted that the Sephardic custom was already in force in *Rambam's* time and is cited by him (see *Be'er HaGolah* and *Chemed Moshe*). Furthermore the Ashkenazic custom resembles *Rambam's* view only in that it favors lighting more than one set of lamps. It differs from *Rambam's* in two points: (a) the Ashkenazim have every member of the household kindle for himself, while according to *Rambam* the head of the household kindles one set of lamps for each of its members; (b) in the Ashkenazic custom, lamps are lit only by the males, while according to *Rambam* lamps are lit even for the women.

13. There are two reasons for this preference; (a) olive oil yields the steadiest and clearest flame (see *Shabbos* 23a ... כָּל הַשְּׁמָנִים יָפִים with *Tos.* s.v. מפוש; cf. *Meiri* to 21a); (b) because the miracle of Chanukah occurred with olive oil (this is the only oil which may be used for the *Menorah* in the Temple; see *Exodus* 27:20). Preferably, the *mitzvah* of kindling should reflect this historical event (*Chayei Adam* 154:5, *Aruch HaShulchan* 673:1).

14. In order to emulate the *Menorah* lamp of the Temple in which [olive] oil was used (MB; see *Meiri Shabbas* 21a). *Maharal MiPrague* [*Ner Mitzvah*] maintains that even *post facto* (בְּדִיעֲבָד) one cannot discharge his obligation with any fuel other than oil, but the *Poskim* do not accept his argument (see *Sha'ar HaTziyun* 673:4).

15. The Talmudic sources speak of a נֵר, *ner*, which refers to a receptacle holding fuel for kindling purposes, i.e., a lamp and not a light. Indeed the benediction recited before kindling uses this word (לְהַדְלִיק נֵר שֶׁל חֲנֻכָּה) indicating that this aspect of the Temple *Menorah* must be represented in the *mitzvah* of kindling. Surely one cannot perform the *mitzvah* by kindling a long burning wood splint; it is not a, נֵר, *lamp.* (Candles, although they seem to resemble splints, actually operate on the same principle as oil lamps. The flame on the wick melts the

the additional lights. If he had already kindled all of the lights he may not recite the first benediction (... *who has commanded us to kindle ...*); he must recite the next two benedictions (on the first night) or the second (on the other nights) while the lights are still burning *(OC 676:2 with MB)*. However, some authorities point out that one cannot recite these benedictions if the lights have already burned half an hour after kindling (see *Teshuvos Hisorerus Teshuvah* 1:67, *Sedei Chemed Maareches Chanukah* cited in *Ner Ish Uveiso* p. 34; *Shoneh Halachos* 676:6)

29. After kindling the first light one recites the formula הַנֵּרוֹת הַלָּלוּ (676:4 with *MB*).

30. According to many authorities, even someone away from home who discharges his obligation by having someone kindle for him at his own home, must nevertheless recite the last two blessings upon seeing burning Chanukah lights. The *Shulchan Aruch* rules that one should *not* recite these blessings in such a case because of the doubt as to whether one is obligated to recite the blessings in this instance *(OC 676:3 with MB)*. [Therefore one should make it a point to be present when the lights are being kindled so as to hear the recitation of the benedictions, and thus to discharge his obligation, for it is a cardinal rule that, שׁוֹמֵעַ כְּעוֹנֶה, *one who hears is considered as if he had recited.*]

31. As already mentioned (§20) the act of kindling is the essence of the *mitzvah* (הַדְלָקָה עוֹשָׂה מִצְוָה). Therefore, if after kindling, the lights were inadvertently extinguished (e.g., while attempting to adjust the wick, one accidentally extinguished the flame), he is not obligated to rekindle them even if this happened during the first half hour of burning. However it is preferable to rekindle the extinguished lights *(OC*

673:2 with *MB* §27). If, however, he placed the lights in a place where they were apt to be extinguished by an ordinary wind, or, he did not put enough oil into the lamp, or, he used a candle too short to burn for half an hour, or the like, he must rekindle the lights [to burn for half an hour], but should not recite the blessings again *(OC 673:2 and 675:2 with MB)*.

◄§ The Shamash

32. One may not derive any benefit from the burning lamps. Therefore an additional lamp or candle is placed alongside the lights in a manner which sets it off from the Chanukah lights (usually it is placed higher than them) so that the number of Chanukah lights can readily be discerned. This light is called the *shamash* (lit. attendant) and serves as a precaution against inadvertent use of the Chanukah lights; in case someone reads or makes some other use of the lights, it can be assumed that he enjoyed the *shamash*. In Ashkenazic communities a candle is used to kindle the lights and it serves as the *shamash*. In some communities the *shamash* is set up with the rest of the lights and all of them — the Chanukah lights and the *shamash* — are kindled with another flame. Nevertheless if someone wishes to do anything needing light, he should refrain from doing it near the menorah, even though the *shamash* is burning *(OC 673:1 with MB)*.

◄§ One Who is Away From Home

33. If one is lodged away from home (see below) and is staying at the home of a fellow Jew he may buy a partnership in his host's candles or oil (a penny's worth is sufficient) and discharge his obligation through the agency of his host. It is preferable, however, that he kindle his own lights, if possible *(677:1 with MB)*.

fuel which is then sucked up through the wick.) The presence of a wick is also presumed to be a necessity. A gas lamp, by comparison, is merely burning gas, *sans* wick or receptacle. The incandescent light is a glowing piece of metal, hardly comparable to a נֵר, lamp (see *Teshuvos Beis Yitzchak, Yoreh Deah* 120; *Teshuvos Yad HaLevi* v. 1; *R' Z.P. Frank, Mikra'ei Kodesh* p. 47).

34. The above holds true for a transient lodger. If one lives with a fellow Jew year round and eats at his table, he is considered as part of the household and is not required to kindle for himself *(MB 377:1; cf. Beur Halachah* there). [He should however kindle his own lights in accordance with the custom that every male member of the household kindles for himself (see above §2).]

35. If the traveler's wife is at home, she must kindle to fulfill her own obligation (her *mitzvah* is not discharged by her husband's kindling away from home, for lights must be kindled in each household; see *Terumas HaDeshen* 101). If she will be lighting at home, the husband may rely on his wife and fulfill the *mitzvah* through her agency. If he wishes to, however, he may also kindle for himself and recite the benedictions *(OC 677:3),* but he must have in mind that he does not wish his obligation to be discharged for him by his wife *(MB 677:15).* However some authorities dispute this ruling and hold that his duty is fulfilled with his wife's kindling in any case. Although one may rely on the first view, it is preferable that he either kindle before his wife does so, or hear the blessings from someone else *(MB 377:16;* see also *Pri Megadim, Mishbetzos Zahav 377:1).*

36. Someone who is merely paying a visit or is invited to a meal by a friend or relative cannot discharge his obligation by kindling at his host's home. The *mitzvah* is fulfilled only with kindling at one's own residence *(MB 677:12).* If one plans to stay at the friend or relative's house for the entire night or until near midnight he should consult a competent halachic authority.

⋖§ The Ritual

Before the performance of any mitzvah, it is proper to state one's intention. The following declaration is from Siddur Otzar HaTefillos. It appears in the Siddur Bais Yaakov with minor variations.

לְשֵׁם יִחוּד קוּדְשָׁא בְּרִיךְ הוּא וּשְׁכִינְתֵּיה, בִּדְחִילוּ וּרְחִימוּ לְיַחֵד שֵׁם י״ה בְּו״ה בְּיִחוּדָא שְׁלִים, בְּשֵׁם כָּל יִשְׂרָאֵל. הֲרֵינִי בָא לְקַיֵּם מִצְוַת הַדְלָקַת נֵר חֲנֻכָּה, לְתַקֵּן אֶת שָׁרְשָׁהּ בְּמָקוֹם עֶלְיוֹן.

יְהִי רָצוֹן מִלְּפָנֶיךָ, יהוה אֱלֹהַי וֵאלֹהֵי אֲבוֹתַי, שֶׁיִּהְיֶה עַתָּה עֵת רָצוֹן לְפָנֶיךָ, לִהְיוֹת עוֹלֶה מִצְוַת הַדְלָקַת נֵר חֲנֻכָּה כְּאִלּוּ הִשַּׂגְתִּי כָּל הַסּוֹדוֹת הַנּוֹרָאִים אֲשֶׁר הֵם חֲתוּמִים בָּהּ, וְתַעֲלֶה לְפָנֶיךָ עִם כַּוָּנַת מַעֲשֵׂה מִצְוָה זֹאת, הַנַּעֲשִׂית עַל יְדֵי בְּנֵי יְדִידֶיךָ, הַמְכֻוָּנִים כָּל שְׁמוֹתֶיךָ הַקְּדוֹשִׁים הָרְאוּיִים לָבוֹא בְּהַדְלָקָה זוֹ, הַמַּעֲלִים יִחוּד וְזִוּוּג מִדּוֹת הַקְּדוֹשׁוֹת הָעֶלְיוֹנוֹת, וּלְהָאִיר בִּשְׁכִינָה עֹז הַמְּאוֹרוֹת הַגְּדוֹלִים וּמִשָּׁם יֻשְׁפַּע שֶׁפַע שֶׁפַע לִי אֲנִי עַבְדְּךָ (Hebrew name) בֶּן [female בַּת] (mother's Hebrew name) לְאוֹר בְּאוֹר הַחַיִּים. כִּי אַתָּה תָּאִיר נֵרִי יהוה אֱלֹהַי יַגִּיהַּ חָשְׁכִּי. שְׁלַח אוֹרְךָ וַאֲמִתְּךָ הֵמָּה יַנְחוּנִי לְיִרְאָה וּלְאַהֲבָה אֶת שְׁמֶךָ לִלְמוֹד וּלְלַמֵּד אֶת תּוֹרָתְךָ הַקְּדוֹשָׁה, תּוֹרָה שֶׁבִּכְתָב וְתוֹרָה שֶׁבְּעַל פֶּה, בְּהַתְמָדָה גְדוֹלָה, וְלִכְבוֹד שִׁמְךָ יִתְבָּרַךְ וְיִתְעַלֶּה. וּבְכֹחַ סְגֻלַּת נֵר חֲנֻכָּה תְּחַכְּמֵנוּ בְּאוֹר תּוֹרָתֶךָ, אָנוּ וְזַרְעֵנוּ וְזֶרַע זַרְעֵנוּ. וִיקֻיַּם בִּי מִקְרָא שֶׁכָּתוּב: לֹא יָמֻשׁוּ מִפִּיךָ וּמִפִּי זַרְעֲךָ וּמִפִּי זֶרַע זַרְעֲךָ, אָמַר יהוה, מֵעַתָּה וְעַד עוֹלָם. וְיִהְיוּ זַרְעִי וְזֶרַע זַרְעִי תַּלְמִידֵי חֲכָמִים וַחֲסִידִים, אֲהוּבִים לְמַעְלָה, וְנֶחְמָדִים לְמַטָּה. וּתְחַזֵּק אֶת לְבָבָם לַתּוֹרָה וַעֲבוֹדָה, הַכֹּל בִּרְצוֹנְךָ הַטּוֹב. וְאֶזְכֶּה לִרְאוֹת בָּנִים וּבְנֵי בָנִים עוֹסְקִים בַּתּוֹרָה וּמִצְוֹת בֶּאֱמֶת. גַּל עֵינֵינוּ וְנַבִּיטָה נִפְלָאוֹת מִתּוֹרָתְךָ הַקְּדוֹשָׁה, לְכַוֵּן לַאֲמִתָּהּ שֶׁל תּוֹרָה וְסוֹדוֹתֶיהָ. וּבִזְכוּת מַתִּיתְיָהוּ כֹהֵן גָּדוֹל וּבָנָיו הַרְאֵנוּ נִפְלָאוֹת, וּבְאוֹרְךָ נִרְאֶה אוֹר, וְטַהֵר אֶת לְבָבֵנוּ לַעֲבוֹדָתֶךָ, וְהַרְחִיקֵנוּ מִמִּדּוֹת רָעוֹת וּמַחֲשָׁבוֹת זָרוֹת, וְתֶחֱזֶינָה עֵינֵינוּ בְּשׁוּבְךָ לְצִיּוֹן בְּרַחֲמִים, בְּהַעֲלוֹתְךָ אֶת הַנֵּרוֹת, וְשָׁם נַעֲבָדְךָ בְּיִרְאָה, כִּימֵי עוֹלָם וּכְשָׁנִים קַדְמוֹנִיּוֹת. יִהְיוּ

לְשֵׁם יִחוּד/Expression of Intent ‏ﹶ

לְשֵׁם יִחוּד — *For the sake of the unification.* This Kabbalistic formulation, similar to that customarily recited before many *mitzvos,* is discussed at

length in the ArtScroll *Bircas HaChammah.* Its basis is that man's sins have caused God's Presence, the *Shechinah,* to be separated from His Essence. This lack of harmony impedes the flow of God's blessings, with detrimental

⋘ Prefatory Prayer

Before the performance of any mitzvah, it is proper to state one's intention. The following declaration is from Siddur Otzar HaTefillos. *It appears in the* Siddur Bais Yaakov *with minor variations.*

For the sake of the unification of the Holy One, Blessed is He, and His Presence, in fear and in love to unify the Name Yud-Kei with Vav-Kei in perfect unity, in the name of all Israel. Behold, I come to fulfill the commandment of kindling the Chanukah light, to perfect its root on High.

May it be your will, HASHEM, my God and the God of my ancestors, that this be a favorable time before you for the observance of the Chanukah lamp lighting, as if I had fathomed all the awesome secrets that are sealed into it. May it ascend before You with the intent of this commandment as it is performed by the children of Your beloved ones, who concentrate on all Your sacred Names that are recalled by this lighting, who elevate the unification and pairing of the holy, supreme Attributes, and illuminate through Your powerful Presence the Great Luminaries. From there may an emanation be directed to me, Your servant (Hebrew name) son/daughter of (mother's Hebrew name) to illuminate through the Lights of Life. 'For it is You Who will light my lamp, HASHEM, my God, Who will illuminate my darkness.'

Dispatch Your light and truth — they shall guide me to fear and love of Your Name, to study and to teach Your holy Torah, the Written Torah and the Oral Torah, with great diligence and to give honor to Your blessed, exalted Name. By virtue of the Chanukah lights' inherent power, make us wise through the lights of Your Torah, us, our children and grandchildren. May this verse be fulfilled, as it is written: ' "It shall not depart from your mouth, from the mouth of your children and from the mouth of your children's children", says HASHEM, "from now to eternity".' May my children and grandchildren be Torah scholars and devout people, beloved above and cherished below, and may You strengthen their resolve in Torah and service, all according to Your good desire. May I deserve to see children and grandchildren engaging in the Torah and commandments with sincerity.

Uncover our eyes that we may perceive the wonders of Your holy Torah to define the truth of the Torah and its mysteries. In the merit of Mattisyahu, the great Kohen, and his sons, show us wonders and through Your light may we see light. Purify our hearts for Your service, distance us from evil traits and foreign thoughts, may our eyes see Your return to Zion with mercy when You will rekindle the lights. There we shall serve You as in days of old and as in former years.

---

results to the entire universe. Man's performance of God's will, however, contributes to the restoration of this harmony. Thus, we dedicate our fulfillment of the commandment to the achievement of this unification. On a simple level, a *mitzvah* should be performed with intent to fulfill the commandment, an intention that is verbally expressed by the לְשֵׁם יְחוּד.

לְרָצוֹן אִמְרֵי פִי, וְהֶגְיוֹן לִבִּי לְפָנֶיךָ, יהוה צוּרִי וְגֹאֲלִי. וַאֲנִי תְפִלָּתִי
לְךָ יהוה, עֵת רָצוֹן, אֱלֹהִים בְּרׇב חַסְדֶּךָ, עֲנֵנִי בֶּאֱמֶת יִשְׁעֶךָ. וִיהִי
נֹעַם אֲדֹנָי אֱלֹהֵינוּ עָלֵינוּ, וּמַעֲשֵׂה יָדֵינוּ כּוֹנְנָה עָלֵינוּ, וּמַעֲשֵׂה יָדֵינוּ
כּוֹנְנֵהוּ.

סדר ההדלקה ‏

On the first night, three blessings are pronounced before kindling the Menorah.
On all subsequent nights the third blessing, שֶׁהֶחֱיָנוּ, is omitted.

בָּרוּךְ אַתָּה, יהוה אֱלֹהֵינוּ, מֶלֶךְ הָעוֹלָם,
אֲשֶׁר קִדְּשָׁנוּ בְּמִצְוֹתָיו וְצִוָּנוּ
לְהַדְלִיק נֵר שֶׁל חֲנֻכָּה.

סֵדֶר הַבְּרָכוֹת/The Blessings ‏

The Talmud [*Shabbos* 23a] rules that on the first night of Chanukah one recites three blessings prior to kindling the lights: לְהַדְלִיק, *to kindle;* שֶׁעָשָׂה נִסִּים, *Who has wrought miracles;* and שֶׁהֶחֱיָנוּ, *Who has kept us alive* (*Orach Chaim* 676:1).

The commentators homiletically derive Scriptural support for this sequence from the verse [*Numbers* 21:8]: *Make yourself a fiery figure* [an allusion to the first blessing, which refers to kindling the flames] and mount it עַל נֵס, *on a standard* [the word נֵס also means *miracle,* the subject of the second blessing], *whoever looks at it will live* [the third blessing thanks God for having kept us alive].

On subsequent nights the third blessing is omitted and only the first two are recited. [See *Laws of Chanukah,* p. 117.]

Rambam (*Hilchos Berachos* 1:4): lists three primary categories of blessings: (1) בְּרָכוֹת הַנֶּהֱנִין, *blessings recited prior to partaking of material enjoyment;* (2) בִּרְכוֹת הַמִּצְוֹת, *blessings recited prior to fulfilling religious duties;* and (3) בִּרְכוֹת הוֹדָאָה, *blessings of thanksgiving,* 'which have the character of praise, thanksgiving, and supplication, the purpose being that we should always have the Creator in mind and revere Him.'

The requirement to recite blessings prior to the performance of *mitzvos* is of Rabbinic origin. The only exception is the blessing recited prior to Torah study which, according to most sources, is of Scriptural mandate, derived from *Deut.* 32:3: *When I call out the Name of HASHEM, ascribe greatness to our God.* Exegetically, the Sages derive that when one studies Torah, which is a manifestation of the Divine Name, one should *ascribe greatness* to God by pronouncing a blessing (*Berachos* 21a). [See also *Devarim Rabbah* 8, where the blessing for Torah study is derived from *Psalms* 119:12: *Blessed are You, HASHEM,* which is followed by *teach me your ordinances.*]

The three Chanukah blessings fall under two of *Rambam's* categories. The first blessing, obviously, is a בִּרְכַּת הַמִּצְוָה, *blessing prior to the performance of a mitzvah.* The last two blessing are בִּרְכוֹת הוֹדָאָה, *blessings of thanksgiving.*

⇥§ First Blessing: The Mitzvah

בָּרוּךְ אַתָּה ה' — *Blessed are You, HASHEM.* All blessings begin by addressing God directly [נוֹכַח] in second person: *Blessed are 'You',* because prayer is so exalted that it enables a mortal human being to turn directly to God, so to speak.

Generally, the blessings then change to third person [נִסְתָּר], *Who has sanctified us with 'His' commandments,* because the blessings conclude by describing His outward manifestation as He guides and controls the universe. Of that aspect of God, we have no clear understanding, only an imperfect perception of outward appearances (*Michtav*

May the expressions of my mouth and the thoughts of my heart find favor before You, HASHEM, my Rock and my Redeemer. For me, my prayer is to You, HASHEM, at an opportune time; O God, in the abundance of Your kindness, answer me with the truth of Your salvation. May the pleasantness of my Lord, our God, be upon us — may He establish our handiwork for us; our handiwork may He establish.

✒ Order of the Kindling

On the first night, three blessings are pronounced before kindling the Menorah. On all subsequent nights the third blessing, שֶׁהֶחֱיָנוּ, is omitted.

Blessed are You, HASHEM our God, King of the universe, Who has sanctified us with His commandments, and commanded us to kindle the Chanukah light.

MeEliyahu; for further discussion of the concept of blessing, see Overviews to the *Siddur* and *Bircas HaMazon*).

This combination of second and third person originates from a Talmudic dispute (*Yerushalmi Berachos* 9:1), in which the Sages Rav and Shmuel disagree whether a blessing should be formulated in the second person אַתָּה, *You* [i.e., בָּרוּךְ אַתָּה, *Blessed are You*]. Rav rules in the affirmative based on *Psalms* 16:8: שִׁוִּיתִי ה' לְנֶגְדִּי תָמִיד, *I have set HASHEM before me always* [i.e., and I therefore address Him in second person]. Shmuel rules that all blessings should be recited in the third person and should read: בָּרוּךְ ה' כו', *Blessed is HASHEM*, etc. [in the 'hidden' third-person], omitting אַתָּה, *You.*

The *Rishonim* [early decisors of Halachah] write that the Sages wished to preserve the opinions of both Rav and Shmuel in the general formula of blessings. Therefore, they composed the first part in second person following Rav — *Blessed are You* — and the rest of the blessing in third person following Shmuel — *who has commanded us* (*Shibbolei HaLeket*; see Responsa of *Rashba* 5:52).

אֱלֹהֵינוּ מֶלֶךְ הָעוֹלָם — *Our God, King of the Universe.* Every blessing must make mention of God's Name and His Kingship (*Berachos* 40b; *Rambam, Hil. Berachos* 1:5). This affirms our recognition of Divine Providence and awareness of Him as God and Sovereign of the entire universe.

That every blessing must mention God's Kingship is derived from the passage [*Psalms* 145:1]: אֲרוֹמִמְךָ אֱלוֹהַי הַמֶּלֶךְ וַאֲבָרְכָה שִׁמְךָ לְעוֹלָם וָעֶד, *I will exalt You, my God, the King, and bless Your name forever* (*Yerushalmi Berachos* 9:1; *Sefer HaManhig*).

As codified in *Shulchan Aruch Orach Chaim* §214, if one forgot to utter God's Name or His Kingship in a blessing — he must repeat the blessing. Furthermore, the word מֶלֶךְ, *King*, without הָעוֹלָם, *of the universe*, is sufficient to convey the idea that God is King of everything that exists. [But see *Even HaOzer* cited in *Be'ur Halachah* who differs. *Be'ur Halachah* concludes that if one said מֶלֶךְ, *King*, it might not be necessary to repeat the blessing.]

אֲשֶׁר קִדְּשָׁנוּ בְּמִצְוֹתָיו — *Who has sanctified us with His commandments.* The performance of *mitzvos* in itself elevates a person and makes him more prone to absorb sanctity. Alternatively, the word קִדְּשָׁנוּ, *sanctified us*, can be related to קִדּוּשִׁין, *betrothal*. God has *betrothed* us, as it were, by allowing us to perform His commandments (*Abudraham*).

בָּרוּךְ אַתָּה, יהוה אֱלֹהֵינוּ, מֶלֶךְ הָעוֹלָם, שֶׁעָשָׂה נִסִּים לַאֲבוֹתֵינוּ בַּיָּמִים הָהֵם בַּזְּמַן הַזֶּה.

וְצִוָּנוּ לְהַדְלִיק נֵר שֶׁל חֲנֻכָּה — *And commanded us to kindle the Chanukah light.* This is the text of this blessing as recorded in the Talmud (*Shabbos* 23a). The Talmud proceeds to record the obvious question: 'Where did He command us?' That is, since the kindling of the Chanukah light is of post-Biblical origin and ordained by the Sages of the pre-Mishnaic period, how can we imply that God *Himself* commanded us to kindle these lights, as if it were ordained by the Torah?

— The Talmud explains that the Torah commands us to follow the ordinances of the recognized Torah leaders — *you shall not turn aside from the sentence which they shall show you* [*Deut.* 17:11]. Accordingly, a Rabbinic observance — such as the requirement to kindle lights on Chanukah — has Biblical sanction, and the term וְצִוָּנוּ, *and He has commanded us*, is quite appropriate.

Rambam (*Hilchos Berachos* 11:3) follows that Talmudic dictum when he explains the connotation of the blessing: *... Who has sanctified us with His commandments, having commanded us to heed those [Sages] who have instructed us to kindle the Chanukah light.*

⧽ Variant versions of the blessing

The wording: לְהַדְלִיק נֵר שֶׁל חֲנֻכָּה is based on most printed versions of the Talmudic passage cited above and many manuscripts. This version is found in tractate *Soferim* chapter. 20, *Rambam*, *Rif*, *She'iltos*, *Halachos Gedolos*, *Siddur R' Amram Gaon*, *Rosh* and *Tur*, and the one most commonly used in Ashkenazic communities [see *Pri Megadim*], and in the Spanish-Portugese Sephardic rite.

Mishnah Berurah §676:1 writes that this is the version accepted by 'all the *Poskim.*'

The standard Sephardic [Syrian] sidurim, however, contain a different version: לְהַדְלִיק נֵר חֲנֻכָּה, *to kindle the Chanukah light* (omitting the preposition שֶׁל, *of*).

This version is recorded by *R' Yosef Karo* in *Shulchan Aruch Orach Chaim* 676:1, and by *Pri Chadash* who maintains this was the original wording. *Birkei Yosef*, too, approves of this version and records that it was the version used by *Arizal*. *Gra* and *R' Yaakov Emden* also prefer it. Moreover it is the version used by the ancient communities in Jerusalem.

The preference for this version is based on the fact that Chanukah lights may not be used for personal pleasure — such as reading — unlike Sabbath lights, which are meant to be enjoyed. There is a fine distinction between the expression נֵר חֲנֻכָּה, *Chanukah light*, which subtly implies total consecration to the *mitzvah* of Chanukah and that the light may be used for no other purpose, and נֵר שֶׁל שַׁבָּת, *light* **of** *Sabbath*. The insertion of שֶׁל gives the implication that the 'light' has a purpose of its own that is unrelated to the Sabbath. Indeed, the Sabbath lights are lit to provide illumination and, as such, their *light* is permitted for personal use. Additionally, they are *of Sabbath* because they are being lit in honor of the Sabbath. In the case of Chanukah lights, such a dual meaning is inappropriate because all private enjoyment of the lights is forbidden. The phrase נֵר חֲנֻכָּה, with the omission of שֶׁל, implies that the lights are exclusively for the *mitzvah* (see *Ba'er Hetev* and *Shaarei Teshuvah* 673).

The version preserved by *Sh'lah* — cited by *Maharshal*, Responsa 85, *Magen Avraham*, *Piskei Rid*; cf. also *Leket Yosher* who maintains that this was the version recited by *R' Yisrael Isserlein* [*Terumas HaDeshen*] — is לְהַדְלִיק נֵר שֶׁלַּחֲנֻכָּה. This combination of

Blessed are You, HASHEM our God, King of the universe, Who has wrought miracles for our forefathers, in those days at this season.

שֶׁל and חֲנֻכָּה to form the word, שֶׁלַחֲנֻכָּה, implies: *totally of Chanukah*, and is preferred for the same reason given by those who prefer נֵר חֲנֻכָּה over the version נֵר שֶׁל חֲנֻכָּה.

Mishnah Berurah (ibid.) cites *Pri Megadim* to the effect that: 'People are not customarily scrupulous about this' [i.e., about pronouncing שֶׁלַחֲנֻכָּה as one word, but generally recite it as two — שֶׁל חֲנֻכָּה — except for those who follow the Sephardic/*Arizal* version, נֵר חֲנֻכָּה].

All agree, however, that we say נֵר, *light*, in singular, even on subsequent nights when we follow the custom of kindling additional lights, although it may technically be more correct to use the plural נֵרוֹת, *lights*. This is because the Sages did not wish to make a distinction between the wording of the first night's blessing and that of subsequent nights. Additionally, the basic precept may be fulfilled with only one candle each night (*Pri Megadim 673*).

⏤§ Second Blessing: The Miracle

The following blessing is recited in connection with only two *mitzvos* all year: on Chanukah when kindling the lights, and on Purim when reading the *Megillah*. It commemorates the great miracles God performed for our ancestors during these respective seasons.

This blessing is in the category of בִּרְכוֹת הוֹדָאָה, *blessings of thanksgiving*. That blessings are said in commemoration of miracles is deduced in the Talmud [*Berachos 54a*] from *Exodus 18:10*: *And Jethro said, 'Blessed be HASHEM Who saved you!'* [The idea is that the Torah, which is not merely a chronicle of events, and which avoids any unnecessary words, would not have recorded Jethro's statement unless it conveyed a general teaching, specifical-

ly that one must bless God for performing an act of salvation.]

The Talmud [*Shabbos 23a*] records that the reason this blessing is said every night of Chanukah (and not only on the first night as is the case with the third blessing), is because 'the miracle applies to every day' [of Chanukah]. That is, because the cruse of oil burnt all the eight days.

The Kabbalists emphasize that while reciting this blessing one should concentrate on his gratitude to God for all the miracles He wrought on behalf of our ancestors throughout history. And he should imagine that he lived at that time, and was the personal beneficiary of the miracle *(Sh'lah)*.

שֶׁעָשָׂה נִסִּים לַאֲבוֹתֵינוּ — *Who has wrought miracles for our forefathers.* *Knesses HaGedolah* cites *Igros HaRambam* (see *Teshuvos HaRambam*, ed., Freiman §43) that a convert to Judaism may also recite this formula 'who has wrought miracles for *our* forefathers.' If he wishes, however, he may modify the wording and substitute 'who has wrought miracles for *Israel* ... ' *(Shaarei Teshuvah, Orach Chaim 676:1)*.

R' Hirsch notes that the use of the word נֵס to mean *miracle* derives from its primary meaning of *banner, signpost* [see *comm.* to ArtScroll *Bereishis 22:1*]. He writes that miracles, 'God's great acts, are termed [נִסִּים] because they are "signposts," and stand out as "banners" to teach and guide us.'

בַּיָּמִים הָהֵם בַּזְּמַן הַזֶּה — *In those days at this season.* This is the version in *Siddur Rav Amram Gaon* and *Shibbolei HaLeket*. See *Leket Yashar* citing *Terumas HaDeshen* and *Maharshal §64* who also cite this version as correct.

Magen Avraham, too, records this version and states categorically: 'בַּזְּמַן

Only on the first night recite:

בָּרוּךְ אַתָּה, יהוה אֱלֹהֵינוּ, מֶלֶךְ הָעוֹלָם,
שֶׁהֶחֱיָנוּ וְקִיְּמָנוּ וְהִגִּיעָנוּ לַזְּמַן הַזֶּה.

*On the first night the light to the extreme right should be kindled. On each
subsequent night a new light is added to the left of the previous night's lights.
The new light is always lit first, the one to its right second, and so on. After one
light has been kindled, הַנֵּרוֹת הַלָּלוּ is recited. The additional lights are kindled
during its recitation.*

הַנֵּרוֹת הַלָּלוּ אֲנַחְנוּ מַדְלִיקִין עַל הַנִּסִּים
וְעַל הַנִּפְלָאוֹת, וְעַל

הַזֶּה at this season, and not וּבַזְּמַן הַזֶּה,
and at this season.'
Aruch HaShulchan infers from
Magen Avraham's need to reject the
reading of וּבַזְּמַן, that the conjunctive
and must have appeared in some earlier
version. [Indeed, the reading is found in
Machzor Vitry.] However, *Aruch Ha-
Shulchan* maintains that the earlier version is preferable to that adopted by
Magen Avraham. In *Aruch HaShulchan's* interpretation, the *vav* [*and*] indicates that the blessing refers to two
periods: (1) *In those days,* meaning
that the struggle resulting in the
Hasmonean victory over Antiochus
took place over an extended period of
time, not only during the eight days of
Chanukah; (2) *and* [we also celebrate
the miracle that was performed] *at this
season.* This refers to the miracle of the
lights, which took place during the
eight-day period we now celebrate as
Chanukah.

The particle *and* connecting the two
expressions also carries a connotation of
prayer, as if to say that God should perform miracles for us nowadays while we
give thanks for the miracles that he performed for our ancestors *at this season.*
As *Siddur R' Saadia* expresses it: 'Just
as You have wrought miracles for the
early ones, so may You do for the later
ones, and save us in these days as You
did in those days' *(N'siv Binah).*

[There is a particular significance in
the date of a miracle, because God visits

the holy emanations of each miracle
upon Israel annually, on the date it occurred. (See *Overview,* ArtScroll edition
of *Eichah.*)]

In the Lubavitch siddur, *Tehillat Hashem,*
p. 339, the word בַּזְּמַן is vowelized בִּזְמַן;
similarly, לַזְמַן in the *Shehecheyanu* blessing
is vowelized לִזְמַן (see below).

◄§ Third Blessing: "Time"

The following blessing is referred to
in Rabbinic literature as בִּרְכַּת הַזְּמַן, *the
Blessing of Time,* or simply as בִּרְכַּת
שֶׁהֶחֱיָנוּ, *the blessing Shehecheyanu*
['Who has kept us alive'].

It is recited: on the festivals; over
fruits of a new season which ripen at
recurring intervals and are not always
available; upon *mitzvos* that are performed at seasonal intervals such as
those connected with the annual
festivals; upon seeing a friend whom
one has not seen for a significant interval; upon purchasing a new article of
importance, or upon a significant
benefit that befalls someone. [See *Talmudic Encyclopedia,* vol. IV, p. 431, s.v.
בִּרְכַּת הַזְּמַן, for an analysis of each of the
above criteria.]

The blessing is recited on Chanukah
because it is an annual festival. That the
blessing is recited only the first night of
Chanukah is explicitly stated in the
Talmud, *Shabbos* 23a. *Rashi* there (s.v.
כל יומי) explains that this is so since the
'reaching' [וְהִגִּיעָנוּ] mentioned in the
blessing refers to the *onset* of the

Blessed are You, HASHEM our God, King of the universe, Who has kept us alive, sustained us, and brought us to this season.

On the first night the light to the extreme right should be kindled. On each subsequent night a new light is added to the left of the previous night's lights. The new light is always lit first, the one to its right second, and so on. After one light has been kindled, הַנֵּרוֹת הַלָּלוּ is recited. The additional lights are kindled during its recitation.

These lights we kindle upon the miracles, the wonders, the salvations, and the battles which You

period. In other words, since the blessing thanks God for allowing us to survive for another year to perform the *mitzvah* again, it is inappropriate to recite it day after day.

However, if for some reason, one did not recite the blessing on the first night, he may do so on a subsequent night (*Orach Chaim* §676:1).

שֶׁהֶחֱיָנוּ וְקִיְּמָנוּ וְהִגִּיעָנוּ לַזְּמַן הַזֶּה — *Who has kept us alive, sustained us, and brought us to this season* [lit. *to this time*]. This is the standard version of the blessing. (See *Berachos* 54a; *Succah* 46a.)

According to *Magen Avraham*, however, the word לַזְּמַן should be vowelized לִזְמַן, and this ruling is cited by *Mishnah Berurah* 676:1 as final. The

Lubavitch siddur, *Tehillat Hashem*, also reads לִזְמַן consistent with its reading בִּזְמַן in the previous blessing. However, most printed siddurim preserve the former vowelization, לַזְּמַן, and it is justified on grammatical grounds in *Avodas Yisrael* siddur, contrary to *Mateh Moshe* §980. The Syrian-Sephardic liturgy concurs with the לִזְמַן reading.

This blessing is technically in the category of בִּרְכוֹת הוֹדָאָה, *blessings of thanksgiving*. It expresses our gratitude to God for having granted us the life and sustenance to celebrate another festive season.

[In the Diaspora the *Shehecheyanu* blessing is recited on 17 mandated occasions each year. See page 107.]

הַנֵּרוֹת הַלָּלוּ ‎⋧/HaNeiros Hallalu

This *zemer* is of very ancient origin. It is mentioned with some variations in the Talmudic 'minor tractate' *Soferim* 20:6 as part of the blessings to be recited when kindling the Chanukah lamp. *Rosh* in tractate *Shabbos* 2:8 mentions its recital, as does *Tur* and *Shulchan Aruch Orach Chaim* 676.

The version in *Soferim* reads:

הַנֵּרוֹת הָאֵלּוּ אָנוּ מַדְלִיקִין עַל הַיְשׁוּעוֹת וְעַל הַנִּסִּים וְעַל הַנִּפְלָאוֹת אֲשֶׁר עָשִׂיתָ לַאֲבוֹתֵינוּ עַל יְדֵי כֹּהֲנֶיךָ הַקְּדוֹשִׁים וְכָל (מִצְוַת) שְׁמוֹנַת יְמֵי חֲנֻכָּה הַנֵּרוֹת הָאֵלּוּ קֹדֶשׁ וְאֵין לָנוּ רְשׁוּת לְהִשְׁתַּמֵּשׁ בָּהֶן אֶלָּא לִרְאוֹתָן בִּלְבָד כְּדֵי לְהוֹדוֹת לְשִׁמְךָ עַל נִפְלְאוֹתֶיךָ וְעַל נִסֶּיךָ וְעַל יְשׁוּעָתֶךָ.

Another version is given in *Abudraham*, and cited by *Tur*. [See *Avodas Yisrael*.] That version contains minor variations, and limits itself to 38 words, which, according to *Maharshal* (*Teshuvos* 85, cited by *Magen Avraham* 676:3), alludes to the total of 36 lights that are kindled during the eight days of Chanukah, plus the two-word superscription הַנֵּרוֹת הַלָּלוּ, the eight letters of which are intended to be a separate allusion to the eight festive days of Chanukah.

The text we have used, however, is found in *Otzar HaTefillos*, *Siddur Bais Yaakov*, and most currently published siddurim. Accordingly, it is the one most customarily recited today.

הַתְּשׁוּעוֹת וְעַל הַמִּלְחָמוֹת, שֶׁעָשִׂיתָ לַאֲבוֹתֵינוּ
בַּיָּמִים הָהֵם בַּזְּמַן הַזֶּה עַל יְדֵי כֹּהֲנֶיךָ הַקְּדוֹשִׁים.
וְכָל שְׁמוֹנַת יְמֵי חֲנֻכָּה הַנֵּרוֹת הַלָּלוּ קֹדֶשׁ הֵם,
וְאֵין לָנוּ רְשׁוּת לְהִשְׁתַּמֵּשׁ בָּהֶם אֶלָּא לִרְאוֹתָם
בִּלְבָד, כְּדֵי לְהוֹדוֹת וּלְהַלֵּל לְשִׁמְךָ הַגָּדוֹל עַל
נִסֶּיךָ וְעַל נִפְלְאוֹתֶיךָ וְעַל יְשׁוּעָתֶךָ.

The recital of this prayer, like the kindling of the lights itself, serves 'to make the miracle known' [פִּרְסוּמֵי נִיסָא] and as a reminder that 'these lights are sacred throughout the eight days of Chanukah, and we are not permitted to make ordinary use of them but only to look at them' (Sh'lah).

הַנֵּרוֹת הַלָּלוּ אֲנַחְנוּ מַדְלִיקִין — *These lights we kindle.* Some versions replace אֲנַחְנוּ with the synonymous אָנוּ, and use the Hebrew suffix-form מַדְלִיקִים instead of the Aramaic מַדְלִיקִין.

עַל הַנִּסִּים וְעַל הַנִּפְלָאוֹת עַל הַתְּשׁוּעוֹת — *Upon the miracles, [and upon] the wonders, [and upon] the salvations.* This is the most popular version recited today by Ashkenazim, and found in most siddurim.

The Sephardic liturgy preserves a different order: עַל הַנִּסִּים וְעַל הַתְּשׁוּעוֹת וְעַל הַנִּפְלָאוֹת. The Lubavitch siddur, *Tehillas Hashem*, reads: עַל הַתְּשׁוּעוֹת וְעַל הַנִּסִּים וְעַל הַנִּפְלָאוֹת, which is the closest to the ancient version recorded in Tractate *Soferim* [see prefatory comment].

Some who follow the Chassidic liturgy add וְעַל הַנֶּחָמוֹת, *and upon the consolations,* an addition borrowed from the parallel phrase in some Chassidic [*Nusach Sfard*] versions of *Al HaNissim*.

נִסִּים, *miracles,* refers to the obvious acts of intervention of His Divine Providence ... The word נֵס means *banner* or *signpost,* and God's miracles are meant to be 'signposts' and symbols that stand out to teach and to guide us ... The expression נִפְלָאוֹת, *wondrous acts,* describes these extraordinary occurrences in terms of their independence from the regular order of things (*R' Hirsch*).

וְעַל הַמִּלְחָמוֹת — *And [upon] the battles,* i.e., the battles against the Syrian-

Greeks, which the Jews won thanks to God's help (*R' Hirsch*).

This phrase — borrowed from *Al HaNissim* — does not appear in many versions of *HaNeiros Hallalu,* but is found in *Siddur Otzar HaTefillos* and that of *R' Yaakov Emden.*

R' Menachem Weldler suggests that the reason it was inserted is to emphasize that the miracle of the lights provided proof that the military victories were as much a Divine miracle as the miracle of the oil, and all the events of Chanukah are accordingly perceived in the context of God's Providential direction.

However, *B'nai Yisas'char* cautions, that many *Acharonim* write that וְעַל הַמִּלְחָמוֹת, *and upon the battles,* should not be recited because all wars are objectionable, 'even the sword that brings peace'.

Indeed the Sephardic liturgy omits it, as does the Lubavitch siddur *Tehillat Hashem.*

שֶׁעָשִׂיתָ לַאֲבוֹתֵינוּ בַּיָּמִים הָהֵם בַּזְּמַן הַזֶּה — *Which You performed for our forefathers in those days at this season.* See commentary to parallel phrase in the second blessing (p. 125).

עַל יְדֵי כֹּהֲנֶיךָ הַקְּדוֹשִׁים — *Through Your holy priests.* The miracle of Chanukah is uniquely that of the *Kohanim.* When the Tabernacle in the Wilderness was dedicated, each of the tribal princes brought a special offering, but Aaron, the leader of the tribe of Levi, had no of-

performed for our forefathers in those days at this season through Your holy priests. During all eight days of Chanukah these lights are sacred, and we are not permitted to make ordinary use of them, but only to look at them in order to express thanks and praise to Your great Name for Your miracles, Your wonders and Your salvations.

fering. He was chagrined, feeling sure that his exclusion was a sign of Divine displeasure, but God consoled him by telling him that his role would be greater than that of the princes, because he would light the flames of the *Menorah*. [This alluded to the 'eternal flame of Torah' that would have been extinguished forever had it not been for the brave struggle of the Hasmonean family of *Kohanim*, who defeated Syria's attempt to replace the Torah with Greek culture] (see *Ramban*, Numbers 8:2; Overview and History).

הַנֵּרוֹת הַלָּלוּ קֹדֶשׁ הֵם וְאֵין לָנוּ רְשׁוּת לְהִשְׁתַּמֵּשׁ בָּהֶם — *These lights are sacred, and we are not permitted to make ordinary use of them.* This phrase is the crux of this entire prayer; it is to emphasize this aspect of the Chanukah lights that the Sages mandate reciting *HaNeiros Hallalu* (R' S. Y. Zevin, *HaMoadim BeHalachah*).

As explained in the section of Laws [p. 118], it is forbidden to use the Chanukah lights for any personal purpose — such as reading or doing work by their illumination 'lest one slight the *mitzvos*' (Shabbos 21b). The prohibition against enjoying the lights makes it manifestly clear to all that they were kindled for the sole purpose of commemorating the miracle.

The *Rishonim* are in disagreement as to whether it is permissible to make use of the illumination for the sake of a *mitzvah* — for example, eating a Shabbos meal or studying Torah. Some say that even such use is a slight to the *mitzvah*, because it gives the impression that since the Chanukah *mitzvah* is not dear to the person, he uses it in the service of

another *mitzvah* (*Ramban* in Milchamos; *Ran; et al*). Others permit the use of the Chanukah lights for such purposes, on the grounds that assisting in the performance of another *mitzvah* is no dishonor to the lights (*Baal HaMaor, et al*; and see *Taz*, 673:4). [See also R' S. Y. Zevin, *The Festivals in Halachah*, Vol. II, p. 80ff.]

In compliance with the prohibition against enjoying the lights, we light a 'shamash' [lit. *servant*] flame, which is not holy, so that any incidental pleasure that comes from the lights can be considered as coming from the *shamash*.

אֶלָּא לִרְאוֹתָם בִּלְבָד — *But only to look at them.* The only activity we are permitted is to gaze upon the lights and thereby contemplate upon the miracles they commemorate.

כְּדֵי לְהוֹדוֹת וּלְהַלֵּל לְשִׁמְךָ הַגָּדוֹל — *In order to express thanks and praise to Your great Name.* That is, by refraining from utilizing the Chanukah lights for anything but the *mitzvah* itself and contemplating them while they burn we make it apparent to all that our intent is to popularize the miracle and to praise God's great Name in acknowledgment of His great miracles.

R' *Hirsch* explains that we give thanks to God's 'Name' by recognizing and acknowledging the miracles wrought in our history by God, and publicizing them to all.

לְהוֹדוֹת וּלְהַלֵּל — *To express thanks and praise.* The Talmud (Shabbos 21b) concludes its narration of the Chanukah miracle with: 'They [i.e., the Sanhedrin] established these [eight days] as יָמִים טוֹבִים בְּהַלֵּל וְהוֹדָאָה, *holidays in praise and thanksgiving.*' Rashi (ad loc) ex-

After the proper number of lights have been kindled Ashkenazim recite
מָעוֹז צוּר, while Sephardim recite Psalm 30 [p. 148].

א   **מָעוֹז צוּר** יְשׁוּעָתִי   לְךָ נָאֶה לְשַׁבֵּחַ,

תִּכּוֹן בֵּית תְּפִלָּתִי   וְשָׁם תּוֹדָה נְזַבֵּחַ,

לְעֵת תָּכִין מַטְבֵּחַ   מִצָּר הַמְנַבֵּחַ,

אָז אֶגְמוֹר בְּשִׁיר מִזְמוֹר   חֲנֻכַּת הַמִּזְבֵּחַ.

plains that the term יָמִים טוֹבִים, *holidays*, does not refer to days on which labor is forbidden — the usual sense of this phrase. Rather it means days set aside for הַלֵּל, the recitation of the *Hallel* prayers [*Psalms* 113-118], וְהוֹדָאָה, and the recitation of *Al HaNissim* during the *thanksgiving* blessings of *Shemoneh Esrei* [מוֹדִים] and *Bircas HaMazon* [נוֹדֶה].

Sfas Emes explains the difference between the *praise* [הַלֵּל] and the *thanksgiving* [הוֹדָאָה] recited on Chanukah: The praise emphasizes the magnitude of the miracle; while the thanksgiving constitutes each individual's recognition of his own shortcomings and that a miracle came, not because of his worthiness, but as a result of God's mercy upon Israel.

◄§ מָעוֹז צוּר/Ma'oz Tzur

Following the kindling of the lights and recital of *HaNeiros Hallalu* it is customary to recite the following *zemer*. In the Sephardic rite, Psalm 30 [see p. 148] is recited before *Ma'oz Tzur*.

The *zemer* consists of six stanzas. The author's name, Mordechai [מרדכי], appears in the acrostic signature in the initial letters of the first five stanzas. The date of its composition seems to have been in the mid-thirteenth century. Whether the last stanza formed part of the original composition or was added later is the subject of some disagreement. (See prefatory comment to stanza VI.)

In the *zemer* the *Payyatan* [liturgical poet] is inspired by the glow of the Chanukah lights to recall various exiles that the Jewish people endured, to praise God for redeeming us from each of them [*Shem MiShmuel* notes that each of the earlier periods of servitude — Egyptian, Babylonian, Persian, Greek — served to prepare the nation for the tribulations it would encounter in the subsequent exiles], and to pray for a restoration of the Temple and for the dawn of the Messianic Redemption.

The commentary is drawn primarily from *Avodas Yisrael*, as well as *N'siv Binah*, *R' S. R. Hirsch*, and *World of Prayer*. The author has offered his own comments to fill in gaps left by the commentators.

◄§ I. Plea for the Reestablishment of the Temple Worship.

מָעוֹז צוּר יְשׁוּעָתִי — *O mighty stronghold of my salvation*. The phrase literally reads: *Fortress, Rock of my salvation*, or *Mighty Rock of my salvation*. The term מָעוֹז צוּר refers to God, and is borrowed from *Psalm* 31:3: הֱיֵה לִי לְצוּר מָעוֹז ... לְהוֹשִׁיעֵנִי, *become for me a Mighty Rock ... to save me.*

God is frequently referred to in Scripture as the *Rock*. The term has the connotation of strength and dependability, and also alludes to Him figuratively as

the Source from which we were hewn, so to speak, and the Cause of everything. We must accordingly strive to emulate His Attributes and follow in His ways. (See *Ibn Ezra* and *R' Hirsch* to *Deut.* 32:4; see also *Rambam, Moreh Nevuchim* 1:16.)

The Talmud [*Berachos* 10a] homiletically interprets צוּר in another sense: וְאֵין צוּר כֵּאלֹהֵינוּ, literally *and there is no Rock like our God*, [I *Samuel* 2:2] is understood homiletically to mean אֵין צַיָּר כֵּאלֹהֵינוּ, there is *no Molder like our God*, meaning that only God can

After the proper number of lights have been kindled Ashkenazim recite מָעוֹז צוּר, while Sephardim recite Psalm 30 [p. 148].

I.
O mighty stronghold of my salvation,
    to praise You is a delight.
Restore my House of Prayer
    and there we will bring a thanksgiving offering.
When You will have prepared the slaughter
    for the blaspheming foe,
Then I shall complete with a song of hymn
    the dedication of the Altar.

fashion all materials and circumstances to correspond to His will. Accordingly, our stich can be understood to mean that God has fashioned even the most disadvantageous circumstances to become Israel's salvation.

לְךָ נָאֶה לְשַׁבֵּחַ — *To praise You is a delight.* In this first stanza, the *Payyatan* acknowledges God as the stronghold of his salvation to Whom it is befitting to offer praise. He is the Protector of Israel throughout our history and no matter how imminent Israel's destruction has often seemed, God always prevented the 'inevitable' from happening (*Avnei Eliyahu* to לְכוּ נְרַנְּנָה).

תִּכּוֹן בֵּית תְּפִלָּתִי — *Restore my House of Prayer,* i.e., rebuild the Temple in Jerusalem and bring on the Messianic era. The reference to the Holy Temple as *House of Prayer* derives from *Isaiah 56:7: For My House shall be called a House of Prayer for all people.*

וְשָׁם תּוֹדָה נְזַבֵּחַ — *And there we will bring a thanksgiving offering.* In the rebuilt Temple we will acknowledge Your beneficence and deliverances by offering the תּוֹדָה, *thanksgiving offering,* as mandated in the Torah [see *Leviticus 7:11ff*].

Most Temple offerings brought by individuals [קָרְבְּנוֹת יָחִיד] are required as atonement. Even burnt offerings, which can be brought voluntarily, *should* be brought to atone for the failure to perform positive commandments. In the world of perfection that will exist in

Messianic times, the urge to sin will no longer exist, so the need for atonement offerings will disappear. But the תּוֹדָה, *thanksgiving offering,* will be required even in Messianic times, because God's miracles and goodness will always be acknowledged. Therefore we look forward to the time when we can offer our thanksgiving offerings in the rebuilt Temple (*Vayikra Rabbah 9:7* according to *Tiferes Zion*).

לְעֵת תָּכִין מַטְבֵּחַ — *When You will have prepared the slaughter.* Compare Isaiah's prophecy concerning evildoers [14:21]: הָכִינוּ לְבָנָיו מַטְבֵּחַ, *prepare slaughter for his children.* Here, too, the *Payyatan* draws from the Biblical idiom and poetically makes reference to the Messianic era when God will wreak final vengeance on Israel's foes.

מִצָּר הַמְנַבֵּחַ — *For [lit. from; i.e. delivering us from] the blaspheming foe.* That is, the foe who blasphemes against God. The expression מְנַבֵּחַ is borrowed from *Isaiah 56:10* where it occurs in its literal sense of *barking.* Here it connotes the blasphemous 'barks' of Israel's enemies (*Avodas Yisrael*).

אָז אֶגְמוֹר בְּשִׁיר מִזְמוֹר חֲנֻכַּת הַמִּזְבֵּחַ — *Then I shall complete with a song of hymn the dedication of the Altar.* — In the rebuilt Temple. Compare *Psalms 30:1:* מִזְמוֹר שִׁיר חֲנֻכַּת הַבַּיִת (see p. 149).

The dedication of the Tabernacle Altar in Moses' days was accompanied by much pomp and by sacrifices offered by the respective Princes [נְשִׂיאִים] of the

בְּנִיגוּן כֹּחִי כִלָּה,　　רָעוֹת שָׂבְעָה נַפְשִׁי　ב

בְּשִׁעְבּוּד מַלְכוּת עֶגְלָה,　　חַיַּי מֵרְרוּ בְקֹשִׁי

הוֹצִיא אֶת הַסְּגֻלָּה,　　וּבְיָדוֹ הַגְּדוֹלָה

יָרְדוּ כְּאֶבֶן בִּמְצוּלָה.　　חֵיל פַּרְעֹה וְכָל זַרְעוֹ

Tribes, as recorded in *Numbers 7:10ff.* Solomon's Temple, too, was dedicated with a seven-day period of special offerings and celebration (*II Chronicles 7:9*). Alternatively the verb אֲגמוֹר, *I shall complete*, refers to the מִזְמוֹר, *hymn*, i.e., *I will sing to its completion the hymn of the Altar dedication.* A similar usage of the root גמר is found in the blessings לִגְמוֹר אֶת הַהַלֵּל, *to recite completely the Hallel.*

The Mishnah (*Shevuos 2:2*) states: They may add to the [boundaries of the] city [Jerusalem] or the Temple Court only with (the consent of) a king and with שִׁיר, *song*. The *Gemara* (*ibid.* 15b) clarifies that this *song* includes the recitation of מִזְמוֹר שִׁיר חֲנֻכַּת הַבַּיִת, *The Song of Dedication* (*Psalms 30*). [*Rambam, Hil. Beis HaBechirah 6:12* mentions *only* this song; see *Kessef Mishneh* there.] We pray that God restore our House of Prayer — the Holy Temple — then we will sing the entire hymn of dedication, psalm 30.

The dedication [Hebrew: *Chanukah*] of the Altar is symbolically related to the Chanukah holiday, for the construction of the Tabernacle in the Wilderness was completed on the twenty-fifth day of Kislev, which should have been the day of its dedication [see p. 98]. Additionally, Chanukah celebrates the resumption of the service in the Temple in addition to the miracle of lights. While the Temple was under Syrian-Greek occupation, they desecrated the altar with pagan offerings. Upon liberating the Temple, the Hasmoneans dismantled the altar and constructed a new, pure one in its place — whereupon they celebrated its inauguration with festive ceremonies and offerings. [See *The Festivals in Halachah*, vol. II, pp. 62, regarding the halachic status of the defiled altar.]

•§ II. The Egyptian Bondage

In the second stanza the *Payyatan* praises God for the liberation from Egyptian bondange.

The deliverance of the Jews at the time of Chanukah stimulates the *Payyatan* to mention another Exile. The glow of the Chanukah lights kindles a fiery feeling of hope as we recall Israel's deliverance from Egypt (*R' Menachem Weldler*).

רָעוֹת שָׂבְעָה נַפְשִׁי — *My soul had been sated with troubles.* The *Payyatan* speaks in first person, as the spokesman for the Israelite nation, which endured the suffering in Egypt.

The phraseology of this stich recalls *Psalms 88:4:* כִּי שָׂבְעָה בְרָעוֹת נַפְשִׁי, *my soul has been sated with troubles* — i.e., it is hardly capable of absorbing additional suffering (*Radak*).

בְּנִיגוּן כֹּחִי כִלָּה — *My strength has been consumed with grief.* Not only had the soul — i.e. Israel's spiritual essence — suffered, but under the rigors of the Egyptian oppression every Jew faced *physical* annihilation as well.

חַיַּי מֵרְרוּ בְקֹשִׁי — *They had embittered my life with hardship.* That is, with hard labor. See *Exodus 1:14: And they* [the Egyptians] *embittered their lives with hard labor ... all their bondage at which they made them slave was rigorous.*

בְּשִׁעְבּוּד מַלְכוּת עֶגְלָה — *With the calf-like kingdom's bondage.* — A poetic reference to Egypt who is so called in *Jeremiah 46:20:* עֶגְלָה יְפֵה־פִיָּה מִצְרַיִם, *Egypt* [by virtue of her natural beauty (*Radak*)] *is like a very fair calf.*

II.

My soul had been sated with troubles,
my strength has been consumed with grief.
They had embittered my life with hardship,
with the calf-like kingdom's bondage.
But with His great power
He brought forth the treasured ones,
Pharaoh's army and all his offspring
went down like a stone into the deep.

וּבְיָדוֹ הַגְּדוֹלָה — *But with His great power* [lit. *arm*]. The allusion is to the exercise and display of God's power in Egypt. See *Exodus* 9:31: *And Israel saw the 'great hand' which HASHEM wrought on the Egyptians.*

[Of course, God is incorporeal and such physical terms as 'arm' cannot be applied to Him in the literal sense. Since God's abstract Attributes cannot be perceived by human intellect, we figuratively apply to Him human physical characteristics to help us express otherwise abstract concepts. For example, in human terms, the 'arm' signifies power and the 'eye' signifies vigilance, so Scripture speaks metaphorically of God's 'arm' or 'eye'. This principle is referred to often in the Talmud as: 'The Torah speaks in the language of man.' Such ascription of human physical terms to God is called anthropomorphism, and is often employed in Scripture and in religious poetry.]

In the verse cited above from *Exodus*, *Rashi* explains *great hand* as: 'The great power which the *hand of God* exercised.' *Ibn Ezra* interprets it as alluding to the severe punishment which God wrought upon the Egyptians. *Ramban* cites the Kabbalistic teaching that the phrase refers to God's display of retributive justice, which became revealed to the Egyptians.

The word should technically be vowelized גְּדוֹלָה, but in order to preserve its rhyme with סְגֻלָּה in the next stich, many printed versions took the poetic liberty of vowelizing the word גְּדֹלָה. Many siddurim, however, do vowelize it גְּדוֹלָה. It is difficult to establish what the original vowelization was.

הוֹצִיא אֶת הַסְּגֻלָּה — *He brought forth the treasured ones*, i.e., the Israelites, of whom God said [*Exod.* 19:5]: *You shall be My treasured possession among all the peoples.*

That is, the Israelites are like a valuable object which a king keeps for himself, not handing over its custody to anyone else *(Ramban)*. Thus, as *Maharal* explains, Israel's destiny as a nation is not dependent on the general natural, physical, social or economic laws that govern the destinies of the other nations; Israel as a nation is placed directly under God's protection. 't was this nation that God brought forth from Egypt, in order that they 'obey faithfully and keep His covenant' [*Exodus, ad loc*].

חֵיל פַּרְעֹה וְכָל זַרְעוֹ — *Pharaoh's army and all his offspring.* See *Exodus* 14:6: *And he* [Pharaoh] *prepared his chariots, and his people he took with him.*

The expression וְכָל זַרְעוֹ, *all his offspring*, poetically implies all his subjects as well as his children. Indeed, the Midrash records that all the Egyptian fighting men — except for Pharaoh himself — drowned in the Sea.

יָרְדוּ כְּאֶבֶן בִּמְצוּלָה — *Went down like a stone into the deep.* Compare the Song at the Sea [*Exodus* 15:4-5]: *Pharaoh's chariots and his army He cast into the sea, and the pick of his officers drowned in the Sea of Reeds. The depths covered them, they went down into the deep like a stone.*

In some versions the preposition בּ, *into*, is omitted to preserve the meter. The interpretation, however, remains the same.

דְּבִיר קָדְשׁוֹ הֱבִיאַנִי   וְגַם שָׁם לֹא שָׁקַטְתִּי,
וּבָא נוֹגֵשׂ וְהִגְלַנִי   כִּי זָרִים עָבַדְתִּי,
וְיֵין רַעַל מָסַכְתִּי   כִּמְעַט שֶׁעָבַרְתִּי,
קֵץ בָּבֶל, זְרֻבָּבֶל,   לְקֵץ שִׁבְעִים נוֹשָׁעְתִּי.

◆§ III. The Babylonian Exile

Fire is endowed with the wonderful property that it may kindle another flame without lessening its own brilliance. Similarly the miracle of Chanukah is not diminished by the recall of other redemptions. In the third stanza the *Payyatan* recalls the Babylonian exile and redemption, which followed the destruction of the First Temple *(R' Menachem Weldler).*

דְּבִיר קָדְשׁוֹ הֱבִיאַנִי — *To the holy abode of His Word* [i.e. the Holy of Holies] *He brought me.* That is, God established the Israelites securely in *Eretz Yisrael,* and during the reign of King Solomon 'brought them into the Holy Sanctuary of the Temple' — the national symbol of peace and tranquility.

The Holy of Holies is referred to as דְּבִיר [*d'vir,* 'word'] in I *Kings* 6:5. *Metzudos* there explains that it is so called because it was from the Holy of Holies abode of the Tablets of the Covenant, that the word [*d'var*] of God emanated. In the broader context of this stanza, *N'siv Binah* suggests that the term *holy d'vir* in this stich might refer to the Holy Land in its entirety. It, too, is termed *d'vir* since it is in *Eretz Yisrael* exclusively that God's prophetic Word may be heard.

וְגַם שָׁם לֹא שָׁקַטְתִּי — *But there, too, I had no rest.* That is, even in the tranquility of *Eretz Yisrael* during Temple times I forfeited my 'rest' and a new Exile befell me.

וּבָא נוֹגֵשׂ וְהִגְלַנִי — *And an oppressor came and exiled me.* — This 'oppressor' was the wicked Babylonian king, Nebuchadnezzar, who entered *Eretz Yisrael,* besieged Jerusalem, and captured the city. He destroyed the Holy Temple and

carried off a large part of Judah into captivity to Babylon. He also blinded King Zedekiah, exiling him and other Judean nobles to Babylon as well. It was in his grief over this disaster, that resulted in the loss of national independence for the ensuing seventy years, that the contemporary Prophet Jeremiah composed the elegy *Eichah* [*Lamentations*].

The description of Nebuchadnezzar as נוֹגֵשׂ, *oppressor,* derives from *Isaiah* 14:4: *And you shall take up this proverb against the king of Babylon and say, How has the oppressor* [נוֹגֵשׂ] *ceased!*

כִּי זָרִים עָבַדְתִּי — *For I had served aliens.* That is, *alien gods.* It was in the sin of idolatry that the Jews and their kings were most steeped at the time, and it was the cause of this exile from their homeland. When Israel descended from its spiritual grandeur to the depths of iniquity — ignoring the calls and exhortations of its Prophets to repent — the Divine Presence ascended from the Temple which had become no more than a shell, beautiful but empty, and returned to the heavens where It had been before Israel fashioned earth into a habitation for God. The Temple was destroyed, Jerusalem lay in ruins, and the populace exiled.

[See *Causes of Destruction,* Overview to ArtScroll *Eichah*/Lamentations pp. xxxix ff.]

The Rabbinic *mussar* leaders often emphasize that it is difficult for us to comprehend how the Israelites who lived during the time of the Temple, when God's Presence dwelt on earth, could have had such base inclinations toward idol worship.

The *Chazon Ish* [letters 108-9] similarly explains that since the time of the Second Temple when God removed these idolatrous inclinations from us, we can no longer perceive the gratification this idol worship

III.   *To the holy abode of His Word He brought me.*
But there, too, I had no rest
And an oppressor came and exiled me.
For I had served aliens,
And had drunk benumbing wine.
Scarcely had I departed
At Babylon's end Zerubabel came.
At the end of seventy years I was saved.

offered our ancestors. Accordingly, we cannot presume to judge the moral standards of our forebears who were lured and often succumbed to this inexplicable temptation which, by God's grace, is nonexistent today. Since our ancestors were so much greater than we, God subjected them to trials which we today would fail entirely to withstand.

וְיֵין רַעַל מָסַכְתִּי — *And [had] drunk* [lit. *prepared for myself*] *benumbing wine.* The stich is attached to the previous one and continues the acknowledgment of Israel's sins that led to the Destruction of the Temple and ensuing Exile: *For I had served aliens* and I indulged myself with the heady wine of pagan error and delusion.

The phrase recalls *Psalm* 60:5: הִשְׁקִיתָנוּ יַיִן תַּרְעֵלָה, *You made us drink benumbing wine.* According to *Avodas Yisrael* the stich introduces what follows and is a figurative allusion to the suffering: we 'drank' the wine of sin, and as a result, our senses became numb [see *Rashi* in *Psalms* ibid.].

כִּמְעַט שֶׁעָבַרְתִּי — *Scarcely had I departed.* The phraseology is based on *Song of Songs* 3:4. In our *zemer* it refers to the exile. Israel says: 'I had scarcely departed my homeland when, in seventy years — a short period in terms of Jewish history — Babylon's reign ended by God's grace and I was saved by Zerubabel.'

Others perceive the syntax differently and interpret this stich not as introduction to the Redemption but as climaxing the suffering mentioned in the previous stich '... And had drunk the benumbing wine [of punishment] — כִּמְעַט שֶׁעָבַרְתִּי, *I had almost perished.*'

Either Israel declared that it nearly perished *physically* from the ordeal of the exile, or it nearly perished *spiritually*, as if to say, 'I had so indulged myself in sin while in Babylon that I nearly lost my spiritual identity through assimilation. Then, just in time, the exile ended and Zerubabel saved me.'

קֵץ בָּבֶל זְרֻבָּבֶל — *At Babylon's end Zerubabel came.* The Hebrew is staccato and literally reads: *Babylon's end, Zerubabel.* The implication is: Babylon's destined period of supremacy came to an end, and Zerubabel emerged to lead the Jews back to *Eretz Yisrael.*

⧓ Zerubabel

Zerubabel, son [or grandson (see *I Chron.* 3:19)] of She'altiel, scion of the House of David, was one of the prominent leaders of the Jews during the last years of the Babylonian exile, and the organizer of the ensuing repatriation and building of the Second Temple. Together with his contemporaries — Yeshua, son of Yehozadak the High Priest, Seraya, Nechemiah, Mordechai, and other leaders — Zerubabel led the original caravan of repatriates to *Eretz Yisrael* to rebuild the Temple [*Ezra* 3:2]. We find in *Haggai* 1:1 that he was governor of Judah.

In the prophecy foretelling the rebuilding of the Temple, Zerubabel is mentioned explicitly. These verses [*Zechariah* 4:6-10] form the climax of the *haftarah* of *Shabbos* Chanukah. In these passages the prophet foretells how Zerubabel would finish work on the Temple and topple mountains: *Not by*

אֲגָגִי בֶּן הַמְּדָתָא,	כְּרוֹת קוֹמַת בְּרוֹשׁ בִּקֵּשׁ
וְגַאֲוָתוֹ נִשְׁבָּתָה,	וְנִהְיְתָה לוֹ [לְפַח וּ]לְמוֹקֵשׁ
וְאוֹיֵב שְׁמוֹ מָחִיתָ,	רֹאשׁ יְמִינִי נִשֵּׂאתָ
עַל הָעֵץ תָּלִיתָ.	רֹב בָּנָיו וְקִנְיָנָיו

אֲזַי בִּימֵי חַשְׁמַנִּים,   יְוָנִים נִקְבְּצוּ עָלַי   ה

might nor by power, but by My Spirit, says HASHEM of Legions.

In the Talmud [*Sanhedrin* 38a] Zerubabel is identified with Nechemiah, the word Zerubabel not being his proper name, but an appellation denoting that he was born in Babylon [זֶרַע־בָּבֶל=זְרוּבָּבֶל, *of Babylonian descent*]. He later served as one of the members of the אַנְשֵׁי כְּנֶסֶת הַגְּדוֹלָה, *Men of the Great Assembly* — the synod of 120 great elders who led Israel at the start of the Second Temple era.

לְקֵץ שִׁבְעִים נוֹשַׁעְתִּי — *At the end of seventy years I was saved.* In fulfillment of Jeremiah's prophecy [25:12]: *... And it shall come to pass, when seventy years are fulfilled, I will punish the king of Babylon ...* [see also *II Chronicles* 2:36].

On the dating of these seventy years, see "The Mysterious Seventy Years" in the Overview to ArtScroll *Esther* pp. xxiii *ff.*

◆§ IV. The Purim Miracle/Deliverance from Haman's plot.

In the fourth stanza the *Payyatan* is stimulated to a remembrance of *Megillas Esther* which vividly preserves Haman's fiendish plans and Israel's miraculous rescue from his threat of extermination *(R' Menachem Weidler).*

כְּרוֹת קוֹמַת בְּרוֹשׁ — *To sever the towering cypress* [i.e., Mordechai]. This is a reference to Haman's mortal hatred of Mordechai, as related in *Esther* 3:2 ff. Mordechai had refused to bow down before Haman, the newly-elevated, self-proclaimed god. Haman's vanity caused him to react to this 'affront' in a manner typical of most rabid anti-Semites throughout the ages. He wanted to punish not only Mordechai as an *individual*, but to destroy all the Jews — the people of Mordechai — for Haman knew that Mordechai's refusal to bow was caused by his religious beliefs. Accordingly, he hated not Mordechai the 'upstart,' but Mordechai the *Jew*.

The metaphor of *cypress*, [בְּרוֹשׁ] as alluding to *Mordechai* is derived from the Talmud, *Megillah*, 10b, where the Sages expound an obscure prophecy in *Isaiah* 55:13: *Instead of the 'thorn' shall come up the 'cypress'* — the Sages interpret the 'thorn' as Haman and the 'cypress' as Mordechai. Haman, the prickly, useless thorn, tried to elevate himself over Mordechai, the stately cypress. But Divine justice prevailed and Haman was hung on the same gallows he had prepared for Mordechai.

בִּקֵּשׁ אֲגָגִי בֶּן הַמְּדָתָא — *Sought the Aggagite, son of Hammedatha* — that is, Haman, son of Hammedatha the Aggagite [=a descendant of Agag, King of Amalek (*I Samuel* 15:9)] (*Esther* 3:1).

[For purposes of the Hebrew meter and rhyme, the word בְּקֵשׁ, *sought,* is grouped with the previous stich. However, in terms of meaning, it belongs with this stich, which is where we have translated it for the sake of clarity.]

וְנִהְיְתָה לוֹ [לְפַח וּ]לְמוֹקֵשׁ — *But it became [a snare and] a stumbling block to him.* — That is, Haman's own sinister plans recoiled on his own head, as related in *Esther* ch. 7, especially 7:9-10: *'Furthermore, the fifty-cubit-high gallows which Haman made for Mordechai — who spoke good for the King — is standing in Haman's house! And the*

IV.

To sever the towering cypress
  sought the Aggagite, son of Hammedatha,
But it became [a snare and] a stumbling block to him
  and his arrogance was stilled.
The head of the Benjaminite You lifted
  and the enemy, his name You obliterated
His numerous progeny — his possessions —
  on the gallows You hanged.

V.

Greeks gathered against me
  then in Hasmonean days.

King said, 'Hang him on it!' So they hanged Haman on the gallows which he had prepared for Mordechai ...

In many versions the bracketed words are omitted.

וְגַאֲוָתוֹ נִשְׁבָּתָה — *And his arrogance was stilled.* As Scripture states: *And Haman trembled in terror before the King and Queen ... And Haman remained to beg Queen Esther for his life; for he saw that the King's evil determination against him was final* (Esther 7:6-7).

רֹאשׁ יְמִינִי נָשָׂאתָ — *The head of the Benjaminite You [O God] lifted.* That is, You promoted from lowly status (see *Radak* and *Ibn Ezra* to *Genesis* 40:13) *the head* of Mordechai who is called אִישׁ יְמִינִי, *Benjaminite*, in *Esther* 2:5.

וְאוֹיֵב שְׁמוֹ מָחִיתָ — *And the enemy's name You obliterated.* Haman was a descendant of the wicked Amalek, and utterly blotting out the memory of Amalek is mandated as a *mitzvah* in the Torah. Compare *Deuteronomy* 25:17 ff: *Remember what Amalek did to you by the way when you went forth from Egypt ... You shall blot out the remembrance of Amalek from under Heaven; you shall not forget.*

רֹב בָּנָיו וְקִנְיָנָיו עַל הָעֵץ תָּלִיתָ — *His numerous progeny — his possessions — on the gallows You hanged.* — See *Esther* 9:7-10

According to the *Talmud* [*Megillah* 16b] Haman's sons were hanged one under the other on a single long pole.

The expression רֹב בָּנָיו — meaning *his numerous progeny* [not: 'most of his progeny'] — occurs in *Esther* 5:11.

The Hebrew literally reads, 'His numerous progeny *and* his possessions, the connotation being that Haman's possessions, too, were hanged on gallows, an expression that obviously, can be taken literally only with great difficulty.

The translation follows *Avodas Yisrael* which explains *his possessions* as synonymous with '*his progeny* who comprised all of his possessions and of whom he boasted greatly.'

In his commentary to Siddur, *R' Hirsch* remarks that 'his possessions' could hardly be the object of 'on the gallows you hanged' — for why would the Jews hang Haman's possessions on a gallows? He suggests that *his numerous progeny and his possessions* is the object of מָחִיתָ, *You blotted out*, in the previous stich. Accordingly he renders the stiches: *The head of the Benjaminite You did raise, but You blotted out the name of the foe, his sons and the abundance of his wealth. And him [Haman] You hanged upon the gallows.*

◄§ V. The Hasmonean Victory/The Miracle of Chanukah

Apparently, this stanza forms the climax of the *zemer* as it was composed originally. [See prefatory comment to stanza VI.]

In it, the *Payyatan* recounts the Divinely orchestrated rescue from the

וּפָרְצוּ חוֹמוֹת מִגְדָּלַי   וְטִמְּאוּ כָּל הַשְּׁמָנִים,
וּמִנּוֹתַר קַנְקַנִּים   נַעֲשָׂה נֵס לַשּׁוֹשַׁנִּים,
בְּנֵי בִינָה יְמֵי שְׁמוֹנָה   קָבְעוּ שִׁיר וּרְנָנִים.

terror of Antiochus, the miracle of the oil, and the reason for the celebration of Chanukah (R' Menachem Weldler).

יְוָנִים נִקְבְּצוּ עָלַי — Greeks gathered against me. Yavanim — Greeks — is here a general description for Antiochus IV Epiphanes, the Seleucid monarch of Syria who was the central foe in the Chanukah story. He advocated an intense campaign of Hellenization [i.e., spreading of Greek culture and ideas] and the Jews of Eretz Yisrael who remained loyal to the Torah, became his main targets. (See "History," p. 44). The broader sense of Yavanim here would be: Hellenizers.

The ancestor of these peoples, Yavan, is listed in the genealogy of Genesis 10:2 as one of the sons of Japheth son of Noah. His descendants are identified with the Ionians, a tribe of the Hellenic race who settled on the mainland of Greece, the islands of the Aegean Sea, and the coast of Asia Minor. According to Targum Yonasan, Yavan is Macedonia. In Talmudic times, the term Yavan connoted the Greek peoples as a whole.

אֲזַי בִּימֵי חַשְׁמַנִּים — Then [אֲזַי being a poetic form of אָז] in Hasmonean days. The term Chashmanim instead of the familiar Chashmonaim is borrowed from Psalms 68:32 (see Radak and Ibn Ezra there). The Payyatan employs it for purposes of the rhyme (Avodas Yisrael).

On the derivation of the term Chashmonaim describing the family of Mattisyahu, see p. 102.

וּפָרְצוּ חוֹמוֹת מִגְדָּלַי — They breached the walls of my towers. The Syrians breached the walls of the Temple Mount, as recorded in Mishnah Middos 2:3: '... There were thirteen breaches in the wall, that had originally been made by the Kings of Greece [i.e., Syria] ... [see "History," p. 47].

וְטִמְּאוּ כָּל הַשְּׁמָנִים — And they defiled all the oils. — That is, all the oils prepared for use in the daily lighting of the Menorah in the Temple. [Cf. Megillas Taanis cited in Shabbos 21b.]

וּמִנּוֹתַר קַנְקַנִּים — And from the one remnant of the flasks. When the Hasmoneans triumphed over Antiochus' armies and succeeded in regaining the Temple, they found only one flask of undefiled oil, stamped with the seal of the High Priest (Shabbos, ibid.).

נַעֲשָׂה נֵס לַשּׁוֹשַׁנִּים — A miracle was wrought for the roses. [That is, for the Jews.] There was only enough oil in this one remaining flask to light the Temple Menorah for one day. A miracle occurred and they were able to light this oil for eight days (Shabbos ibid.). [See: "The Miracle," p. 91.]

The use of 'roses' as an appellation for the Jewish people derives from Song of Songs 2:2: As a rose among thorns, so is My beloved among the daughters. That passage is an allegorical dialogue between God and His beloved nation, Israel, the connotation being that God says of Israel: Like the rose maintaining its beauty among the thorns, so is my faithful beloved among the nations. As Rashi there explains: 'Just as the rose retains it beauty, so does My beloved people, Israel, maintain her faith despite the torments of her neighbors [i.e., the thorns] who try to sway her after their strange gods.' [See ArtScroll ed. Shir HaShirim.]

בְּנֵי בִינָה — Men of insight. — The Sages and Torah leaders of that generation.

יְמֵי שְׁמוֹנָה קָבְעוּ שִׁיר וּרְנָנִים — Eight days established for song and jubilation. Blessed with the insight to recognize the impact of the miracle for future generations, the Sages established it as an eight-day holiday.

They breached the walls of my towers
and they defiled all the oils;
And from the one remnant of the flasks
a miracle was wrought for the roses.
Men of insight — eight days
established for song and jubilation

As the Talmudic citation from *Shabbos* 21b concludes: '... The following year, these days were fixed and established as a festival of praise and thanksgiving' [marked by the kindling of lights and daily recital of *Hallel*].

[On the popular question of why *eight days* were instituted when there was enough oil for one day and the ensuing miracle was needed only for *seven* days, see p. 94.]

◄§ Plea for the Final Redemption

This following stanza is generally regarded to be a later addition [about 1500] by a different author. The first three words form the acrostic חזק, *be strong*. This stanza is omitted from some *siddurim*, e.g., *Avodas Yisrael, R' Hirsch Siddur*, and all Sephardic *siddurim*, but occurs in many early *siddurim*.

According to R' Munk [*World of Prayer*], several later authors among them R' Moshe Isserles [Rama], R' Yirmiyah of Wuerzburg, R' Shmuel, author of *Nachalas Shiv'ah*, — composed different versions of the sixth stanza. We have included a sampling below.[1]

1. These are alternate versions of the sixth stanza:
Rabbi Moshe Isserles *(Rama):* the first three lines spell the acronym מֹשֶׁה, *Moshe*.

מעולם היית ישעי, כבודי ומרים ראשי./ שמע נא קול שועי, מלכי אלהי קדשי./ ה עביר חטאתי ופשעי, גם בגלות השלישי./ חזק ישראל, הכניע ישמעאל, ומארם תפדה נפשי.

You have always been my salvation, my honor, and raiser of my pride./ Harken, please to the sound of my plea, my King, my God, my Holy One./ You forgave my sin and my iniquity, even during the third [i.e., Greek] exile./ Strengthen Israel, humble Ishmael, and from Aram redeem my soul.

Rabbi Yirmiyah of Wuerzburg: the name יִרְמְיָה, *Yirmiyah*, is contained in the initials of the first five words.

יהי רצון מלפניך, יחיד הוד והדר./ גאל שארית צאנך, מארם ישמעאל וקדר./ רחום בקודש נאדר, רווח תשים לעדר./ נחלתך הודיע, אל נקמות הופיע, בעמלק מדור דור.

May it be Your desire, Unique One, Who is Glorious and Beautiful,/ Save the remnants of Your flock, From Aram, Ishmael and Kedar [a descendant of Ishmael]./ Compassionate One, glorified in holiness, establish relief for the flock./ Inform Your heritage, that the God of retribution shall appear, against Amalek, from generation to generation.

Rabbi Shmuel, author of "Nachalas Shiv'ah": the acronym here spells שְׁמוּאֵל הַלֵּוִי חָזָק, *Shmuel HaLevi Chazak*.

שמך יברך לעולם, מתוך קהל אמונים./ וכסאך יהי שלם, אם תנקום בזדונים./ ל נפשות נענים, הסכת ממעונים./ להושיע עמך, ולהציל שרידך, ידידך כאז בימי חשמנים.

חי זקוף קרן ישועה, וקרב קץ הגאולה./ ומלכות זדון הרשעה, יהי מעיר מפלה./ בנפול בני עולה, ולעמך תעשה הצלה./ בצדקת אתנים, גאל בנים, ותבנה העיר על תלה.

Your Name is blessed eternally, among the congregation of the faithful,/ Your throne will become complete, if You take vengeance upon the wanton./ For the sake of the oppressed souls, listen from the Heavens,/ To save Your people, to rescue Your remnant, Your beloved one — as in the days of the hasmoneans.

O Living One, stand erect the horn of salvation, and hasten the day of salvation./ And the wanton, wicked empire — may its capital become debris,/ when the iniquitous people fall. To Your people, bring rescue./ For the sake of the Patriarchs' righteousness, Redeem the descendants, and rebuild the city (i.e., Jerusalem) on its hilltop.

וְקָרֵב קֵץ הַיְשׁוּעָה,   חֲשׂוֹף זְרוֹעַ קָדְשֶׁךָ

מֵאֻמָּה הָרְשָׁעָה,   נְקוֹם נִקְמַת דַּם עֲבָדֶיךָ

כִּי אָרְכָה לָנוּ הַיְשׁוּעָה   וְאֵין קֵץ לִימֵי הָרָעָה,

דְּחֵה אַדְמוֹן בְּצֵל צַלְמוֹן   הָקֵם לָנוּ רוֹעִים שִׁבְעָה.

Containing, as it does, a strong plea for Divine vengeance against Israel's foes and for our ultimate redemption, this stanza was subject to much censorship by Christian authorities. Accordingly some *siddurim* have replaced certain stiches with others less offensive to the censors, as will be noted in the commentary. The version presented here is from *Siddur Otzer HaTefillos.*

חֲשׂוֹף זְרוֹעַ קָדְשֶׁךָ — *Bare Your holy arm.* That is, display your Divine power. [See commentary to וּבְיָדוֹ הַגְּדוֹלָה in Stanza II.]

The expression is borrowed from *Isaiah* 52:10: *HASHEM has bared His holy arm in the sight of all the nations, and all the extremes of the earth shall see the salvation of our God.*

וְקָרֵב קֵץ הַיְשׁוּעָה — *And hasten the End for salvation.* The word קֵץ, *End*, refers to the deadline beyond which God will not permit the exile to extend. This 'End' of our tribulation and Exile is prophesied in the Book of Daniel. We conclude our thanks for God's past salvations with a prayer that he hasten the 'End' and bring the Messianic age when we will have relief from all subjugation, and be free to serve Him unhindered.

[For a philosophical presentation of the concept of 'End', see Overview to ArtScroll *Daniel*, p. xlvii: "The Scripture and the 'End'."]

Some versions read וְקָרֵב יוֹם הַיְשׁוּעָה, *and hasten the day of salvation.*

נְקוֹם נִקְמַת דַּם עֲבָדֶיךָ מֵאֻמָּה הָרְשָׁעָה — *Avenge the vengeance of Your servants' blood from the wicked nation.*

Compare *Deut.* 32:43: *For He will avenge the blood of His servants, and wreak vengeance on His foes ...* Also *Psalms* 79:10: *Why should the nations say, 'Where is their God?' — let the revenging of the spilled blood of Your servants become apparent among the nations and before our eyes!*

Some versions read מִמַּלְכוּת הָרְשָׁעָה, *from the wicked kingdom,* i.e., from the wicked authorities who subjugate their Jewish citizens.

In many siddurim this stich has been the victim of the censor's pen. It has occasionally been softened by substituting the following stich: עֲשֵׂה נָא לְמַעַן שְׁמֶךָ לִהְיוֹת לָנוּ תְּשׁוּעָה, *Act for the sake of Your Name to provide us with a triumph,* that is, since our suffering can be interpreted as a disgrace to the God we serve, we ask Him to deliver us for His sake, even if we are undeserving.

כִּי אָרְכָה לָנוּ הַיְשׁוּעָה — *For the triumph is too long delayed for us.* Many versions read כִּי אָרְכָה הַשָּׁעָה, *for the hour has grown long,* i.e., the 'hour' of our tribulations has been extended greatly.

וְאֵין קֵץ לִימֵי הָרָעָה — *And there is no end to days of evil,* i.e., the suffering seems unending and is of unspecified duration. Compare the description of hopelessness and despair which would accompany periods of suffering in *Deut.* 28:66-67: *And you shall be afraid day and night, without faith in your survival. In the morning you shall say, 'If only it were evening!' and in the evening you shall say, 'If only it were morning!' — because of things your*

VI.
Bare Your holy arm
and hasten the End for salvation —
Avenge the vengeance of Your servants' blood
from the wicked nation.
For the triumph is too long delayed for us,
and there is no end to days of evil,
Repel the Red One in the nethermost shadow
and establish for us the seven shepherds.

heart shall dread and your eyes shall see.

דְּחֵה אַדְמוֹן בְּצֵל צַלְמוֹן — *Repel the Red One in the nethermost shadow.* The exact allusion of 'Red One' is the subject of some doubt. The most common interpretation is that it refers to Esau who in *Genesis* 25:25 is described as אַדְמוֹנִי, *of red complexion.* In Rabbinic literature, Esau-Edom is identified as the ancestor of Rome, which destroyed the Second Temple, and hence of the Roman Empire, i.e. Christian-Western Civilization, under whose influence the Jewish people lingers and is still 'exiled' today. It is from this 'Edomite' subjugation [גָּלוּת אֱדוֹם] — the last of the Four Exiles Israel was to endure before the final dawn of Messianic redemption (see footnote to ArtScroll *Genesis* p. 474; *Rambam* ibid. 15:12, and *comm.* ibid. p. 1225)] — that the *Payyatan* begs Almighty God to release us.

There is also an opinion that this stanza *was* part of the original work and *Admon* is to be understood as a reference to the contemporary German Emperor Frederic Barbarossa (1121-90) who was nicknamed 'Redbeard', and who was perceived as symbolic of general gentile oppression.

The term צַלְמָוֶת, *nethermost shadows,* occurs often in Scripture. For purposes of rhyme, however, the *Payyatan* chose the less common form צַלְמוֹן drawn from *Psalms* 68:15.

An alternative stich — obviously inserted to placate Christian censors who objected to the specific reference to Edom-Rome — is preserved in some *siddurim.* It reads: מְחֵה פֶּשַׁע וְגַם רֶשַׁע, *blot out willful sin as well as wickedness.*

This version is an appeal that God remove from us the primary impediments to the onset of the Messianic era — intentional sin and wickedness.

Note that this stich is not a prayer that God blot out *sinners,* but sinfulness. 'When sins will cease, sinners will be no more' (see *Berachos* 10a).

הָקֵם לָנוּ רוֹעִים שִׁבְעָה — *And establish for us the seven shepherds.* The 'seven shepherds' are those who, as prophesied in *Micah* 5:4, *will graze the land of Assyria with the sword, and the land of Nimrod with the keen blade.*

The Sages [*Succah* 52b] elaborate on this and identify the 'seven shepherds': David will be in the center [representing the Messianic monarchy]. Adam, Seth, and Methuselah will flank him on his right [representing mankind as a whole], and Abraham, Jacob, and Moses to his left [representing the 'Shepherds' of Israel; see *Maharsha* and *Ein Yaakov*]. These will lead the battle to bring on the promised redemption and renew our days as of old.

Some versions read רוֹעֶה שִׁבְעָה, *shepherd of the seven,* but the reference is obscure.

Customs vary regarding the recitation of further psalms and prayers.
The order presented here follows that of Siddur Bais Yaakov.
(Many recite ויהי נעם and ישב בְּסֵתֶר seven times.)

יז **וִיהִי נֹעַם** אֲדֹנָי אֱלֹהֵינוּ עָלֵינוּ, וּמַעֲשֵׂה יָדֵינוּ כּוֹנְנָה
עָלֵינוּ, וּמַעֲשֵׂה יָדֵינוּ כּוֹנְנֵהוּ.

א־ב **ישֵׁב** בְּסֵתֶר עֶלְיוֹן, בְּצֵל שַׁדַּי יִתְלוֹנָן. אֹמַר לַיהוה
ג מַחְסִי וּמְצוּדָתִי, אֱלֹהַי אֶבְטַח בּוֹ. כִּי הוּא יַצִּילְךָ
ד מִפַּח יָקוּשׁ, מִדֶּבֶר הַוּוֹת. בְּאֶבְרָתוֹ יָסֶךְ לָךְ, וְתַחַת כְּנָפָיו
ה תֶּחְסֶה, צִנָּה וְסֹחֵרָה אֲמִתּוֹ. לֹא תִירָא מִפַּחַד לָיְלָה,
ו מֵחֵץ יָעוּף יוֹמָם. מִדֶּבֶר בָּאֹפֶל יַהֲלֹךְ, מִקֶּטֶב יָשׁוּד

ᴈ∗ ויהי נעם/Psalm 90:17

The Midrash teaches that when the Tabernacle was completed, Moses prayed that it might endure and be blessed by God. His brief prayer *(Psalms 90:17)*, ... ויהי נעם, *May the pleasantness ...,* has been borrowed to preface the performance of other *mitzvos* as well, for it expresses the wish that our service of God be pleasing to Him and that its effects be permanent.

Moses composed Psalm 91, ישב בְּסֵתֶר, on the day he completed construction of the Tabernacle, and its opening verse describes Moses himself, who entered the Divine clouds and was enveloped in the shadows of the Almighty.

Since the psalm refers to the completion of the Tabernacle, it is appropriate for Chanukah, as well. A further reason for its recitation on Chanukah may be verse 7, which describes how God helps his devout ones to prevail over overwhelming armies, just as the small Hasmonean force defeated the huge Syrian armies of Antiochus.

[The commentary to the Psalms that follow have been adapted and abridged from the ArtScroll Tehillim by Rabbi Avrohom Chaim Feuer.]

17. ויהי נעם ה׳ אֱלֹהֵינוּ — *May the pleasantness of my Lord, our God.* The term נעם, *pleasantness,* refers to the bliss someone feels when he has done something that achieved its purpose. When man has this feeling of accomplishment, he is not alone — God, too, feels satisfaction that His will has been done *(Malbim).*

וּמַעֲשֵׂה יָדֵינוּ כּוֹנְנָה עָלֵינוּ — *May He establish our handiwork for us.* This is a plea that we be independent of any man or government. Let us be free to serve God as we wish *(R' Hirsch).*

In any material activity, a craftsman *shapes* his creation, but remains dependent on it, in a sense. Architects and builders can erect a structure, but it rests on the earth, not on them, and *they* must depend on *it* for shelter. In the spiritual world, the opposite is true. One's Torah study develops in his own mind and his performance of a *mitzvah* has as much spiritual content as he puts into it. We pray now that our deeds be worthy of God's pleasure and that he 'establish' them as being significant on the basis of our own spiritual handiwork *(Malbim).*

ᴈ∗ ישב בְּסֵתֶר/Psalm 91

1. ישֵׁב בְּסֵתֶר עֶלְיוֹן — *Whoever sits in the refuge* [lit. *hidden* or *secret place*] *of the Most High.* The person who scorns conventional forms of protection and seeks only the refuge provided by the Most High will find his faith rewarded. He will be enveloped by God's providence so that he can continue to seek holiness and wisdom without fear

◈ Additional Psalms and Prayers

Customs vary regarding the recitation of further psalms and prayers.
The order presented here follows that of Siddur Bais Yaakov.
(Many recite וִיהִי נֹעַם and יֹשֵׁב בְּסֵתֶר seven times.)

Psalm 90 17 May the pleasantness of my Lord, our God, be upon us — may He establish our handiwork for us; our handiwork may He establish.

Psalm 91 Whoever sits in the refuge of the Most High — he shall dwell in the shadow of the Almighty. ² I will say of HASHEM: He is my refuge and my fortress, my God — I will trust in Him. ³ That He will deliver you from the ensnaring trap and from devastating pestilence. ⁴ With His pinion He will cover you, and beneath His wings you will be protected; His truth will be a shield and armor. ⁵ You shall not fear the terror of night, nor the arrow that flies by day; ⁶ Nor the pestilence that walks in gloom,

---

of those who would seek to do him harm: *He shall dwell in the shadow of the Almighty (Rashi).*

[As explained in the *Prefatory Remarks*, this psalm was composed on the day Moses completed the construction of the Tabernacle. The final verse of the preceding psalm (90:17) was also composed then, when the work was done. Moses blessed Israel, and they responded by echoing his earlier wish: '*May the pleasantness of my Lord, our God, be upon us — may He establish our handiwork for us; our handiwork may He establish.*' The Tabernacle is not considered to be truly 'established' until the *Most High* dwells there and makes it His own *refuge*.]

Tehillos Hashem notes that the customary superscription giving the author's name is omitted from this psalm and that Moses' authorship is left unstated. This is due to his unsurpassed humility; he submerged his entire being in God and gave himself no credit. Since Moses 'secreted' himself in the *Most High*, this psalm does not mention his name.

בְּצֵל שַׁדַּי יִתְלוֹנָן — *He shall dwell in the shadow of the Almighty.* The architect and builder of the Tabernacle was בְּצַלְאֵל, *Bezalel,* whose name is com-

posed of the words בְּצֵל אֵל, *in the shadow of God.* Bezalel anticipated aspects of the Divine blueprint even before Moses gave him the necessary information. So amazed was Moses that he asked Bezalel, 'Perhaps you reside *in the shadow* of God?' *(Berachos 55a; see Tanchuma, Vayakhel 3.)*

2. אֹמַר לַה' מַחְסִי וּמְצוּדָתִי — *I will say of HASHEM: He is my refuge and my fortress.* The devout man *who dwells in the secret place of the Most High* declares publicly that God is his *refuge* from all physical dangers, and his *fortress,* protecting him from all human enemies *(Radak; Sforno).*

5. לֹא תִירָא מִפַּחַד לָיְלָה — *You shall not fear the terror of night.* If you put your faith in God, fear will be banished from your heart *(Rashi).* The person who walks alone in the dark is usually terrified of the unknown forces he imagines to be lurking in the shadows [but he who walks with God never walks alone] *(Radak).*

מֵחֵץ יָעוּף יוֹמָם — *[Nor] the arrow that flies by day.* Man is most vulnerable to the sudden tragedies and misfortunes that 'fly at him' without warning like swift *arrows (Radak).*

Targum identifies חֵץ as the *arrow*

ז צָהֳרָיִם. יִפֹּל מִצִּדְּךָ אֶלֶף, וּרְבָבָה מִימִינֶךָ, אֵלֶיךָ לֹא יִגָּשׁ.

ח-ט רַק בְּעֵינֶיךָ תַבִּיט, וְשִׁלֻּמַת רְשָׁעִים תִּרְאֶה. כִּי אַתָּה יהוה

י מַחְסִי, עֶלְיוֹן שַׂמְתָּ מְעוֹנֶךָ. לֹא תְאֻנֶּה אֵלֶיךָ רָעָה, וְנֶגַע

יא לֹא יִקְרַב בְּאָהֳלֶךָ. כִּי מַלְאָכָיו יְצַוֶּה לָּךְ, לִשְׁמָרְךָ בְּכָל

יב-יג דְּרָכֶיךָ. עַל כַּפַּיִם יִשָּׂאוּנְךָ, פֶּן תִּגֹּף בָּאֶבֶן רַגְלֶךָ. עַל שַׁחַל

יד וָפֶתֶן תִּדְרֹךְ, תִּרְמֹס כְּפִיר וְתַנִּין. כִּי בִי חָשַׁק וַאֲפַלְּטֵהוּ,

טו אֲשַׂגְּבֵהוּ כִּי יָדַע שְׁמִי. יִקְרָאֵנִי וְאֶעֱנֵהוּ, עִמּוֹ אָנֹכִי בְצָרָה,

טז אֲחַלְּצֵהוּ וַאֲכַבְּדֵהוּ. אֹרֶךְ יָמִים אַשְׂבִּיעֵהוּ וְאַרְאֵהוּ

בִּישׁוּעָתִי. אֹרֶךְ יָמִים אַשְׂבִּיעֵהוּ, וְאַרְאֵהוּ בִּישׁוּעָתִי.

---

unleashed by the Angel of Death; since he fears no one, he cuts a man down even in broad daylight.

7. יִפֹּל מִצִּדְּךָ אֶלֶף וּרְבָבָה מִימִינֶךָ — *A thousand will fall at your side and a myriad at your right hand.* According to Rashi, this means that thousands and myriads of demons will fall before the man who is shielded by God's truth. Radak perceives this as a description of the enemies of Israel who fall before them in battle.

Radak interprets this verse: Despite the fact that the pestilence ... and destroyer will lay waste (*v.* 6) to thousands who fall at your right side and tens of thousands who fall at your left side, *it* [i.e., the pestilence] *shall not come near you.*

8. רַק בְּעֵינֶיךָ תַבִּיט — *You will merely peer with your eyes.* You will behold the destruction of the wicked who spurned God and refused to *sit in the refuge of the Most High* (Radak), but they will be helpless to harm you (Metzudos).

Alshich cites Talmudic instances that the Rabbis could punish someone by training their holy eyes on him, and the sinner would disintegrate into a heap of bones. Thus, *Only with your eyes you will behold the wicked,* for that will suffice to decimate them.

וְשִׁלֻּמַת רְשָׁעִים תִּרְאֶה — *And you will see the retribution of the wicked.* Only a person who is delivered from danger because of his own merit is accorded the privilege of witnessing the downfall of his enemies. If he was saved only because of the merits of others [like Lot, who was saved from Sodom because of Abraham], the man is forbidden to witness the suffering that he, too, deserved to share (Olelos Yehudah).

9. כִּי אַתָּה ה' מַחְסִי — *Because 'You, HASHEM, are my refuge.'* These are the Psalmist's words to the man of faith. The statement is recorded here in abbreviated form, as if it read: 'Because you said, "HASHEM is my refuge", you thereby made the Most High the *dwelling place* [i.e., the repository] of your faith' (Rashi; Ibn Ezra; Radak).

10. וְנֶגַע לֹא יִקְרַב בְּאָהֳלֶךָ — *Nor will any plague come near your tent.* The Talmud (Sanhedrin 103a) perceives this as a blessing for domestic bliss [for *tent* signifies 'household']. 'May you raise worthy children and students, who will not shame you by acting improperly in public.'

11. לִשְׁמָרְךָ בְּכָל דְּרָכֶיךָ — *To protect you in all your ways.* The Talmud (Chagigah 16a) teaches that these angels are not merely guardians, but witnesses as well. They observe every action and they are destined to testify for or against the man under their protection when he comes before the heavenly tribunal after death.

12. עַל כַּפַּיִם יִשָּׂאוּנְךָ — *They will carry you on palms.* The angels created by the mitzvos that you perform with your

nor the destroyer who lays waste at noon. ⁷ *A thousand will fall at your side and a myriad at your right hand, but to you it shall not approach.* ⁸ *You will merely peer with your eyes and you will see the retribution of the wicked.* ⁹*Because 'You, HASHEM, are my refuge,' You have made the Most High Your dwelling place.* ¹⁰ *No evil will befall you, nor will any plague come near your tent.* ¹¹ *He will charge His angels for you, to protect you in all your ways.* ¹² *They will carry you on palms, lest you strike your foot against a stone.* ¹³ *You will tread upon the lion and the viper, you will trample the young lion and the serpent.* ¹⁴ *For he has yearned for Me and I will deliver him; I will elevate him because he knows My Name.* ¹⁵ *He will call upon Me and I will answer him, I am with him in distress, I will release him and I will honor him.* ¹⁶ *I will satisfy him with long life and show him My salvation.*

palms [i.e., giving charity and doing acts of kindness] will raise you above all dangers that lurk in your path (Zera Yaakov).

13. תִּרְמֹס כְּפִיר וְתַנִּין — *You will trample the young lion and the serpent.* These two dangerous creatures hate each other. When they see each other they are aroused to murderous fury. Furthermore, if someone tramples upon them they are infuriated and poised to kill.

Despite the double danger of trampling on both of them at the same time, God will be at your side and you will pass through these perils unscathed (Akeidas Yitzchak).

14. כִּי בִי חָשַׁק וַאֲפַלְּטֵהוּ — *For he has yearned for Me and I will deliver him.* Earlier the Psalmist promised that HASHEM *will charge His angels for your sake* (v. 11). This verse records how God actually fulfilled His promise, telling His angels why He shows special favor to the man of faith (Ibn Ezra; Sforno).

15. יִקְרָאֵנִי וְאֶעֱנֵהוּ — *He will call upon Me and I will answer him.* Yerushalmi (Berachos 9:1) explains that if a man in distress seeks the help of a human being, he will not storm into his potential protector's home abruptly. Rather he will go to the protector's gates and re-

quest an audience from the gatekeeper. There is no guarantee that the audience will be granted. However, no such procedure need be followed by those who seek protection from God. The Holy One, Blessed is He, declares, 'If misfortune should befall you, do not cry out to the ministering angel Gabriel or to the ministering angel Michael! Cry out to Me, and I will answer you immediately!'

עִמּוֹ אָנֹכִי בְצָרָה — *I am with him in distress.* This may be likened to a mother who was angry at her pregnant daughter. The mother went upstairs, leaving her daughter below. When the daughter went into labor and began to scream in pain, the mother, too, began to cry out.

The neighbors were amazed by the mother's anguish and asked, 'Are you giving birth with her?'

The mother replied, 'Although my daughter angered me, I cannot bear to hear her scream, because her pain is my pain!'

So, too, when God was angered by Israel, He abandoned them and ascended to heaven. When He destroyed the Temple, however, He heard Israel's anguished cries. Then He cried with them, telling His ministering angels, 'My children are suffering and I am suf-

לַמְנַצֵחַ בִּנְגִינֹת מִזְמוֹר שִׁיר. אֱלֹהִים יְחָנֵּנוּ וִיבָרְכֵנוּ,

יָאֵר פָּנָיו אִתָּנוּ סֶלָה. לָדַעַת בָּאָרֶץ דַּרְכֶּךָ,

בְּכָל גּוֹיִם יְשׁוּעָתֶךָ. יוֹדוּךָ עַמִּים אֱלֹהִים, יוֹדוּךָ עַמִּים

כֻּלָּם. יִשְׂמְחוּ וִירַנְּנוּ לְאֻמִּים, כִּי תִשְׁפֹּט עַמִּים מִישֹׁר,

וּלְאֻמִּים בָּאָרֶץ תַּנְחֵם סֶלָה. יוֹדוּךָ עַמִּים אֱלֹהִים, יוֹדוּךָ

עַמִּים כֻּלָּם. אֶרֶץ נָתְנָה יְבוּלָהּ, יְבָרְכֵנוּ אֱלֹהִים אֱלֹהֵינוּ.

יְבָרְכֵנוּ אֱלֹהִים, וְיִירְאוּ אוֹתוֹ כָּל אַפְסֵי אָרֶץ.

fering with them' (Midrash Shocher Tov).

16. אֹרֶךְ יָמִים אַשְׂבִּיעֵהוּ — I will satisfy him with long life [lit. length of days]. I will fill out the days of the man of faith. His life will not be cut short in this world (Ibn Ezra; Radak).

[Moreover, some men live long lives that are full of frustration and disappointment, but this man will live a satisfying, meaningful life.]

וְאַרְאֵהוּ בִּישׁוּעָתִי — And show him My salvation. He will witness the salvation I will bring about at the advent of the

Messiah, at the time of the revival of the dead, and at the salvation of the World to Come (Radak).

Indeed, it is not God who needs salvation, but Israel; yet God calls Israel's victory 'My salvation' to emphasize that Israel's salvation is His as well (Midrash Shocher Tov). It is God's desire to display His Presence in this world, but if there were no Israel, no community of faith, then there would be no place for God to reveal His glory and no one to appreciate Him. Therefore, God, Himself, is the beneficiary of Israel's salvation (Tehillos Hashem).

◆§ לַמְנַצֵחַ/Psalm 67

This psalm — after the introductory verse — has a total of forty-nine words, corresponding to the days of counting. According to tradition, its text was revealed to both Moses and David in a vision of a seven-branched Menorah on a golden tablet, with the words of the psalm etched on its branches and stem (see illustration on next page). The seven verses allude to the seven branches of the Menorah which stood in the Holy Temple. This Menorah is the source of intellectual illumination for Israel. Consequently, the psalm is appropriate for Chanukah, the festival of the Temple Menorah.

1. לַמְנַצֵחַ בִּנְגִינֹת מִזְמוֹר שִׁיר — For the Conductor, upon Neginos, a song with musical accompaniment. The Conductor was the Levite in charge of the Temple orchestra that accompanied the Temple service; Neginos was a type of musical instrument (Radak).

The four musical references of this introductory verse correspond to the four realms (mineral, vegetable, animal, and human) of the world. All four were in a state of imperfection until the Torah was given at Sinai (Alshich).

2. אֱלֹהִים יְחָנֵּנוּ וִיבָרְכֵנוּ — May God favor us and bless us. Favor us although we are undeserving; bless us with fer-

tility, for the persecutions of exile have decreased our population (Sforno).

יָאֵר פָּנָיו אִתָּנוּ סֶלָה — May He display His luminous countenance with us, selah. May He illuminate our minds so that we may perceive the wondrous lessons of Torah (Sforno).

3. לָדַעַת בָּאָרֶץ דַּרְכֶּךָ — To make known Your way on earth. We ask for intellectual enlightenment so that we can spread Your teachings throughout the world. We yearn to guide mankind to appreciate Your way of kindness and mercy (Rashi; Sforno).

Mankind is baffled by the seemingly

Psalm 67 For the Conductor, upon Neginos, a song with musical accompaniment. ² May God favor us and bless us, may He display His luminous countenance with us, selah. ³ To make known Your way on earth, among all the people Your salvation. ⁴ The nations will acknowledge You, O God, the nations will acknowledge You, all of them. ⁵ Nations will be glad and sing for joy, because You will judge the nations fairly and guide the nations on earth, selah. ⁶ The nations will acknowledge You, O God, the nations will acknowledge You, — all of them. ⁷ The earth has yielded its produce, may God, our own God, bless us. ⁸ May God bless us and may all the ends of the earth fear Him.

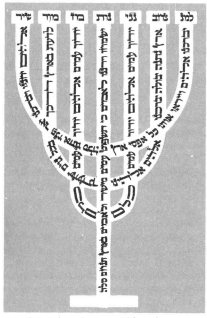

A traditional rendering of the psalm as it was revealed in the form of a menorah to Moses and David.

chaotic development of human affairs. If You shine Your countenance upon Israel, You will demonstrate that You guide world events towards a clear-cut goal. Then mankind will recognize Your way in all affairs *on earth (R' Hirsch).*

R' Hirsch notes that God's *way* includes two concepts, both the manner in which God guides world events and the pattern of conduct which He demands of man. By shining His countenance upon the Jewish nation, God will make

known both facets of His *way.* Mankind will recognize that human history is guided toward the fulfillment of God's goals, and His blessings upon Israel will lead mankind to follow God's Law as exemplified by Israel.

בְּכָל גּוֹיִם יְשׁוּעָתֶךָ — *Among all the people Your salvation.* God is concerned with the welfare and salvation of all peoples. One purpose of Israel's dispersion is to expose many nations to the Torah's teaching so that they too can learn and accept the truth *(Shaarei Chaim).*

4. יוֹדוּךָ עַמִּים כֻּלָּם — *The nations will acknowledge You, all of them.* Ultimately, God's message will penetrate every corner of the world and all nations will worship Him *(R' Hirsch).*

5. יִשְׂמְחוּ וִירַנְּנוּ לְאֻמִּים — *Nations will be glad and sing for joy.* Both עַם and לְאֹם mean *nation:* לְאֹם refers to the *state* that governs a people and represents its particular striving. So long as nations are selfish and acquisitive, their nationalistic posture will reflect selfishness; but ultimately, all national governments will discard selfish isolation and recognize that the welfare of all men depends on a harmonious community of nations joyously united in the worship of God. עַם is a *national community* that keeps itself separate from all other nations. International animosity is inevitable so long as each nation seeks only its own welfare *(R' Hirsch).*

6. יוֹדוּךָ עַמִּים אֱלֹהִים — *[The] nations will acknowledge You, O God.* This

אַבַּ"ג יִתַּ"ץ

אָנָּא בְּכֹחַ, גְּדֻלַּת יְמִינְךָ, תַּתִּיר צְרוּרָה.

קְרַ"ע שַׂטַ"ן

קַבֵּל רִנַּת, עַמְּךָ שַׂגְּבֵנוּ, טַהֲרֵנוּ נוֹרָא.

נַגַּ"ד יְכַ"שׁ

נָא גִבּוֹר, דּוֹרְשֵׁי יִחוּדְךָ, כְּבָבַת שָׁמְרֵם.

בַּטַּ"ר צַתַּ"ג

בָּרְכֵם טַהֲרֵם, רַחֲמֵם צִדְקָתְךָ, תָּמִיד גָּמְלֵם.

חֲקַ"ב טְנַ"ע

חֲסִין קָדוֹשׁ, בְּרוֹב טוּבְךָ, נַהֵל עֲדָתֶךָ.

יְגַ"ל פְּזַ"ק

יָחִיד גֵּאֶה, לְעַמְּךָ פְנֵה, זוֹכְרֵי קְדֻשָּׁתֶךָ.

שַׁקַּ"ו צִַ"ת

שַׁוְעָתֵנוּ קַבֵּל, וּשְׁמַע צַעֲקָתֵנוּ, יוֹדֵעַ תַּעֲלֻמוֹת.

בָּרוּךְ שֵׁם כְּבוֹד מַלְכוּתוֹ לְעוֹלָם וָעֶד.

א-ב **מִזְמוֹר שִׁיר** חֲנֻכַּת הַבַּיִת לְדָוִד. אֲרוֹמִמְךָ יהוה כִּי

ג דִלִּיתָנִי, וְלֹא שִׂמַּחְתָּ אֹיְבַי לִי. יהוה

---

verse has appeared before. Each time it introduces a new reason for thanksgiving. First it tells that the nations will give thanks for the fairness of God's judgment and the resultant harmony of the social order. The second time it tells that the nations will give thanks for the world's abundant produce and prosperity (*Rashbam; Sforno*).

According to R' Hirsch, the psalm is divided into three parts corresponding to the three phases in which mankind will fulfill its mission. First (*vs.* 1-2), only the Jewish people will come to recognize and to obey God's Will. Second (*vs.* 3-5), the leaders of all the nations will submit to God's authority and worship Him. Third and finally (*vs.* 6-8), *all* people will learn to worship God directly; at this point their leaders will give up their positions of privilege and power because the people will no longer need them.

אָנָּא בְּכֹחַ/Ana B'Choach

Tradition ascribes this mystical prayer to the tanna R' Nechuniah ben Hakanah. It contains forty-two words, the initials of which form the secret forty-two letter Name of God. Moreover, the six initials of each of its seven verses form Divine Names. The Kabbalists teach that it should be divided into phrases of two words each, but our translation follows the division indicated by a simple reading of the phrases. The commentary will not attempt to delve into the mystical connotations of the prayer.

The commentary to this prayer has been adapted and abridged from the ArtScroll *Siddur*, "Friday Evening Service", by Rabbi Nosson Scherman.

תַּתִּיר צְרוּרָה — *Untie the bundled sins.* The accumulated sins of Israel are bound together like a barrier that prevents our prayers from ascending to the Heavenly Throne. We ask God to remove this impediment (*Iyun Tefillah*).

דּוֹרְשֵׁי יִחוּדְךָ — *Those who foster Your Oneness.* The acknowledgment of God's *Oneness* is a paramount part of God's mission [see comm. to *Shema*, ArtScroll *Siddur*]. As the nation that accepts this obligation upon itself, Israel pleads for God's protection (*Iyun Tefil-*

lah). *Etz Yosef* comments that Israel pursues this goal through the study of Torah.

בָּרְכֵם — *Bless them.* With financial security to ease their way (*Etz Yosef*).

טַהֲרֵם — *Purify them.* By helping them avoid impure thoughts (*Etz Yosef*).

תָּמִיד גָּמְלֵם — *Always recompense them.* [Even in giving recompense, which, by definition, means dealing with someone according to his deeds, there is room for mercy. We ask God to be merciful even

The Ritual [148]

*W*e beg You! With the strength of Your right hand's greatness, untie the bundled sins. Accept the prayer of Your nation; strengthen us, purify us, O Awesome One. Please, O Strong One — those who foster Your Oneness, guard them like the apple of an eye. Bless them, purify them, show them pity, may Your righteousness always recompense them. Powerful Holy One, with Your abundant goodness guide Your congregation. One and only Exalted One, turn to Your nation, which proclaims Your holiness. Accept our entreaty and hear our cry, O Knower of mysteries.

Blessed be the Name of His glorious Kingdom forever and ever.

Psalm 30 A song with musical accompaniment for the inauguration of the Temple; by David. ² I will exalt You, HASHEM, for You have raised me up from the depths, and not let my foes rejoice

when weighing our deeds in the scales of justice.]

שׁוְעָתֵנוּ ... צַעֲקָתֵנוּ — *Our entreaty ... our cry.* An *Entreaty* [שַׁוְעָה] is a call for help that is directed to someone who is

capable, or thought to be capable, of helping. A cry [צְעָקָה], on the other hand, is a cry of pain directed to no one. We ask God to respond to our call for salvation, or, at least, to have compassion for our suffering (*Iyun Tefillah*).

מִזְמוֹר שִׁיר חֲנֻכַּת הַבַּיִת/Psalm 30 ≈§

King David composed this psalm to be sung when his son, Solomon, dedicated the Temple. The Sages prescribed that whenever new land was added to Jerusalem, this psalm be chanted throughout the city to musical accompaniment (*Shavuos* 15b). It is recited almost universally on Chanukah, both because of its origin as a celebration of the Temple's dedication and because tractate *Soferim* 18:2 designates it as the שִׁיר שֶׁל יוֹם, *Song of the Day*, of Chanukah.

An obvious difficulty is how the psalm, which seems to deal only with David's illness, recovery, and exultant gratitude to God, is related to the dedication of the Temple. *Radak* explains that the eventual inauguration of the Temple by Solomon represented David's vindication against the taunts and charges of his enemies. If David was truly a doomed sinner, as they claimed, his offspring could not have gained the privilege of realizing David's dream of building the Temple.

R' Hirsch explains that the most basic purpose of the Temple is to show God's closeness to Israel. This purpose is best achieved when each individual Jew recognizes God's presence and help in his personal life. Accordingly David's representation of himself as hopelessly ill and beset by foes — but never losing his faith in God, and finally being vindicated by God's deliverance — is the perfect embodiment of the Temple's role in the life of the nation.

[In the *Sefardic* rite this psalm is recited immediately after הַנֵּרוֹת הַלָּלוּ, pp. 126-8.]

1. מִזְמוֹר שִׁיר — *A song with musical accompaniment.* Each of these words, when used alone, can be translated simply as 'song'. When they are used together, however, the word שִׁיר refers to the lyrics of the composition, be it poetry or prose, and the word מִזְמוֹר describes the accompaniment of כְּלֵי זֶמֶר, *musical instruments (Siddur Baal HaTanya).*

Midrash Shocher Tov comments: Two terms describing song are used here because the Temple was built and inaugurated twice — once in the days of Solomon and again in the days of Ezra. מִזְמוֹר refers to the First Temple, שִׁיר refers to the Second.

חֲנֻכַּת הַבַּיִת לְדָוִד — *For the inauguration of the Temple; by David.* [Since it was

ד אֱלֹהָי, שִׁוַּעְתִּי אֵלֶיךָ, וַתִּרְפָּאֵנִי. יהוה הֶעֱלִיתָ מִן שְׁאוֹל
ה נַפְשִׁי, חִיִּיתַנִי מִיָּרְדִי בוֹר. זַמְּרוּ לַיהוה חֲסִידָיו, וְהוֹדוּ
ו לְזֵכֶר קָדְשׁוֹ. כִּי רֶגַע בְּאַפּוֹ, חַיִּים בִּרְצוֹנוֹ, בָּעֶרֶב יָלִין בֶּכִי,
ז וְלַבֹּקֶר רִנָּה. וַאֲנִי אָמַרְתִּי בְשַׁלְוִי, בַּל אֶמּוֹט לְעוֹלָם.

Solomon, not David who built the Temple, why is the inauguration ascribed to David?]

Rashi explains: David composed this psalm to be sung later, in Solomon's days, at the inauguration.

Alshich cites the fact that Solomon's entire inauguration ceremony was halted by the refusal of the Temple gates to open for him until he appealed to them to open in honor of David (*Shabbos* 30a. See *Psalms* 24:7,9 and ArtScroll *comm.*). Thus, it was David who was responsible for the successful completion of the inauguration.

Ibn Ezra mentions an opinion that David composed his psalm not for the inauguration of the First Temple, but for a later Temple. [See *Maharsha, Shavuos* 15b.] *Tehillos Hashem* explains this according to the *Yalkut Shimoni* (*II Sam* 145): David asked God, 'Why can I not build the Holy Temple?'

God answered, 'Because if you build it, it will endure and never be destroyed.'

Said David, 'That is certainly all the better!'

God replied, 'It is clearly revealed to me that Israel is destined to sin, but instead of destroying them I will vent my rage on the beams and stones of the Temple, and Israel will be spared.'

Therefore, David could not participate in the first construction and inauguration, and his psalm of dedication was reserved for the eternal Temple of the future.

[Another problem arises here. The psalm discusses David's sickness and mourning but does not deal at all with the Temple or its inauguration.]

— According to the opinion cited in *Ibn Ezra* that this psalm refers to a future Temple, the 'sickness' describes the tragic, downtrodden state of Israel during the exiles preceding its construction.

— The Temple is the most profound demonstration that God is always near to man and that His Presence rests on earth. In David's personal life, this spiritual phenomenon was demonstrated by his constant faith in God even during the painful, draining illness he describes in this psalm, and God's ultimate salvation. Thus, this psalm depicts in microcosm what the Temple represents on the universal level (*R' Hirsch*).

2. דליתני — *For You have raised me up from the depths.* [This word is derived from דָּלָה, *to draw up* water from the deep well.]

David's reputation sank low when his enemies claimed he had no portion in the World to Come. But when Solomon dedicated the Temple and the gates did not open until David's name was invoked, his honor [cf. *Psalms* 24:7,9] was restored (*Rashi*).

In normal usage, the word הֶגְבַּהְתָּנִי would be more appropriate. David used the obscure form דְּלִיתָנִי, as an allusion to the דַּלְתֵי הַבַּיִת, *the doors of the Temple*, whose miraculous opening was the means by which his prestige was elevated (*Yosef Tehillos, Baal HaTanya*).

Ibn Ezra observes that if we wish to appreciate the threat which David's enemies posed against him in his sickness we should study psalm 41 [where the invalid is described as דַּל, *impoverished* (v. 2). Here David gives thanks כִּי דְלִיתָנִי, *for You have raised me up from that lowly state'...*]

3. שִׁוַּעְתִּי אֵלֶיךָ — *I cried out to You.* I

over me. ³ *HASHEM, my God, I cried out to You and You healed me.* ⁴ *HASHEM, You have raised up my soul from the lower world, You have preserved me lest I descend to the Pit.* ⁵ *Sing to HASHEM, His devoted ones, and give thanks to His holy Name.* ⁶ *For His anger endures but a moment; life results from His pleasure; in the evening one lies down weeping, but with dawn — a cry of joy!* ⁷ *I had said in my serenity, 'I would never falter'.*

sought a cure for my ills only from You and not from any physician, because I realized that the source of my misfortunes was spiritual, not physical (*Ibn Ezra; Malbim*).

וַתִּרְפָּאֵנִי — *And You healed me.* You accepted my repentance and forgave my sin, as it says, וְשָׁב וְרָפָא לוֹ, *he shall repent and be healed* [*Isaiah 6:10*] (*Rashi*).

[According to those who comment that David composed the psalm with reference to his own grave illness, this verse, as well as several others, can best be understood literally.]

4. ה' הֶעֱלִיתָ מִן שְׁאוֹל נַפְשִׁי — *HASHEM, You have raised up my soul from the lower world.* שְׁאוֹל, *lower world,* describes Gehinnom, as does the word בּוֹר, *pit* (*Radak*).

Harav Yerucham Levovitz asks: David was still alive when he uttered these words — how could he speak as if he had already descended to Gehinnom which is a place of punishment for sinners after death? From this we learn that one can suffer in purgatory even while alive! As the Talmud (*Nedarim* 22a) teaches, כָּל הַכּוֹעֵס כָּל מִינֵי גֵיהִנָּם שׁוֹלְטִין בּוֹ, *Whoever becomes angry is subjected to all types of Gehinnom.* The flames of frustration, anguish, and melancholy are the equivalent of the fires of Gehinnom. Throughout the Book of Psalms, most references to '*falling into the lower world*' refer to this type of inferno.

5. זַמְּרוּ לַה' חֲסִידָיו — *Sing to HASHEM, His devoted ones.* Upon witnessing my salvation, all men devoted to God

should rejoice over the power of repentance and the magnitude of His mercy which redeems the righteous repenter, despite the seriousness of his transgression (*Radak*).

6. כִּי רֶגַע בְּאַפּוֹ — *For His anger endures but a moment* [lit., *for a moment in His anger*]. The devoted ones should sing God's praises, for His anger, although thoroughly justified, lasts only a brief moment. For example, all of the י"ג מִדּוֹת הָרַחֲמִים, *The thirteen Attributes of God's Mercy,* depict God's kindness. Following them there is only one Attribute that is threatening: *He remembers the sins of the fathers to their children,* and even this goes no further than *the third and fourth generation.* However, God's kindness is לָאֲלָפִים, *for two thousand generations* (*Radak*). Thus God's anger literally lasted only a few brief moments!

חַיִּים בִּרְצוֹנוֹ — *Life results from His pleasure,* i.e. by pleasing God and gaining His good will, one assures long life (*Rashi*).

Even during that brief flash of anger, God intends the punishment to make the sinner worthy of eternal life (*Shaloh*). [Compare *Isaiah 5:7,8.*]

7. וַאֲנִי אָמַרְתִּי בְשַׁלְוִי בַּל אֶמּוֹט לְעוֹלָם — *I had said in my serenity 'I would never falter.'* But I was mistaken because continued serenity is not in my hands, only in the hands of God, Who can *support my greatness with might* or *conceal His face* (*v. 8*), i.e., withdraw His support from me, as He wishes (*Rashi*).

ח יהוה בִּרְצוֹנְךָ הֶעֱמַדְתָּה לְהַרְרִי עֹז, הִסְתַּרְתָּ פָנֶיךָ הָיִיתִי

ט-י נִבְהָל. אֵלֶיךָ יהוה אֶקְרָא, וְאֶל אֲדֹנָי אֶתְחַנָּן. מַה בֶּצַע

יא בְּדָמִי בְּרִדְתִּי אֶל שָׁחַת, הֲיוֹדְךָ עָפָר הֲיַגִּיד אֲמִתֶּךָ. שְׁמַע

יב יהוה וְחָנֵּנִי, יהוה הֱיֵה עֹזֵר לִי. הָפַכְתָּ מִסְפְּדִי לְמָחוֹל לִי,

יג פִּתַּחְתָּ שַׂקִּי, וַתְּאַזְּרֵנִי שִׂמְחָה. לְמַעַן יְזַמֶּרְךָ כָבוֹד וְלֹא

יִדֹּם, יהוה אֱלֹהַי לְעוֹלָם אוֹדֶךָּ.

א **שִׁיר הַמַּעֲלוֹת** לְדָוִד, הִנֵּה מַה טּוֹב וּמַה נָּעִים, שֶׁבֶת

ב אַחִים גַּם יָחַד. כַּשֶּׁמֶן הַטּוֹב עַל

---

8. הִסְתַּרְתָּ פָנֶיךָ הָיִיתִי נִבְהָל — *Should You but conceal Your face, I would be terrified.* There were moments when You concealed Your truth from my intellect, either because I boasted of my righteousness and You sought to test me (see 26:2), or in order to punish me for my sins. At those times my mind became confused and overcome with fright, and my better judgment was overwhelmed by my Evil Inclination (*Radak*).

11. שְׁמַע ה' וְחָנֵּנִי — *Hear, HASHEM, and favor me.* David appealed to HASHEM, the Divine Name which depicts the Divine Attribute of *Mercy*, and asked for an undeserved favor, and not strict judgment (*Alshich*).

12. הָפַכְתָּ מִסְפְּדִי לְמָחוֹל לִי — *You have changed for me my lament into dancing.* The translation of מָחוֹל as *dancing* follows *Targum* and *Metzudos.* [However from the commentary of *Radak* it would seem that מָחוֹל may be related to מְחִילָה, *forgiveness.*]

I was mourning over the spectre of my soul perishing because of my sins, but You gladdened me by sending the Prophet Nathan with good tidings: *HASHEM has also forgiven your sin,*

you shall not die (II Samuel 12:13). Accordingly, our verse would be rendered: *You have changed my lament to forgiveness (Radak).*

In times of tragedy, Scripture reverses the idiom of dancing as a representation of joy (*Lamentations* 5:15): שָׁבַת מְשׂוֹשׂ לִבֵּנוּ נֶהְפַּךְ לְאֵבֶל מְחֹלֵנוּ, *Gone is the joy of our hearts, our dancing has turned into mourning (Tehillos Hashem).*

13. כָּבוֹד — *Soul* [lit. *glory*]. The translation follows *Radak* and *Metzudos* who explain that the soul is called כָּבוֹד, *glory,* because it is the most glorious part of a human being. Thus: My soul will sing to You forever if You will not drag me down to the dust (a reference to *will the 'dust' acknowledge You, v. 10).*

כָּבוֹד is a description of the soul because it emanates from God's כִּסֵּא הַכָּבוֹד, *Throne of glory.*

Iyun Tefillah maintains that כָּבוֹד, *glory,* refers to the glory of God's Presence which will dwell forever in the Temple as a result of the inauguration, as it says, כִּי מָלֵא כְבוֹד ה' אֶת בֵּית ה', *For the glory of HASHEM filled the House of HASHEM (I Kings 8:11).*

◆§ שִׁיר הַמַּעֲלוֹת/Psalm 133

The penultimate verse of the previous psalm reads, *There I shall cause the glory of David to sprout, I prepared a lamp for my anointed* (132:17). In his role as monarch, David's greatest 'glory,' like that of any king, is to bring harmony and unity to his nation. King David sought to bind up the wounds of his strife-torn people, and his all-embracing personality knitted together the many-colored fabric of the diverse segments that make up a nation.

The Ritual [152]

⁸ But, HASHEM, it was Your good will alone that supported my greatness with might. Should You but conceal Your face, I would be terrified. ⁹ To You, HASHEM, I would call and to my Lord I would appeal. ¹⁰ What gain is there in my death, in my descent to the Pit? Will the dust acknowledge You? Will it tell of Your Truth? ¹¹ Hear, HASHEM, and favor me; HASHEM, be my helper! ¹² You have changed for me my lament into dancing; You undid my sackcloth and girded me with joy. ¹³ So that my soul might sing to You and not be stilled, HASHEM my God, forever will I thank You.

Psalm 133 A Song of Ascents, by David. Behold how good and how pleasant is the dwelling of brothers in unity. ² Like the precious oil upon the head running down upon the beard, the

---

David's dream of harmony within Israel was realized during the reign of his son Solomon, whose name שְׁלֹמֹה means שֶׁלּוֹ מִי שֶׁהַשָּׁלוֹם, *He to Whom peace belongs.* Solomon made peace with all of his royal brothers and transformed even the jealous ones from rivals into allies. This psalm extols the glory of such brotherly love *(Ibn Ezra).*

Moses and Aaron provide an example of fraternal love, *par excellence.* Though different in nature and action, Moses and Aaron complemented one another, and together they formed a perfectly balanced leadership for the Jewish nation. This psalm lauds their virtues and declares, *'Behold how good and how pleasant to dwell together in unity'.* Thus, this psalm alludes to the greatness of the Davidic dynasty, which will bring the final renewal of the Temple with the coming of Messiah; and it alludes to the holiness of Aaron the first *Kohen Gadol* and ancestor of the Hasmoneans who restored holiness to the Temple.

1. הִנֵּה מַה טּוֹב וּמַה נָּעִים — *Behold how good and how pleasant.* Certain things are טוֹב, *good*, but not נָּעִים, *pleasant*, such as a potent medicine that tastes bitter. On the other hand, many foods and experiences are *pleasant* to the taste or senses, but not *good* or healthy for the body. However, brotherhood and harmony are both *good* and *pleasant (Mizmor L'Todah).*

שֶׁבֶת אַחִים גַּם יָחַד — *The dwelling of brothers in unity.* We look forward longingly to the idyllic future, when all Jews will be united, like שֶׁבֶת אַחִים, the *dwelling of brothers.* [The words גַּם, literally *also,* may be taken to imply that someone in addition to the *brothers* will join them in their unity. Therefore Rashi interprets:] When God sees that Jews live in harmony, He joins them by placing His Presence in the Temple *(Rashi).*

[The Jewish nation functions on two levels: the political and the spiritual. Moses, who had the status of king, headed the judicial, legislative and executive affairs of the Jews, while Aaron, the High Priest, led them in their spiritual service. Instead of being rivals, Moses and Aaron acted together in respect and affection to fuse the two estates into one harmonious unit.]

Radak explains that both the King and the High Priest are anointed with oil, which symbolizes the smooth and pleasant. [As a lubricant, oil prevents friction.] In the future, Messiah will live in total harmony with the High Priest of his day. Such a relationship existed between Zerubabel, the temporal leader of Israel, and Joshua, the High Priest, who jointly led Israel in the beginning of the Second Temple era, as Zechariah prophesied, וַעֲצַת שָׁלוֹם תִּהְיֶה בֵּין שְׁנֵיהֶם, *And the counsel of peace shall be between them both (Zechariah 6:13).*

2. כַּשֶּׁמֶן הַטּוֹב עַל הָרֹאשׁ יֹרֵד עַל הַזָּקָן זְקַן אַהֲרֹן — *Like the precious oil upon the head running down upon the beard, the beard of Aaron. Rav Vidal HaTzorfati*

הָרֹאשׁ, יֹרֵד עַל הַזָּקָן זְקַן אַהֲרֹן, שֶׁיֹּרֵד עַל פִּי מִדּוֹתָיו.
ג כְּטַל חֶרְמוֹן שֶׁיֹּרֵד עַל הַרְרֵי צִיּוֹן, כִּי שָׁם צִוָּה יהוה אֶת
הַבְּרָכָה, חַיִּים עַד הָעוֹלָם.

א־ב רַנְּנוּ צַדִּיקִים בַּיהוה, לַיְשָׁרִים נָאוָה תְהִלָּה. הוֹדוּ
ג לַיהוה בְּכִנּוֹר, בְּנֵבֶל עָשׂוֹר זַמְּרוּ לוֹ. שִׁירוּ לוֹ שִׁיר

interprets this incident allegorically: Through Moses, God bestowed upon Aaron abundant blessings that would help him in his sacred mission of bringing Israel closer to God. Aaron was given the gifts of wisdom and charm in ample proportions. Oil symbolizes blessing and light. The oil that descended from Aaron's head onto his beard symbolized that God's blessing was not merely an intellectual gift confined to Aaron's mind, but that the 'oil' of blessing spread out and permeated his entire personality — to the very tips of the hairs of his beard, as it were.

Aaron had a warm smile and a friendly word for everyone. He showed concern for anything that mattered to his fellow man, even though the topic was less than lofty. He gave them his heart and they in turn surrendered their minds to him. Since they accepted his advice with regard to their material affairs, they accepted his guidance in affairs of the soul as well.

Yet Moses and Aaron were deeply troubled lest Aaron had used his God-given gifts — his 'oil' — improperly. Perhaps he should not talk about mundane matters? Perhaps he was degrading the exalted dignity of his office by mingling with the lowest levels of society? Therefore the drops of oil 'ascended', so to speak, to the roots of his beard. This demonstrated that Aaron had not misused his gifts. Quite the contrary, he had elevated his talents and brought them back to the 'roots' — the source of all blessing — God Himself.

Finally the Heavenly voice declared that Moses and Aaron were like one. Moses ascended Mount Sinai and dwelled like an angel among real angels

for forty days; Aaron descended to the company of very ordinary people. Yet both brothers were deemed equal — for both *dwelled*, i.e., lived out their lives in the service of God. [See *Aggadah* in *Horayos* 12a.]

זְקַן אַהֲרֹן — *The beard of Aaron. Radak* questions why the Psalmist makes specific reference only to the anointing of the *Kohen Gadol*, but not to the anointing of the king.

Radak explains that Aaron was the first Jewish leader to be anointed, and that this was done in conjunction with the construction of the Tabernacle. This symbolizes the future redemption, for Messiah and the *Kohen Gadol* will be anointed in conjunction with the erection of the Third Temple.

שֶׁיֹּרֵד עַל פִּי מִדּוֹתָיו — *Running down over the hem of his garments.* First Moses dressed Aaron in his priestly vestments, and then anointed him. Then the oil dripped from Aaron's beard onto his garments.

[The word מִדּוֹתָיו literally means *his measurements*. This is an appropriate description of the High Priest's vestments, because Jewish law requires that these garments fit him precisely.]

Maharsha (Comm. to *Horiyos* 12a) explains that the word מִדּוֹת, literally *measurements*, is also used to mean 'character traits' because every aspect of human character is valuable to the extent it is used in proper measure. Aaron was the greatest בַּעַל מִדּוֹת, *Master of good character*, of his time.

God blessed Aaron with the 'oil' of wisdom and talent. This blessing fell upon Aaron's character traits; with all of his intellectual attainments, he attempted to develop his character.

beard of Aaron, running down over the hem of his garments.
³ Like the dew of Hermon descending upon the mountains of
Zion, for there HASHEM has commanded the blessing. May there
be life forever!

Psalm 33 *Sing joyfully, O righteous, because of HASHEM; for the upright,*
praise is fitting. ² Thank HASHEM with the kinor, with the
neivel assor sing to Him. ³ Sing Him a new song, play well with

3. כְּטַל חֶרְמוֹן שֶׁיֹּרֵד עַל הַרְרֵי צִיּוֹן — *Like the dew of Hermon descending upon the mountains of Zion.* Radak explains that Mount Hermon is one of the highest peaks in the Holy Land. Its height makes it an appropriate symbol of closeness to heaven and God. Elsewhere, the Psalmist says: *Tabor and Hermon shall rejoice in Your Name* (89:12). Hermon's massive proportions also make it an appropriate symbol of royal stature and strength. The dew of Hermon symbolizes the blessings that

God pours upon the monarch, and which he, in turn, passes on to his subjects. So said King Solomon (*Proverbs* 19:12): *The King's wrath is like the roaring of the lion, and his favor is like dew upon the grass.* Similarly, the blessings that God bestows upon the land are intended ultimately to flow to Mount Zion, because it is for the sake of the holiness symbolized by Zion, home of the Temple, that God commanded His blessings to descend upon mankind.

רַנְּנוּ צַדִּיקִים/Psalm 33 ◆§

This psalm's connection to Chanukah seems to be its pervasive theme of praise, gratitude, and recognition of God's power and kindness. More specifically, verses 16-19 are a virtual description of the Chanukah era. Mighty King Antiochus IV relied on his huge armies and mounted troops, but they availed him not at all. On the other hand, God turned His attention to help the small band of righteous Jews who learned about and trusted Him. This theme is reminiscent of the *haftarah* of *Shabbos Chanukah,* in which God proclaims: לֹא בְחַיִל וְלֹא בְכֹחַ כִּי אִם בְּרוּחִי אָמַר ה׳ צְבָאוֹת, *'Not by might nor by power, but by My spirit'*, said HASHEM *of Legions* (*Zechariah* 4:6).

1. צַדִּיקִים — *O righteous.* Malbim explains: The יָשָׁר, *upright, straight,* man is on a higher level than the צַדִּיק, *righteous,* man. In the *upright* person's mind, God's control over the universe is plain and obvious; consequently, he never deviates from his chosen path of following God's ways. However, the צַדִּיק, *righteous one,* has not yet attained that level of stability. In his mind there are still doubts. In his heart, conflicting emotions and desires are still at war. Nevertheless, to his great credit, he disciplines himself rigidly and so his external deeds are in complete conformity

with the Divine dictates.

לַיְשָׁרִים נָאוָה תְהִלָּה — *For the upright, praise is fitting.* The *upright* can best judge God's greatness; therefore they should praise him most (*Radak*).

2. בְּכִנּוֹר — *With the kinor.* [Although there are many opinions concerning the exact translation of *kinor* most commentaries agree that it is a harp.][1]

The Psalmist refers to the use of instruments in praising God because music arouses the inner spirit of the intellect and enhances its faculties (*Radak*).

1. In support of this translation, *Shiltei Hagibborim* (chapter 9) cites *Berachos* 3b: A *kinor* was suspended over David's bed. At midnight the north wind would blow through its strings and it would play by itself. The only known instrument whose strings could be strummed by the wind is a harp.

The author goes on to say that the name כִּנּוֹר is derived from כֵּן, *straight* (see *I Kings* 7:31), because the harpstrings are positioned with great precision. כֵּן also means *base* (*Exodus* 38:8), referring to the wide base of the harp which provides stability for this heavy instrument.

Eretz HaChaim and *Zera Yaakov* note that, kabbalistically, *kinor* symbolizes the soul. Rear-

ד חָדָשׁ, הֵיטִיבוּ נַגֵּן בִּתְרוּעָה. כִּי יָשָׁר דְּבַר יהוה, וְכָל

ה מַעֲשֵׂהוּ בֶּאֱמוּנָה. אֹהֵב צְדָקָה וּמִשְׁפָּט, חֶסֶד יהוה מָלְאָה

ו הָאָרֶץ. בִּדְבַר יהוה שָׁמַיִם נַעֲשׂוּ, וּבְרוּחַ פִּיו כָּל צְבָאָם.

ז-ח כֹּנֵס כַּנֵּד מֵי הַיָּם, נֹתֵן בְּאוֹצָרוֹת תְּהוֹמוֹת. יִירְאוּ מֵיהוה

ט כָּל הָאָרֶץ, מִמֶּנּוּ יָגוּרוּ כָּל יֹשְׁבֵי תֵבֵל. כִּי הוּא אָמַר וַיֶּהִי,

י הוּא צִוָּה וַיַּעֲמֹד. יהוה הֵפִיר עֲצַת גּוֹיִם, הֵנִיא מַחְשְׁבוֹת

יא עַמִּים. עֲצַת יהוה לְעוֹלָם תַּעֲמֹד, מַחְשְׁבוֹת לִבּוֹ לְדֹר

יב וָדֹר. אַשְׁרֵי הַגּוֹי אֲשֶׁר יהוה אֱלֹהָיו, הָעָם בָּחַר לְנַחֲלָה

יג-יד לוֹ. מִשָּׁמַיִם הִבִּיט יהוה, רָאָה אֶת כָּל בְּנֵי הָאָדָם. מִמְּכוֹן

בְּנֵבֶל עָשׂוֹר — *With the neivel assor.* *Rashi* comments that *neivel* and *assor* [lit. *ten*] are both descriptive names for the same instrument, i.e., it is called *neivel* and it produces עָשׂוֹר, *ten* different tones. *Targum* describes it as having ten strings. *R' Moshe* quoted by *Ibn Ezra* says it was a wind instrument with ten holes. However, *Ibn Ezra* himself holds that the *neivel* and the *assor* are two separate instruments.

The Talmud (*Arachin* 13b) says that the כִּנּוֹר, *harp*, of the Temple had seven strings; in Messianic times it will have eight; and in the World to Come, ten. It derives the last fact from our verse and explains it thus: 'That which is now a seven-stringed *kinor* will then become a ten-stringed *assor*, of a beauty rivaling that of the hitherto unsurpassed *neivel*. *Rashi* (*ibid.*) says that the name *neivel* derives from נֵבֶל יַיִן, *leather wine bag* (filled with air and squeezed to produce sound).

3. שִׁירוּ לוֹ שִׁיר חָדָשׁ — *Sing Him a new song.* Continue to compose new songs of praise at all times (*Radak*).

Rashi (*Arachin* 13b) quotes the Midrash that throughout Scripture the word for song is שִׁירָה in the feminine form, for in This World of misery, after every song of joy, a new tragedy is born, just as the female gives birth to one child after another. But the song of

the World to Come is called שִׁיר in a masculine form, because this will be the final song after which no more misfortunes will be born.

4. וְכָל מַעֲשֵׂהוּ בֶּאֱמוּנָה — *And His every deed is done with trust.* This refers to the natural forces that God set up to guide the world. They are reliable and unchanging, so that one need not live in constant fear of upheaval and disaster (*Malbim*).

6. בִּדְבַר ה' שָׁמַיִם נַעֲשׂוּ — *By the word of HASHEM the heavens were made.* As we find throughout the story of Creation: וַיֹּאמֶר אֱלֹהִים, *and God said* (*Radak*).

[The *word of God* refers to the Torah which has been transmitted to Israel. Without the constant study of Torah, the universe would cease to exist as the prophet said: *If not for My covenant day and night* (i.e., the constant study of Torah) *I would not have set up the order of heaven and earth* (Jeremiah 33:25). This process of Creation continues, for the word of God, in the form of Torah, continues to perpetuate Creation.]

7. כֹּנֵס כַּנֵּד מֵי הַיָּם — *He assembles like a mound the waters of the sea.* Originally, water covered the face of the entire earth. Afterwards, God gathered the waters into the seas, and commanded

ranged, the letters of כִּנּוֹר can be made to form כ"ו and נר: כ"ו, *twenty-six,* is the numerical value of God's Four-Letter Name, and נר, *flame,* is the soul, as we find נֵר ה' נִשְׁמַת אָדָם, *a flame of HASHEM is the soul of man* (Proverbs 20:27).

sounds of deepest feeling. ⁴ *For upright is the word of HASHEM,*
and His every deed is done with trust. ⁵ *He loves charity and*
justice; the kindness of HASHEM fills the earth. ⁶ *By the word of*
HASHEM the heavens were made, and by the breath of His mouth
all their host. ⁷ *He assembles like a mound the waters of the sea;*
He places in vaults the deep waters. ⁸ *Fear HASHEM, all the earth;*
of Him be in dread, all inhabitants of the world. ⁹ *For He spoke*
and it became; He commanded and it stood firm. ¹⁰ *HASHEM*
annuls the counsel of peoples, He balks the designs of nations.
¹¹ *But the counsel of HASHEM stands forever, the designs of His*
heart for all generations. ¹² *Praiseworthy is the people whose*
God is HASHEM, the nation He chose for His own estate. ¹³ *From*
heaven HASHEM looks down, seeing all of mankind. ¹⁴ *From His*

---

them to remain there. The seas and
oceans contain enough water to cover
the entire face of the earth, but God
confines them, as if the water were piled
up in an immovable mound *(Radak)*.

נָתַן בְּאוֹצָרוֹת תְּהוֹמוֹת — *He places in*
vaults the deep waters. Rashi refers this
to the waters deep beneath the earth's
surface. In the subterranean world there
are both sweet- and salt-water pools, yet
God stores them so that they never mix
(Bamidbar Rabbah 18:22). Alshich also
notes that if the huge underground
reservoirs should ever erupt and shoot
to the surface, they would flood the
earth [*Succah* 51b]. It is God who keeps
them pent up.

9. הוּא צִוָּה וַיַּעֲמֹד — *He commanded and*
it stood firm. When God created the
world, it expanded like the threads
stretching out through the loom until
God roared and the earth stood firm
(Chagigah 12a). This is why God
is called שַׁדַּי, *Shaddai* [lit. *it is enough*],
because it was He who halted the ex-
pansion of the world by roaring דַּי,
enough!

10. ה' הֵפִיר עֲצַת גּוֹיִם — *HASHEM*
annuls the counsel of peoples. Now that
we understand that the command of
God stands firm and invincible forever
(v. 9) we realize that every effort to
challenge Him is futile and will be nullified [as demonstrated, too, by the
Chanukah miracle] *(Ibn Ezra).*

11. עֲצַת ה' ... מַחְשְׁבוֹת לִבּוֹ — *But the*
counsel of HASHEM ... the designs of
His heart. This verse contrasts God's
counsel to that of humans (*v.* 10). The
counsel of the peoples is nullified, but
God's counsel stands forever. Their
designs are balked, but the designs of
God endure eternally *(Ibn Ezra; Radak).*

12. אַשְׁרֵי הַגּוֹי אֲשֶׁר ה' אֱלֹהָיו —
Praiseworthy is the people whose God is
HASHEM. Any people which would put
their faith in God would be
praiseworthy, for then He would
provide them with His הַשְׁגָּחָה, *supervi-*
sion (Malbim).

הָעָם בָּחַר לְנַחֲלָה לוֹ — *The nation He*
chose for His own estate. But Israel is
even more fortunate than others. For
not only has Israel made HASHEM their
God, but He has also chosen them for
His nation. He reveals Himself to them
with miraculous Providence *(Malbim).*

13. מִשָּׁמַיִם הִבִּיט ה' רָאָה אֶת כָּל בְּנֵי הָאָדָם
— *From heaven HASHEM looks* [lit.
looked] *down, seeing* [lit. *He saw*] *all of*
mankind. In this verse and the next, the
Psalmist discusses the two forms of
Divine supervision. In describing God
as 'looking down', our verse implies
that He is distant and relatively unin-
volved in earthly affairs. This is הַשְׁגָּחָה
טִבְעִית, *supervision through nature,* i.e.,
the law of nature by which heavenly
forces exercise control over the universe
within a set of fixed laws *(Malbim).*

טו שִׁבְתּוֹ הִשְׁגִּיחַ, אֶל כָּל יֹשְׁבֵי הָאָרֶץ. הַיֹּצֵר יַחַד לִבָּם,

טז הַמֵּבִין אֶל כָּל מַעֲשֵׂיהֶם. אֵין הַמֶּלֶךְ נוֹשָׁע בְּרָב חָיִל,

יז גִּבּוֹר לֹא יִנָּצֵל בְּרָב כֹּחַ. שֶׁקֶר הַסּוּס לִתְשׁוּעָה, וּבְרֹב

יח חֵילוֹ לֹא יְמַלֵּט. הִנֵּה עֵין יהוה אֶל יְרֵאָיו, לַמְיַחֲלִים

יט-כ לְחַסְדּוֹ. לְהַצִּיל מִמָּוֶת נַפְשָׁם, וּלְחַיּוֹתָם בָּרָעָב. נַפְשֵׁנוּ

כא חִכְּתָה לַיהוה, עֶזְרֵנוּ וּמָגִנֵּנוּ הוּא. כִּי בוֹ יִשְׂמַח לִבֵּנוּ, כִּי

כב בְשֵׁם קָדְשׁוֹ בָטָחְנוּ. יְהִי חַסְדְּךָ יהוה עָלֵינוּ, כַּאֲשֶׁר יִחַלְנוּ לָךְ.

14. מִמְּכוֹן שִׁבְתּוֹ הִשְׁגִּיחַ אֶל כָּל יֹשְׁבֵי הָאָרֶץ — *From His dwelling-place He oversees all inhabitants of earth*. From the more general הַבִּיט, *looks*, of the previous verse the Psalmist changes to the more intense הִשְׁגִּיחַ, *oversees*, which implies הַשְׁגָּחָה פְּרָטִית, *individual supervision*, of all inhabitants of earth. God observes each person, not from the distant heavens, but rather מִמְּכוֹן שִׁבְתּוֹ, *from His dwelling-place*, i.e., where He sits in judgment on each individual according to his unique situation (*Malbim*).

16. אֵין הַמֶּלֶךְ נוֹשָׁע בְּרָב חָיִל — *A king is not saved by a great army*. History furnishes ample proof of God's intervention on behalf of His chosen ones. By the laws of nature and logic, the mighty army should always crush the tiny one, yet many a king has been defeated despite the superiority of his forces. For

example, King Sennacherib of Assyria conquered almost all of the inhabited world, and he arrogantly blasphemed God and besieged Jerusalem. Then, in a single night, the angel of God smote the entire Assyrian army of 185,000 men (*Radak*).

גִּבּוֹר לֹא יִנָּצֵל בְּרָב כֹּחַ — *Nor is a hero rescued by great strength*. Though his entire army was annihilated, the mighty Sennacherib was spared, only to be assassinated by his own sons. All his strength was of no avail. Similarly, the giant Goliath fell before the young shepherd David. Thus, history shows that victory depends not on physical strength but on the will of God (*Radak*).

[As noted in the Prefatory Comment, these passages form the psalm's connection with the Chanukah theme. It was not Antiochus and his huge armies who

dwelling-place He oversees all inhabitants of earth, 15 He Who fashions their hearts all together, Who comprehends all their deeds. 16 A king is not saved by a great army, nor is a hero rescued by great strength; 17 A sham is the horse for salvation; despite its great strength, it provides no escape. 18 Behold, the eye of HASHEM is on those who fear Him, upon those who await His kindness, 19 to rescue from death their soul, and sustain them in famine. 20 Our soul longed for HASHEM — our help and our shield is He. 21 For in Him will our hearts be glad, for in His Holy Name we trusted. 22 May Your kindness, HASHEM, be upon us, just as we awaited You.

were ultimately victorious, but the small band of righteous Jews who feared and trusted in God.]

17. שֶׁקֶר הַסּוּס לִתְשׁוּעָה — *A sham is the horse for salvation.* The horse's might emanates from God who can deprive him of it at will (*Radak*).

וּבְרֹב חֵילוֹ לֹא יְמַלֵּט — *Despite its great strength, it provides no escape.* The strength of the horse provides no assurance that it will carry its rider away from danger (*Radak*).

The mighty horse may not even be able to save itself from destruction (*Ibn Ezra*).

18. הִנֵּה עֵין ה' אֶל יְרֵאָיו — *Behold, the eye of HASHEM is on those who fear Him.* Those who trust in their military prowess stumble, but those who place their trust in God merit His protection (*Radak*).

The *Midrash* observes: When the Israelites perform according to God's will, He looks at them with two eyes, as it says: עֵינֵי ה' אֶל צַדִּיקִים, *The eyes* [plural] *of HASHEM are upon the righteous ones* (34:16); but when they do not perform according to His will, He looks only with one eye, as in our verse, *Behold, the eye of HASHEM is on those who fear Him* (*Shir HaShirim Rabbah* 8:12).

21. כִּי בוֹ יִשְׂמַח לִבֵּנוּ — *For in Him will our hearts be glad.* When He will save us from all the evils that threaten us, we will rejoice in the knowlege that our salvation stems from Him (*Radak*).

22. יְהִי חַסְדְּךָ ה' עָלֵינוּ כַּאֲשֶׁר יִחַלְנוּ לָךְ — *May Your kindness, HASHEM, be upon us just as we awaited You.* [This re-emphasizes the concept that God's beneficence rests upon man in proportion to his sincere trust in God.]

This volume is part of
THE ARTSCROLL SERIES®
an ongoing project of
translations, commentaries and expositions
on Scripture, Mishnah, liturgy,
the classic Rabbinic Writings and thought.

For a brochure of current publications
visit your local Hebrew bookseller
or contact the publisher:
Mesorah Publications, Ltd.
1969 Coney Island Avenue
Brooklyn, New York 11223
(212) 339—1700